Islands of the
SOUTH PACIFIC

By the Editors of
Sunset Books and
Sunset Magazine

Lane Publishing Co.
Menlo Park, California

Cascade *of snowy feathers marks lesser bird of paradise, one of many colorful species brightening Papua New Guinea's tropical forests.*

Research and Text: Joan Erickson
Supervising Editor: Cornelia Fogle

Special Consultant: Frederic M. Rea
    Editor & Publisher, Pacific Travel News

Design and Illustrations: Joe Seney

Cover: Over-the-water thatch hotel bungalows on Tahiti stand silhouetted against vibrant colors of South Seas sunset. Photographed by Morton Beebe.

Acknowledgments
We are grateful to the many people and organizations that helped in the preparation of this travel guide. We wish to acknowledge the assistance and cooperation of the editorial staff of *Pacific Travel News,* especially Phyllis Elving, James Gebbie, Jane Keator, and Victoria Wolcott.

For assistance on individual countries, we thank the following:

American Samoa: The Office of Tourism, especially Vaeotagaloa Maaka Nua. **Cook Islands:** Cook Islands Tourist Authority, especially Ian Fogelberg; and Anne DeWolfe, Air New Zealand, Los Angeles. **Easter Island:** LAN-Chile Airlines. **Fiji:** Fiji Visitors Bureau, especially Sitiveni Yaqona; and John and Joan Holmes, Holmes Associates. **Gilbert Islands:** Broadcasting and Publications Division, Chief Minister's Office; and N.P. Jones, Manager, Otintai Hotel. **Lord Howe Island:** Lord Howe Island Tourist Center. **Micronesia:** Guam Visitors Bureau, especially Martin Pray; Marianas Visitors Bureau, especially J. M. Guerrero; Economic Development Division, Trust Territory of the Pacific; Mike Ashman, Pacific Area Travel Association, San Francisco; and Tom Talamini, Daily and Associates, San Francisco. **Nauru:** Office of Consulate General of Nauru, San Francisco, especially Carlton Skinner. **New Caledonia:** Office du Tourism, especially Bruno Tabuteau. **New Hebrides:** Tourist Information Bureau, especially Joe Mulders. **Norfolk Island:** Norfolk Island Tourist Board; and Australian Tourist Commission, New York. **Papua New Guinea:** Office of Tourism, especially David Bamford; and Peter Barter, Melanesian Tourist Services. **Solomon Islands:** Solomon Islands Tourist Authority, especially Bara Buchanan; C. B. Grey, Air Niugini; and Jack Banley, Guadalcanal Travel Service. **Tahiti and French Polynesia:** Tahiti Tourist Development Board, especially Patrick Picard-Robson; Charlotte Hyde and Loretta Iannalfo, Transportation Consultants International, Los Angeles. **Tonga:** Tonga Visitors Bureau; especially Semisi Taumoepeau; and Charlotte Hyde and Loretta Iannalfo, Transportation Consultants International, Los Angeles. **Tuvalu:** Office of Ministry of Commerce and Natural Resources. **Western Samoa:** Western Samoa Visitors Bureau, especially Vensel Margraff.

Editor, Sunset Books: David E. Clark

First Printing August 1979

Contents

INTRODUCTION 4

POLYNESIA 10
TAHITI & FRENCH POLYNESIA   14
THE SAMOAS   30
TONGA   42
COOK ISLANDS   50

MELANESIA 54
FIJI   58
NEW CALEDONIA   74
NEW HEBRIDES   82
PAPUA NEW GUINEA   90
SOLOMON ISLANDS   98

MICRONESIA 106
GUAM   112
NORTHERN MARIANAS   114
CAROLINE ISLANDS   119
MARSHALL ISLANDS   120

OTHER ISLANDS 122
EASTER ISLAND   122
LORD HOWE ISLAND   124
NORFOLK ISLAND   124
NAURU   125
GILBERT ISLANDS   125
TUVALU   125

ADDITIONAL READINGS 126

INDEX 127

SPECIAL FEATURES
Captain Cook:
    He Mapped the Pacific   17
Say It In Tahitian:
    A Pronouncing Primer   19
Le Truck:
    It's Fun and Inexpensive   25
Pacific Architecture:
    It's Eclectic   32
Tapa Making:
    A Lengthy Process   45
Yaqona:
    It's a Drink of Welcome   61
Fijian Pronouncing Primer:
    Mind Your Bs and Qs   63
Firewalking:
    A Mystifying Ceremony   69
Ladies' Cricket:
    In Mother Hubbards   77
Land Diving:
    Pentecost Island-style   85
Tok Pisin:
    Talk Pidgin   93
The Coconut Palm:
    A Tropical Supermarket   101
Diving:
    A Fascinating Underwater
    World   109
Nan Madol:
    A World of Mysterious Islets   117

ISLANDS OF THE SOUTH PACIFIC

Mention the South Seas, and myriad enchanting tropical images float through your mind. Picture yourself strolling along a palm-shaded, white sand beach beside a lagoon so dazzling blue it hurts your eyes. Pause in the mist below a cascading waterfall, then plunge into its greenery-rimmed pool for a swim. Saunter down a curving path bordered by lush plants laden with blooms. At sunset, linger to enjoy the glowing skies as they fade into twilight. Everywhere you are greeted by friendly people whose relaxed life style you sometimes envy.

Immortalized in song and art, in poetry and prose, the islands of the Pacific have lured travelers for generations. Today, you can explore these islands yourself to experience their bewitching allure and beauty.

Three Regions

Strewn across the sun-warmed waters of the vast Pacific—the earth's largest ocean—lie thousands of tropical islands whose charms have been recounted by generations of travelers. Scattered between the Tropic of Cancer and the Tropic of Capricorn, these islands generally are divided into three regions—Polynesia, Melanesia, and Micronesia.

Nesia means island. Polynesia translates as *many islands,* an apt description of the numerous islands bounded within the Polynesian triangle. Melanesia means *black islands,* a name derived from the darkness of island vegetation or the dusky skin tones of the region's inhabitants. Micronesia, or *small islands,* concisely describes the diminutive islands in this Pacific area.

Mountain peaks, coral atolls

Island topography varies within Polynesia, Melanesia, and Micronesia. You'll find mountainous volcanic islands with craggy, towering peaks, deep valleys, broad plains, and rushing streams, contrasted with low patches of coral with a few palm trees and no running water.

High islands. The high islands are exposed summits of partially submerged volcanoes. Some thrust numerous jagged peaks out of the sea; others are no more than lumps of rock. Most of the high, volcanic islands are drained by rushing rivers that tumble into dramatic waterfalls or empty into broad flatland swamps. Protective coral reefs usually surround at least part of the island.

Low islands. These are coral reefs or atolls built by coral polyps. Ring or horseshoe shaped, most of them enclose salt-water lagoons. Some low islands are nearly submerged; others are uplifted coral masses.

Colorful flora, interesting fauna

The rich fertile soil of the high islands supports the most abundant tropical vegetation, but you'll find fascinating plant life on most of the Pacific islands.

A host of brilliant blossoms brighten the islands—fragrant frangipani and plumeria, cascading flamboyants, multihued orchids, and carpets of bougainvillea. The people of these tropical lands adorn themselves with flowers, tucking blooms in their hair and wearing floral leis around their necks.

The islanders enjoy the fruits of island plants such as breadfruit and mangoes, and weave the leaves of the pandanus into fine mats and baskets as well as walls for their thatch-roofed houses. The coconut palm provides both food and building materials.

In addition to fascinating tropical flora, the Pacific has interesting wildlife. Of particular note are tropical birds such as the multicolored birds of paradise in Papua New Guinea and New Caledonia's *cagou* bird, a rare flightless bird that barks like a dog.

Marine life, of special interest to snorkelers and scuba divers, features multihued coral gardens and a dazzling array of colorful tropical fish.

Island People

You'll also find variety in the peoples of Polynesia, Melanesia, and Micronesia. Each island group has its distinctive physical characteristics, languages, social systems, and dress. Yet all Pacific peoples have one thing in common—the sea. The sun, winds, tides, and dependence on the ocean for food influence their attitudes and ways of life.

Early migration

The people of Polynesia—brown skinned with straight hair—live within the archipelagoes of a vast triangle extending from Hawaii southwest to New Zealand and eastward to Easter Island. Melanesia's people—dark skinned with curly hair—occupy islands on the western fringe of the South Pacific. On the small Micronesian islands in the northwest Pacific, you'll find a variety of brown-skinned people with Malaysian and Polynesian traits.

Ancestors of these island people migrated to the different regions from Asia by way of the Malay Peninsula. The first to migrate were the Melanesians, who may have settled in New Guinea as early as 8000 B.C. Next to arrive were the Micronesians. Carbon dating indicates the Marianas were inhabited by 1500 B.C. The final group to migrate were the Polynesians. These skilled navigators journeyed the farthest, settling as far east as Easter Island, as far south as New Zealand, and as far north as Hawaii.

Europeans discover the Pacific islands

The Pacific migration had ended several centuries before the first European laid eyes on the Pacific Ocean.

In 1513, Vasco Nuñez de Balboa sighted the Pacific after hacking his way through the jungle of Panama's isthmus. Naming his discovery the Great South Sea, he claimed all the land touching it for Spain. Little did he know that the body of water covered one-third of the earth's surface—181 million square km/70 million square miles. Ferdinand Magellan learned of the Pacific's vastness in 1521 when he sailed across the ocean for 3 months without seeing land until he discovered Guam.

The 17th and 18th centuries brought more European explorers. Most notable was Captain James Cook who charted Tahiti, the Marquesas, New Hebrides, New Caledonia, Easter Island, the Cooks, Tonga, Fiji, Norfolk, and Niue. Other seamen to explore the Pacific included Captain Samuel Wallis, Louis Antoine de Bougainville, Jean La Perouse, Abel Tasman, Captain William Bligh, Fletcher Christian, Pedro de Quiros, and Alvaro de Mendaña.

These first travelers returned to Europe with tales of their discoveries. The explorers' reports excited adventurers who sailed to the area. Traders wanted the precious sandalwood that grew in abundance on the islands. Others sought men to work as slave labor in distant sugar cane fields. The missionaries arrived full of zeal to save the souls of the errant natives who wore minimal clothing, sang and danced with abandon, and lived a carefree existence.

Finally, foreign governments asserted their influence and rule on the Pacific islands. These foreign powers introduced their foods, apparel, and architecture. Only in recent years have many Pacific island countries achieved the right to self-government.

Life today in the Pacific

After generations of relative isolation, today's Pacific islanders must cope with more rapid change. Airplanes and ships bring the modern world to them quickly—a modern world to which it is sometimes difficult to adjust. Some old customs fade as new ideas are accepted. Yet amid this change many islanders strive to maintain traditional practices.

Communal life style. Most islanders still live a communal existence in small villages. To satisfy their needs they harvest vegetables from their gardens and fish from the nearby sea. They spend their free time weaving mats, making tapa, or socializing. Evenings are filled with songs and dances that have been passed down for generations. The family unit is still important in village life, and chiefs are respected.

Western civilization has made some impact on these village people. Instead of walking or riding horses, islanders now prefer to travel around on motorscooters. Many canoes are motorized, and meals are sometimes supplemented with canned foods from the local store.

Getting together. The jet age has helped Pacific Island people learn of each other. Every 3 years—next in 1982 —athletes from all over the western Pacific compete in the South Pacific Games, an island Olympics. Every 4 years—next in 1980—an Arts Festival attracts performers from many Pacific islands.

Visiting the Pacific

Today's visitors to Polynesia, Melanesia, and Micronesia can choose from a wide variety of experiences ranging from the very primitive to the modern.

You can enjoy a touch of French sophistication while shopping in the boutiques of Nouméa, New Caledonia, or Papeete, Tahiti. The latest stereo equipment is offered for sale in duty-free shops in Suva, Fiji, and Agana, Guam. If you want an interesting shopping experience, rise early and stroll through the public market. Here you'll mingle with islanders in native dress.

When you leave the town to venture into the countryside, you'll see villages of thatch-roofed huts and white-steepled churches. Here, too, are remnants of early island culture—*maraes* (temples) in Tahiti, the Ha'amonga Trilithon in Tonga, and *latte* stones in the Marianas.

Traditional customs remain

Primitive rituals and traditions still exist in parts of the Pacific. On Pentecost Island in the New Hebrides, men still dive once a year from tall towers with nothing to break their fall but vines wrapped around their ankles. They believe this tradition ensures a good harvest.

The Highlanders of Papua New Guinea paint their faces in bright colors and don elaborate headdresses made of bird of paradise feathers to participate in sing sings where they perform ancient chants and dances.

A time and place to relax

The islands of the Pacific offer you not only the experiences of interesting sights and cultural events, but also a warm and relaxing tropical climate and unhurried pace. Water sports provide the most popular form of recreation. Beautiful beaches and calm, clear lagoons are abundant throughout the Pacific.

Modern resorts or thatch bungalows

In accommodations, the Pacific islands offer something for everyone. You can stay at modern resorts like The Fijian in Fiji, Chateau Royal Hotel in Nouméa, or various high rises along Tumon Bay near Agana, Guam.

Perhaps you prefer a "get-away-from-it-all" refuge; if so, you might choose an over-the-water thatch bungalow on Bora Bora or a simple hut at an island retreat like Toberua Island in Fiji. Nostalgia seekers will enjoy the colonial ambiance of Suva's Grand Pacific Hotel or Aggie Grey's comfortable hostelry in Apia, Western Samoa.

Cosmopolitan dining experiences

Throughout the Pacific, you'll find island restaurants offering French, Chinese, Italian, Indian, and other international dishes. At a native feast you can sample local foods such as chicken, fish, and pork that have been wrapped in banana leaves and baked slowly on hot stones in an underground oven. Raw fish marinated in lime juice and coconut milk is a popular item in nearly every Pacific island country.

Following the feast, local performers dressed in colorful native costumes will entertain you with traditional music and dances.

Traveling to Pacific islands

Travelers can reach the islands of the Pacific from virtually any direction: from Honolulu and the U.S. west coast, from Australia and New Zealand, from the Orient, from Southeast Asia, and from Chile.

Major airlines serving the South Pacific include Continental, Pan American, Air New Zealand, Qantas, UTA French Airlines, Japan Air Lines, and LAN-Chile. Regional carriers like Air Pacific, Air Micronesia, Air Niugini, Polynesian Airlines, Air Nauru, and South Pacific Island Airways operate regular service between Pacific islands. Some also link Australia and New Zealand with Pacific points.

Sea transportation. Cruise ships departing from United States, Australia, and New Zealand ports stop at several islands during South Pacific voyages. Cargo/passenger lines carrying a limited number of passengers also call at South Seas ports and destinations in Micronesia.

Tours. A number of organized tours include islands in the Pacific. From the United States, Tahiti and Fiji can both be stopovers on excursions to Australia and New Zealand. Other tour operators feature the islands of French Polynesia or arrange for visitors to live part of the time with local villagers. Special interest packages focus on Micronesia for scuba diving and on Tahiti for yachting holidays.

Destinations, length of stay, and special features vary with each package. Many include accommodations, land arrangements, entertainment, and even local feasts.

Ask an expert. Since South Pacific travel offers such a wide array of destinations and choices of accommodations and transportation, prospective travelers should seek the advice of a knowledgeable travel agent to help plan the trip.

Peoples of the Pacific *share a love of flowers, bright colors, and traditional music and dance.* **Above:** *Trio of young Polynesian women fashion blooms into floral crowns.* **Top right:** *Musician entertains visitors with Melanesian melodies.* **Bottom right:** *Colorful headband adorns Micronesian performer.*

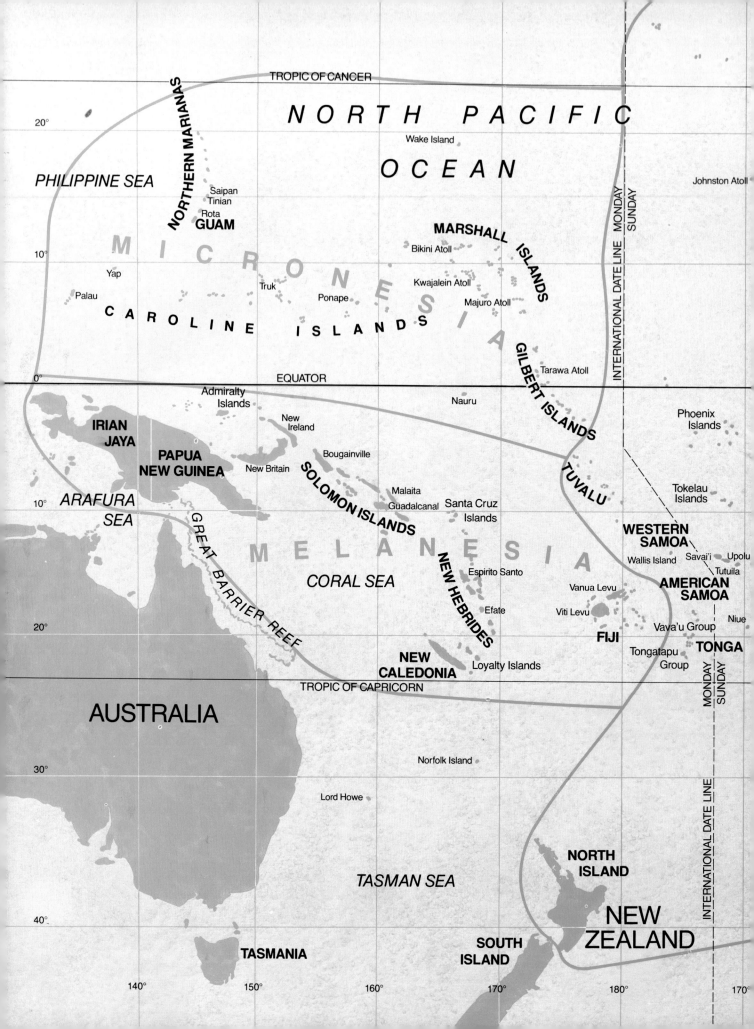

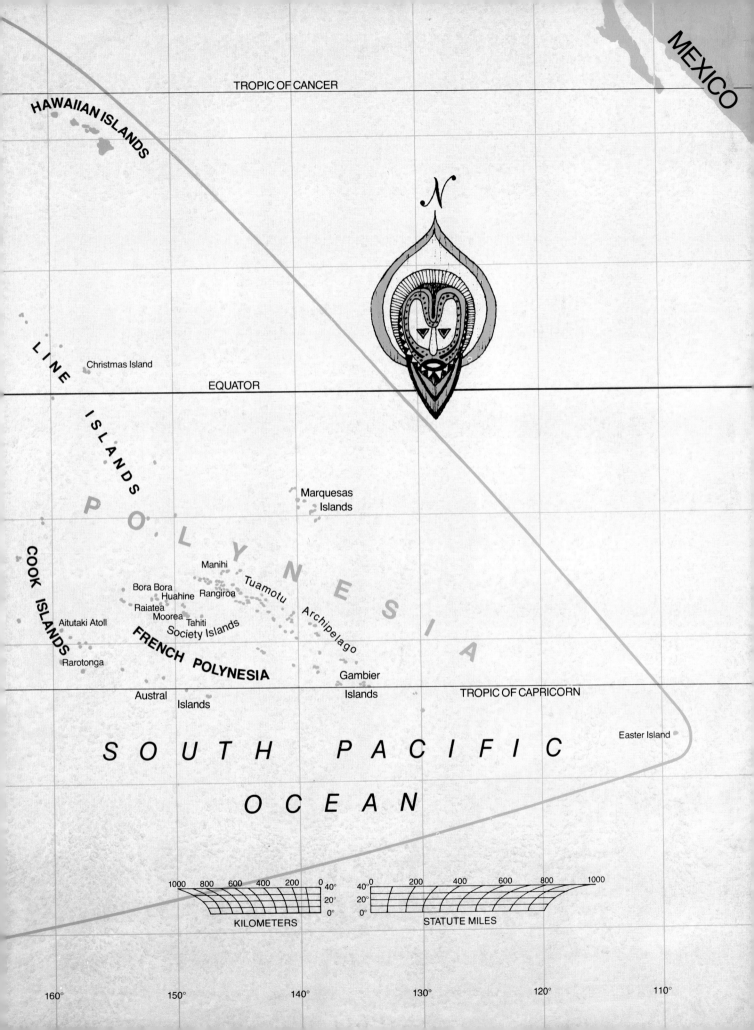

MEXICO

TROPIC OF CANCER

HAWAIIAN ISLANDS

N

Christmas Island

EQUATOR

L
I
N
E

I
S
L
A
N
D
S

P O L Y N E S I A

Marquesas
Islands

COOK
ISLANDS

Manihi

Bora Bora
Huahine   Rangiroa
Raiatea
Moorea   Tahiti
Aitutaki Atoll
Society Islands

Tuamotu

Archipelago

FRENCH POLYNESIA

Rarotonga

Gambier

Austral   Islands   TROPIC OF CAPRICORN
Islands

Easter Island

S   O   U   T   H   P   A   C   I   F   I   C

O   C   E   A   N

1000 800 600 400 200 0 40°   40° 0   200   400   600   800   1000
                              20°   20°
                               0°   0°
KILOMETERS   STATUTE MILES

160°   150°   140°   130°   120°   110°

POLYNESIA

Tahiti and French Polynesia, The Samoas, Tonga, Cook Islands

When people yearn for the romantic South Seas and deserted tropical isles, they usually think first of Polynesia—a word that has become synonymous with a carefree way of life. Since European mariners discovered these islands more than 200 years ago, adventurers, missionaries, traders, writers, painters, and other travelers have been lured by Polynesia's charms—its smiling brown-skinned people, balmy trade winds, palm-trimmed beaches, and unbelievably blue lagoons sheltered by coral reefs.

The word Polynesia means "many islands." These island groups lie scattered across the Pacific Ocean within a vast triangle, stretching from Hawaii southwest approximately 8,000 km/5,000 miles to New Zealand, and a similar distance southeast from Hawaii to Easter Island—an area covering some 39 million square km/15 million square miles.

Inside the Polynesian triangle, you'll find Tahiti, American and Western Samoa, Tonga, the Cooks, and smaller island groups. Living under different governments and in diverse surroundings, the Polynesian people share similar languages and a common heritage and physical appearance—brown eyes, straight hair, and golden-brown skin.

Pacific Migrations

Long before the first European explorers dared to sail beyond the horizon of a world many felt was flat, double-hulled Polynesian canoes plied the waters of the Pacific Ocean. Today archeologists, anthropologists, and linguists are just beginning to unravel the amazing story of these first brave migrations into the unknown. Countless theories exist regarding the path of these early Polynesian migrations.

First explorations

Many scientists believe that the first Polynesians sailed from Asia's South China coast sometime after 2000 B.C. Some authorities think they came in two separate migrations by way of the Malay Peninsula, stopping at various Melanesian and Micronesian islands on their journey. They continued on to Tonga and the Samoas, where they remained for several thousand years before venturing farther eastward. During this period of relative isolation, Polynesian islanders developed their languages, physique, and culture.

Samoans disagree with this theory. In Samoa no legends have been handed down recounting the arrival of the first Samoans or telling of an ancient homeland. Therefore, many Samoans believe that their islands have been populated since the dawn of history. According to this theory, all Polynesians descend from the first Samoans.

Voyages of discovery

Sometime around the birth of Christ, Polynesians once more climbed into their double-hulled canoes and sailed eastward in search of new islands. These migrations continued for another 1,000 years.

Their first stop was probably the Marquesas in French Polynesia. From here, some scientists theorize they journeyed southeast to Easter Island around A.D. 400. Other sailing canoes headed northward toward Hawaii and south to other islands in French Polynesia. From Raiatea, Polynesians continued south to New Zealand and also made a second trip to Hawaii.

By the time the first Europeans arrived in the Pacific

Island fishermen *toss float-rimmed net into shallow lagoon waters near Bora Bora's shore. Traditional ways persist in outer islands.*

in the 16th century, the Polynesian migrations had ended. The Polynesians had explored and colonized nearly all the islands in the Polynesian triangle.

Why did they migrate?

There are as many theories about the reasons for the early migrations as there are about the routes they took. In the past, some scientists believed that the voyages were accidental. They thought the Polynesians were blown off course while traveling between neighboring islands, and that they then drifted for days until sighting land.

However, today many scientists think the trips were intentional. Women, children, animals, and plant cuttings always accompanied the men on these journeys. In most cases canoes were sailed upwind and against the currents.

Many reasons are possible for departure on the long voyages. One theory is that a group defeated in war had to leave its territory to avoid being killed or enslaved.

Another reason might have been lack of food because of overcrowding. Only limited amounts of food could be grown on many of the smaller islands, and when the population increased, food became scarce, forcing groups to leave in search of new islands to settle on.

Sometimes, wars were fought over agricultural land and lagoon fishing rights. The losing group had to leave the island or starve to death.

Navigating unknown seas

These early Polynesian adventurers were skilled navigators. In their sailing canoes they traveled thousands of miles across treacherous, uncharted waters. On these voyages they discovered hundreds of tiny islands that were mere specks in the giant Pacific Ocean.

They made these epic journeys in large twin-hulled canoes. Built up to 30 meters/100 feet long, these canoes could accommodate 60 or more people plus pigs, dogs, fowl, coconuts, and tuber crop cuttings. The large platform linking the twin hulls held both people and supplies. In the center of this platform, a thatch hut provided shelter from sun and rain.

The canoes were powered by paddlers and by pandanus mat sails. The Polynesian navigators observed the stars and the sea. They studied crisscrossing wave patterns generated by distant islands, observed the direction birds flew when returning to land in the evening, and sighted clouds forming over distant land.

European Influences

When the first European explorers arrived in Polynesia, they were greeted by descendants of the ancient Polynesians. Following the traditions of their forefathers, these people lived in harmony with the wind, sea, and sun. They worshipped the gods of their ancestors and recalled legends in song and poetry. As a people they were fierce in battle and gentle in love.

When the European adventurers returned home, they recounted wondrous tales of a tropical paradise—lush green, mountainous islands rich in scenic beauty and gracious people. Soon other travelers arrived. Some stayed, and left a lasting impression on Polynesia.

The missionaries brought Christianity, and soon the Polynesian gods and idols were forsaken. Islanders adopted European dress, and European-style houses were built. From the foreigners who eventually ruled most of the islands, the Polynesians acquired new languages, new food, and new customs.

Polynesia Today

Modern Polynesia is changing. Many of these island countries have been governed by foreign powers which have left a cultural impact. International visitors require facilities and bring new ideas. But despite the influences of the outside world, most Polynesians still retain many of the traditions and customs of their ancestors.

As you travel through Polynesia, you'll discover the charms that have long lured visitors to the islands—beautiful scenery and gracious people who are proud of their heritage.

French Polynesia, a fabled paradise

Anyone seeking a tropical island paradise might well pause here—and wonder whether there's need to look farther. Since its discovery by 18th century European explorers, French Polynesia (Tahiti and its sister islands) has been the destination of countless wanderers, writers, and painters.

When you visit French Polynesia, you'll understand why these islands have become legendary. Green mountains rise to lofty, cloud-piercing peaks. Clear aquamarine lagoons lap white sand shores. Cascading waterfalls plunge into deep, sparkling pools. Aromatic flowering shrubs and trees add color to lush tropical forests.

French Polynesia is a delightful blend of cultures. You'll hear both French and Tahitian spoken. On the streets, smiling pareu-wrapped women pass beret-hatted men carrying long loaves of French bread. They'll both shop in Chinese-owned stores. One night you can enjoy a French dinner by candlelight, the next afternoon Tahitian delicacies traditionally cooked in an earth oven.

Tahiti. Of all the islands in French Polynesia, Tahiti has been the most influenced by modern western civilization. Here, you'll find most of the major resort hotels, the international airport, and rush hour traffic in Papeete rivaling that of large metropolitan cities.

But on Tahiti you can also visit a museum honoring artist Paul Gauguin, who produced some of his best work in the islands. You can visit the site where Captain Cook landed, see the tombs of Polynesian royalty, and view interesting *maraes* (ancient Polynesian temples). Perhaps best of all, you can relax and enjoy Tahiti's beaches, lagoons, and waterfalls.

Outer islands. To experience the French Polynesia of yesteryear, take a trip to the outer islands. Here you'll find a few small resorts and a quiet way of life that has changed little over the years.

Sitting in a beachside bungalow, you'll be aware of silence broken only by the lapping of waves and the rustle of palm fronds caressed by trade winds. At dawn you may be awakened by a noisy rooster eager for the day to begin. After a breakfast of fresh fruit, stroll leisurely down the one main street of a lazy, sunbaked island town, or perhaps bicycle down a dirt road uncluttered by traffic.

Each outer island has its own special magic. Moorea offers you spectacular views of Cook's Bay and Tahiti. On Bora Bora (considered by some to be the most beautiful island in the world), you may want to spend hours snorkeling in a large lagoon filled with spectacular coral formations and brilliantly colored fish. The maraes of Raiatea and Huahine recall a time when Polynesian gods and idols were worshipped. Venturing to Rangiroa or Manihi, you'll experience life on an atoll where land barely rises above the crashing waves of the sea.

Relaxed life style. Wherever you travel in French Polynesia, you'll be intrigued by the people. Proud and happy, they live a relaxed life, generally ignoring the rushed pace of the intruding outside world. They love to sing and dance and revel, and these parties can go on for days.

This relaxed pace, combined with the beauty of the landscape, makes French Polynesia a refuge where you can unwind and escape from urban pressures.

The Samoas, land of tradition

Like other islands in the South Pacific, American and Western Samoa offer visitors a warm climate cooled by the trade winds; volcanic greenery-clad mountains; plummeting waterfalls; unpeopled beaches; and inviting lagoons.

The Samoan people are dignified protectors of their Polynesian heritage. You'll find that these islands—considered by many the cradle of the Polynesian race—are rich today in ancient Polynesian myths, ceremonies, and customs.

Since American Samoa became a United States territory, American institutions and features have gradually filtered into these islands. Yet beneath the thin western overlay, American Samoa still clings to its Samoan traditions.

Fa'a Samoa. Wherever you travel in the Samoas, you'll experience *fa'a Samoa*—the Samoan Way. Tradition plays an important part in Samoan life.

One of the charms of the Samoas is their villages. In both countries clusters of thatch-roofed *fales* dot sandy island shores.

The basic unit of the village community is still the *aiga* (family). A complex hierarchy of chiefs still governs these families and villages.

Each village has at least one imposing church. The Samoans are very proud of their churches, and they pursue Christianity with fervor.

Hospitable people. You'll find the village people warm and friendly. Hospitality is part of *fa'a Samoa*. Robert Louis Stevenson, whom the Samoans affectionately named "Tusitala" (teller of tales), spent his final years here. Margaret Mead, at age 27, arrived in Samoa in 1925 to spend a year studying adolescent girls in a primitive society. Both wrote of the Samoans with love and respect.

Tonga, a Polynesian kingdom

Located just west of the International Date Line, Tonga is the first country in the world to greet each new day.

At first glance, Tonga's scattered island groups resemble most other South Pacific island countries, but they differ in one important way. Tonga is a constitutional monarchy—the last remaining Polynesian kingdom. King Taufa'ahau Tupou IV traces his ancestry to ancient ruling chiefs whose names have been preserved in art and legend. He resides in an elegant Victorian Royal Palace that dates from 1867; it is topped by a stately cupola.

A friendly land. After meeting the people of Tonga, Captain Cook named the country "The Friendly Islands." These gentle people live a traditional way of life in a country rich with ancient history.

Touring Tongatapu, Tonga's main island, you'll see centuries-old ruins of archeological interest. The massive upright coral slabs of Ha'amonga Trilithon, thought to be a kind of South Pacific Stonehenge, were erected around A.D. 1200. Scientists believe the trilithon was used as a seasonal calendar by Tonga's early inhabitants. The nearby terraced tombs known as Langi are the final resting place for royalty dating back to A.D. 950.

Natural beauty. Of equal fascination is Tonga's natural beauty. The country has its full share of coral reefs, clear blue skies, sandy beaches, and inviting atolls.

On Tongatapu, you can watch spouting water jet high into the air at the Houma Blow Holes. In the Vava'u Group, the Port of Refuge is reached by a 13-km/8-mile fiordlike passage—one of the most beautiful waterways in the South Pacific.

The Cook Islands, unspoiled and friendly

Long isolated from major travel routes, the Cook Islands have preserved much of the romance and charm of old Polynesia. Life in these islands moves at a slow, pleasant pace. Most people still farm the land and fish the seas for their basic foods. This peaceful existence offers a welcome relief from the complex demands of modern society.

The main island of Rarotonga is only 34 km/21 miles in circumference, small enough to explore thoroughly at a leisurely pace. You'll enjoy meeting the people of the Cook Islands, who smile, wave, and converse easily with visitors. (Bilingual, they speak both English and Maori.) They will welcome you to their country as a guest, not a tourist.

The friendly people of the Cooks will entertain you with their harmonious church choirs, fantastic drumbeats, and dance performances acclaimed as some of the best in the South Pacific. If relaxation is your goal, you will be pleased to find beautiful unspoiled beaches and lagoons.

TAHITI & FRENCH POLYNESIA

The islands of French Polynesia (Tahiti and its sister islands) have long been acclaimed as the most beautiful in the South Pacific. Explorers Samuel Wallis, Louis Antoine de Bougainville, and James Cook described them in their journals, and Paul Gauguin painted them on canvas.

What are the lures of fabled Tahiti and her neighboring islands? Spectacular mountains plunge into an ocean reflecting every shade of blue. Tropical rain forests teem with brilliant flowering shrubs and trees. Deserted beaches and quiet lagoons lure you to stroll and swim undisturbed. Colorful markets offer an opportunity to mingle with the local people. In candlelit restaurants you can dine on French-inspired specialties.

The atmosphere of French Polynesia blends French sophistication and Polynesian gaiety. The people love to laugh and sing; they approach life with a joyous spirit. As you pause on French Polynesia's shores, relax, and enjoy what many visitors consider to be paradise.

Four Island Groups

The 130 islands of French Polynesia lie in the South Pacific about midway between Australia and the United States. Divided into four groups, these islands encompass an ocean area about the size of western Europe.

Best known of these groups is the Society Islands, consisting of the Windward group (Tahiti, Moorea, Meheitia, Tetiaroa, and Maiao) and the Leeward group (Huahine, Raiatea, Tahaa, Bora Bora, and Maupiti). Other island groups include the Tuamotu Archipelago (including the Gambier Islands), the Austral Islands, and the Marquesas Islands.

Volcanic islands, coral atolls

Geographically, French Polynesia has two types of islands—high islands that are volcanic in origin and low islands that are coral atolls. All the island groups except the Tuamotus have high islands.

Steep, jagged mountains with plummeting waterfalls characterize the high islands. With narrow coastal strips forming the shoreline, most of the islands (except the Marquesas) are protected by an encircling coral reef.

On the low islands, a thin ring of coral surrounds a lagoon with no mountainous island center. Standing on one of these atolls, you hear the ocean waves crashing against the outer shore behind you while you gaze at a quiet, blue-green lagoon.

Island flora. Flowers abound in the rich volcanic soil of the high islands. The sweet, heady scent of tiare-tahiti (Tahitian gardenia) and frangipani fills the warm, tropical air. You'll delight in seeing red, yellow, and orange flamboyants in cascading clusters; delicate multihued orchids; colorful carpets of bougainvillea; and brilliant red poinsettias.

A variety of trees and shrubs thrive in the humid climate and rich soil of the high islands. They include *fei* (wild bananas), *mape* (Tahitian chestnut), pandanus, coconut, breadfruit, mango, casuarina, and tree fern.

In contrast the calcareous, dry soil of the low islands produces little vegetation beyond a few coconut palms and some pandanus and breadfruit trees. Few flowers grow on these islands.

Underwater life. Aquatic life teems in the numerous temperate lagoons of French Polynesia. Exploring these waters, you'll discover a fairyland of multishaped corals and rainbow-colored fish. Parrotfish, bonitos, lobsters, crabs, clams, bass, and groupers all thrive in these waters.

Lovely shells such as conch, cone, cowrie, and triton can be found in lagoon and reef areas. Shells have become an integral part of Tahitian life. Shell necklaces are a traditional farewell gift.

Wildlife. French Polynesia has no dangerous or poisonous animals. Many of its animals—including pigs, dogs, and chickens— were brought to the islands in outriggers by migrating Polynesians. Coconut rats and lizards were stowaways on these first voyages. Europeans later introduced horses, cows, cats, and turkeys.

Discovered by the English and the French

Captain Samuel Wallis, an Englishman, had been at sea for 8 months searching for Terra Australis Incognita when he and his crew accidentally came upon the island of Tahiti in June 1767. Anchoring the H.M.S. *Dolphin* in Matavai Bay off the peninsula now called Point Venus, he claimed Tahiti for England, naming it King George III Island.

Also searching for Terra Australis Incognita, French explorer Louis Antoine de Bougainville anchored off Tahiti in April 1768. Unaware of Wallis's visit, Bougainville claimed the island for France, calling it Nouvelle Cythère—New Island of Love. Bougainville's botanist named the scarlet and violet, paperlike flowers he saw on the island "bougainvillea" after his captain.

A year later Lieutenant James Cook, commanding the H.M.S. *Endeavor,* was directed to take an astronomer to the South Pacific to view the planet Venus as it crossed the disk of the sun. Upon Wallis's suggestion, Cook chose King George III Island as the observation point, building a fort on Point Venus.

During Cook's 3-month stay, he recorded information

Brilliantly costumed *entertainers break into pulsating rhythm of the tamure, Tahiti's famed native dance. Native songs and dances highlight Polynesian feast entertainment.*

Verdant *tropical islands provide scenic vistas for yachters who sail annually to Tahiti, anchoring in calm, protected waters.*

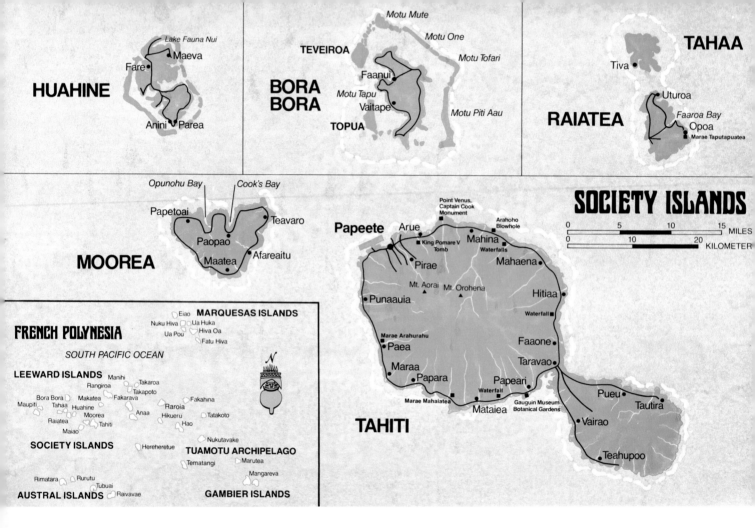

about native customs, manners, religion, and law, and charted Tahiti's coastline. After leaving Tahiti in July 1769, Cook discovered Huahine, Raiatea, Tahaa, and Bora Bora. He named these islands the Society Islands because of their contiguous location. Cook returned to Tahiti in 1773, 1774, and 1777 during further exploratory voyages.

Hearing tales of Tahiti's Garden of Eden, a variety of adventurers flocked to the islands in the years that followed. In March 1797, a large group from the London Missionary Society landed on Tahiti, but they soon found that converting the fun-loving Polynesians to a puritanical life was not easy—it took them 15 years to win their first convert.

During the first half of the 19th century, the islands were torn by wars brought about largely by rival Protestant and Catholic missionaries and their supporting governments (England and France). Tahiti became a French protectorate in 1846 during the reign of Queen Pomare IV. In 1880 King Pomare V made a gift of his kingdom to France, ending the century-old Pomare dynasty.

The country's status changed from colony to territory in 1957, and it became known as French Polynesia. Recently it has been granted internal autonomy. A 7-member council and a local Territorial Assembly of 30 elected members govern the country's internal matters. A High Commissioner, appointed by France, oversees external affairs.

French Polynesia's People

With a culture that blends its ancient Polynesian beginnings with more than 200 years of contact with the outside world, French Polynesian society is a dynamic one. Its population of 137,000 is a composite of 77 percent Polynesian, 14 percent European, and 9 percent Asian (mainly Chinese).

Easygoing people

The indigenous Tahitians are a fun-loving people who believe that life should be lived in the pursuit of happiness. Their easygoing philosophy is summed up in their phrase *aita pea pea*—a kind of happy "Who cares?"

Sharing a love of singing, Tahitians join together in song on almost any occasion. It's not unusual to see several youths sitting along the roadside, strumming their guitars and singing. You'll hear both traditional folk songs and the latest American and European hits—all sung in Tahitian.

They also love to dance. Whether dancing in Papeete's smoke-filled bars or at a village feast, they never seem to tire or become bored with it. One of the best known traditional dances is the *ori-tahiti* or *tamure*. To the accompaniment of wooden drums, the female performs tantalizing, fast-moving hip motions while the male executes equally rapid knee movements.

Urban and rural life styles

Life styles in French Polynesia range from the busy activity of urban Papeete to the relaxed pace of lightly populated rural areas, especially on islands other than Tahiti. Westernization intrudes more slowly on these outer islands than on Tahiti.

Papeete's citizens work for businesses, factories, the government, and the tourist industry. They live in modern homes built of wood and concrete. At the local supermarket they can purchase not only staples but also imported items such as French cheeses and wines. Judging from the traffic on Papeete's main thoroughfares, it appears that nearly everyone owns a motorbike or automobile.

Elsewhere on Tahiti—and especially on the outer islands—you still find vestiges of a slower paced, more traditional life style. But even on these outer islands, western civilization has made inroads.

You'll still see some *fares*—Tahitian dwellings with thatch roofs. However, many have been replaced with houses of concrete block—painted in bright colors of yellow, orange, red, green, and blue—topped by corrugated metal roofs. Cooking is now done inside on a butane stove, not in the *ahimaa,* the traditional hole-in-the-ground oven heated with hot stones.

Villagers still grow their own root crops, fruits, and coconuts. They fish with traps, nets, and harpoons, but night fishing is now done by *mori gaz* (pressure lamps) rather than by torch. Today's diet is supplemented with canned corned beef from the village store.

Walking, outrigger canoes, and horses remain popular forms of transportation, but both motorscooters and motorboats are beginning to infiltrate the outer islands.

Western dress. Tahitians have adopted an informal western style of dress. (Traditional grass skirts appear only on special occasions.) Men wear brightly patterned shirts and shorts or slacks; women don colorful, flower-printed dresses. The *pareu,* a wraparound garment made in a bright *pareo* print fabric, is worn by both men and women. The Tahitians love their flowers—they wear floral leis and *couronnes* (flower crowns) both on special occasions and just for the fun of it.

Speak Tahitian. French and Tahitian are the country's official languages. Tourist industry employees and some shopkeepers also speak English. (If you want to learn more about the Tahitian language, see page 19.)

Religion important. Religious worship plays an important part in the Tahitian daily life. Women don their finest dresses and broad-brimmed straw hats, and men their best suits, to go to church. People sometimes attend services several times a week, participating enthusiastically in a capella congregational hymn singing and in *himene* (trained choir).

More than half of the French Polynesian people are Protestants. There are also a number of Catholics and a few Mormons, Seventh-Day Adventists, Jehovah's Witnesses, and Buddhists.

Copra is prime export. French Polynesia's main agricultural product is copra. Vanilla and coffee add

CAPTAIN COOK
He Mapped the Pacific

Of all the explorers who sailed the Pacific following Magellan's voyage in the early 1500s, the man who traveled the farthest and left the most lasting impression was Captain James Cook. Entering the British navy as a common seaman in 1755, he later became one of England's most renowned explorers.

Between 1768 and 1779, he made three voyages totaling almost nine years. Cook touched nearly every island group in the South Pacific: Easter, the Marquesas, Tahiti, the Cooks, Tonga, Fiji, New Caledonia, Norfolk, Niue, Hawaii, New Hebrides, and Pitcairn. In addition, he charted 2,000 miles of Australia's east coast, circumnavigated and charted New Zealand, charted the west coast of North America, and was the first European to cross the Antarctic Circle.

Today, some 200 years later, Cook is still a name to be reckoned with in the South Pacific. You'll find numerous geographical points named for him—islands, straits, mountains, coves, headlands, and streams.

In addition to all his accomplishments, Cook was known as a kind and gentle person, a considerate commander, and a courteous and understanding student of the native inhabitants of the lands he discovered. Ironically, he met his death in his 50th year (1779) at the hands of Hawaiians at Kealakekua Bay, Hawaii. He was killed during a fracas that followed the theft of one of his small boats.

To the lords of the Admiralty, he had been a source of amazement: a man who overcame "the social handicap of lowly birth" to rise to the rank of Post Captain in the Royal Navy.

Greenery *brightens Papeete's business district, where modern structures housing shops, offices, restaurants have sprouted among older wooden buildings.*

Thatch-roofed *bungalows provide resort accommodations in tropical garden or seaside setting. At Hotel Bali Hai Moorea, guests relax on decks built over lagoon.*

SAY IT IN TAHITIAN
A Pronouncing Primer

French is Tahiti's main language, but most Polynesian residents speak Tahitian.

You'd have to be quite a linguist to learn enough Tahitian to carry on a whole conversation, but you can learn some basics of pronunciation and a few common phrases. If you do, it will make your visit more meaningful, and Tahitians will be pleased with your attempt to use their language.

The Tahitian alphabet has only 13 letters with 5 vowels (a, e, i, o, u) and 8 consonants (f, h, m, n, p, r, t, v).

First, let's tackle vowel pronunciation. More emphasis is placed on pronouncing the vowels in Tahitian than in English.

a—pronounced as in *father*
e—usually pronounced as *a* in *may,* but sometimes as a shorter *eh* sound.
i—pronounced as *e* in *be*
o—pronounced as *o* in *go*
u—pronounced as *u* in *dude*

Each syllable in Tahitian ends with a vowel. Each vowel, when following another vowel, should be pronounced as a separate syllable. Frequently three vowels will be grouped together, in which case all three should be distinctly pronounced. An example is *Faaa* (the international airport)— pronounced "Fah-*ah*-ah."

In general, Tahitian words are accented on the next-to-last syllable, except when an apostrophe separates the final vowel from the vowel preceding it. Then both vowels are given equal emphasis. For example, *mataura'a* (meaning custom) is pronounced "mah-tah-oo-*rah*-ah."

Tahitian consonants are pronounced the same as in English.

Now for a few words and phrases:

Hello—*"Ia-ora'na"* (ee-ah-oh-*rah*-nah)
How are you?—*"Maita'i oe"*
(Mah-ee-*tah-ee oh*-ay)
I am fine—*"Maita'i vau"*
(mah-ee-*tah-ee vah*-oo)
Thank you very much—*"Mauruuru roa"*
(mah-oo-roo-oo-roo *roh*-ah)
Goodbye—*"Parahi"* (pah-*rah*-hee)
To your health—*"Manuia"* (Mah-noo-*ee*-ah)
Please repeat—*"Tapiti"* (Tah-*pee*-tee).

Now go back and practice saying Papeete (Pah-peh-*ay*-tay) a few more times, and it will all come naturally.

---

some revenue. On atolls like those of the Tuamotu Archipelago, mother-of-pearl and pearl-bearing oysters provide much of the income.

The country has a few small factories producing palm oil, soap, ice cream, corned beef, soft drinks, and beer. The tourist industry is also an important source of income.

A sports loving country

The Tahitian people have always loved sports. Ancient Polynesians were avid sports fans enjoying competitions in foot races, wrestling, boxing, javelin throwing, and archery. Today, other sports have been added. There are stadiums on Tahiti and some of the outer islands.

Soccer is the number one spectator sport. Enthusiastic fans gather in a number of locations every Saturday and Sunday during the season (January–July) to watch district teams compete, and the rivalry is keen. Occasional games are played against visiting international teams from New Caledonia, New Hebrides, New Zealand, France, and Chile.

Horse racing has also become a popular sport. From April through November, races take place on the first Sunday of each month at the track in Pirae (5 km/ 3 miles from Papeete). Many of the jockeys race Tahitian style—bareback, wearing only a brightly colored pareu and crown of flowers. Spectators come not only to watch the races and do a little betting, but also to catch up on local news and drink some beer.

Other spectator sports include archery, bicycle races, boxing, outrigger canoe and sailboat races, volleyball, and various track events. If you are in French Polynesia during the July Bastille Day celebrations, you'll see a number of festive events including outrigger canoe races, bicycle races, and javelin throwing contests.

Planning Your Trip

For some prospective visitors, this tropical paradise may seem far away. However, Papeete on the island of Tahiti lies just 6,612 km/4,109 miles southwest of Los Angeles; 5,311 km/3,300 miles northeast of Sydney, and 4,094 km/ 2,544 miles northeast of Auckland.

Papeete can be easily reached by direct or connecting flights of major Pacific international and regional airlines. Planes land at Faaa International Airport, just 5 km/3 miles southwest of Papeete. Transport to hotels is by taxi or Le Truck (the public bus).

(Continued on page 20)

Several passenger liners cruising the Pacific dock at the quay in central Papeete. A few also stop at Bora Bora and Moorea.

Getting around French Polynesia

Once you have arrived in Papeete, you can explore both Tahiti and the outer islands by rental vehicle or public transportation.

The larger tourist hotels on Tahiti are located at least 8 km/5 miles from downtown Papeete. Taxis are relatively expensive, and their rates double between 11 P.M. and 5 A.M. The cheapest—and most colorful—form of island transport on Tahiti is Le Truck. Passengers can ride any number of miles for just a small charge. (For more information on Le Truck, see page 25.)

Taxis are also available on the outer islands. However, they don't run after 5 P.M. unless previous arrangements have been made. Most hotels have airport shuttle service. Le Truck service is limited. For around-the-island exploration, your best mode of transportation on outer islands is a rental motorbike, jeep, or car.

Plane travel. From Tahiti, the fastest way to visit the outer islands is by air. Air Polynésie, the local airline, flies regularly from Papeete to Moorea, Huahine, Raiatea, Bora Bora, Maupiti, and the remote islands (the Marquesas, Australs, and Tuamotu Archipelago). Since fewer flights operate to the remote islands, it may be more difficult to get plane space.

Air Tahiti flies between Papeete and Moorea in an "air bridge" shuttle service daily between dawn and dusk (approximately 6 A.M. to 6 P.M.). Planes depart from Faaa International Airport every 5 to 15 minutes, or whenever there is a planeload of passengers. Reservations are not necessary.

Interisland boats. Daily interisland boat service links Papeete with Moorea. Copra boats and schooners provide regular scheduled service from Papeete to Huahine, Raiatea, and Bora Bora. These boats also make unscheduled trips to the Marquesas, the Austral Islands, and the Tuamotu Archipelago. Adventurous travelers not inclined to clock watching or creature comforts might enjoy a trip on a copra boat or schooner.

Rental vehicles. If you prefer to explore the islands on your own, you can rent a car or jeep, or you can hire a car and English-speaking driver. Rental cars are available on Tahiti and many of the outer islands. To rent a car you must be 21 years old and have a valid driver's license. Traffic keeps to the right.

Many hotels have bicycles available for use by hotel guests.

Taking a tour. Tour operators offer a variety of excursions to and around some of French Polynesia's many islands. For information on flightseeing tours, glass-bottomed boat rides, and bus tours, check with your hotel or a local travel agency.

Accommodations, Tahitian-style

French Polynesia's favorite form of resort hotel architecture is the *fare,* the Tahitian-style, thatch-roofed bungalow. Both modern and comfortable, these bungalows usually are situated in a tropical garden setting near the beach or overlooking a lagoon. All the resort hotels on Tahiti's outer islands have this type of architecture, and most are small—about 50 rooms.

On Tahiti you'll find larger, several-story resort hotels (some also offering bungalow accommodations) as well as a few small bungalow-type hotels. According to the French Polynesian building code, no hotel can be higher than the tallest coconut palm tree—a ruling that has produced some interesting architecture. The Hotel Tahara'a near Papeete could be termed a "downrise," since its seven stories stretch down the side of a steep cliff. The lobby is on the top floor.

Most of the hotels on Tahiti are within a few miles northeast or southwest of Papeete, though a few are located downtown on the waterfront. You'll also find comfortable resort hotels on Moorea, Bora Bora, Raiatea, Huahine, Rangiroa, and Manihi.

Less expensive, family-style accommodations with housekeeping facilities are also available on many of French Polynesia's main islands. In the more remote areas where there are no hotels, you can arrange to stay with a local family; these accommodations may be spartan.

For information on staying with a family or for a list of hotels and their rates, write to the Tahiti Tourist Development Board, B.P. 65, Papeete.

You will find it easier to get accommodations during the low seasons—April to June and September to November. During peak seasons, there is a hotel room shortage. It is especially important to book rooms on the outer islands ahead of time all year, since these islands have only a few hotels.

Dining and entertainment

Dining in French Polynesia can be an exciting experience. All the resort hotels have at least one restaurant, and you'll also find excellent dining at various French, Italian, Chinese, and Vietnamese restaurants outside the hotels, especially on Tahiti. You can savor French soufflé Grand Marnier, Chinese sweet and sour pork, or Tahitian *ei'a ota* (raw fish marinated in lime juice, and smothered with coconut milk, tomatoes, and hard-cooked egg). If you prefer less exotic food, you can also order American milk shakes and hamburgers.

For French dining on Tahiti, try Le Bélvèdere, high in the mountains overlooking the Papeete Harbor (complimentary hotel pickup); Moana Iti, on the Papeete waterfront just past Avenue Bruat; and Taiarapu, in Taravao 60 km/37 miles from Papeete. Waikiki on Rue le Boucher features popular Chinese specialties; La Saigonaise on Pont de l'Est offers Vietnamese dishes; and La Pizzeria on the Papeete waterfront on Boulevard Pomaré has excellent Italian pizzas.

Desiring a brief respite while exploring Papeete, you can stop at a *salon de thé* for a reviving cup of coffee or tea and a pastry. These casual snack shops open around 6 A.M. and close about 6 P.M. If you're hungry, try one of their minipizzas, quiches, or pâtés. Favorite *salons de thé* include Hilaire on Rue General de Gaulle; Le Pam Pam on Place Notre-Dame; and La Marquisienne on Rue Colette.

Resort hotels on Tahiti and the outer islands feature barbecues or buffet-style dinners with Tahitian specialties at least once a week.

The tamaaraa. One of the best ways to sample Tahitian foods and enjoy Tahitian entertainment is to attend a *tamaaraa*—a Tahitian feast. The traditional Polynesian meal is followed by Tahitian music and group dances. Tamaaraas are offered at the Hotel Aimeo and Bali Hai on Moorea. A package trip from Papeete to the feast includes transportation and sightseeing.

Much of the food for the tamaaraa is cooked in an *ahimaa*—an underground earthen oven. The menu usually consists of pig, fish, breadfruit, and bananas. To this basic list may be added chicken, fish, taro, fresh fruit, and Tahitian *poe*. Poe is a dessert made of papayas, taros, pumpkin, manioc, or bananas with sugar, vanilla, and coconut milk.

Following this lavish meal—traditionally eaten with the fingers—guests are entertained by grass-skirted Tahitians who perform harmonious songs and pulsating dances. Don't be surprised if you are invited to learn the hip-jolting *tamure*.

Other entertainment. Many hotels schedule Tahitian entertainment several times a week and music for dancing nightly. Papeete has several discotheques.

Shopping in Papeete

Visitors discover some of the best shopping opportunities in Papeete. Small shops are scattered around

FESTIVAL TIME

Perhaps the best known of French Polynesia's enthusiastic celebrations is Bastille Day. However, the Tahitians' love for revelry is not restricted to this celebration. You can see numerous other festivals throughout the year.

January—April

New Year's Day. On January 1, Tahitians all over the country gather with their families and friends for singing, dancing, and guitar playing.

Chinese New Year. French Polynesia's Chinese community celebrates this traditional holiday in late January or early February with legendary dances and fireworks.

Coronation Ball. In March, Tane Tahitian—handsomest Tahitian of the Year—is selected in Papeete. A ball follows.

Miss Bora Bora Contest. A contest winner is selected and crowned at the end of April on Bora Bora.

May—August

Annual "Maire" Day. Exhibitions of ferns are on display in Papeete in May. There is a ball at day's end.

Miss Moorea Contest. A winner is selected and crowned on Moorea in early June.

Miss Tahiti and Miss Tiurai Contest. In early July, Tahiti's prettiest girl of the year—who will represent the country of French Polynesia in all international beauty events—is selected. Also chosen is her local representative, who reigns over the Bastille Day celebrations.

Bastille Day. This celebration of France's independence officially lasts one week beginning July 14. However, the merriment of this event—called La Fête by the French and Tiurai by the Polynesians—sometimes continues for another 2 weeks.

There's a carnival atmosphere day and night with games, contests, and dances at the fair grounds near Papeete. You'll see bareback horse races, fruit carrier races, javelin throwing contests, canoe races, and singing and dancing contests. Celebrations are also held on Raiatea, Tahaa, Huahine, and Bora Bora.

Night of the Guitar and Ute. In August, local musicians compete in playing guitar French Polynesian-style and in performing the *Ute* (satirical improvisation songs) on Tahiti.

September—December

Te Vahine e te Tiare (the Woman and the Flower). Tahitian women dress up for this floral theme ball at the beginning of September on Tahiti.

Old Tahiti Ball. Near the beginning of October, participants dress up in costumes of a bygone era to attend this ball on Tahiti.

All Saints Day. Cemeteries (particularly in Papeete, Faaa, Arue, and Punaauia on Tahiti) are illuminated with candles on November 1. There are religious services and hymn singing.

Thousand Flowers Contest and Pareu Day. Prizes are given for exhibitions of French Polynesian flowers at a ball in November in Papeete. Attendees wear pareu dress.

Tiare Tahiti (National Flower) Day. Tiare flowers are distributed to everyone on the streets of Papeete, in the hotels, and on departing planes. Arriving passengers receive a *hei* (Tahitian wreath). The Tiare Ball is held in the evening.

New Year's Eve. The Papeete waterfront is illuminated on December 31. Competitors run through the Papeete streets in the "Cross de la Saint Sylvestre."

the town, and you'll find several shopping centers as well as Marché Papeete, the municipal market.

One of the most attractive local handicrafts is pareo cloth, a brightly colored, handblocked fabric. Tahitians use a variety of pareo fabrics to make curtains, bedspreads, shirts, dresses, bathing suits, scarfs, and ties. If you can't find what you want ready-made, a tailor or dressmaker can quickly make it for you. (Note: Some pareo cloth is imported from Japan.)

Other handmade Tahitian items include shell garlands, costume jewelry made of black and gold lip-pearl shells, woven hats and Marquesan woodcarvings.

You can shop Monday through Friday from 7:30 to 11:30 A.M. and 2 to 5 P.M., and Saturdays from 7:30 to 11 A.M.

Recreational opportunities

Not surprisingly, recreational activities focus on the water. Inviting warm, tropical lagoons and bays surround islands trimmed by beautiful sand beaches. Resort hotels cater to water sports; equipment is available for fishing, snorkeling, scuba diving, sailing, canoeing, water-skiing, and glass-bottomed boat touring. In addition, several local companies have equipped fishing boats, diving boats, and sailboats available for charter for day trips as well as for longer excursions.

Fishing. Deep-sea fishing in French Polynesia gained worldwide prominence in the 1930s when Zane Grey hooked record and near-record game fish in the area. The sport remains popular today. Big game fish you can catch include black marlin, sailfish, mahi mahi (dolphin), wahoo, ocean bonito, barracuda, red snapper, and red bass. Peak season is November through April.

Fully equipped deep-sea fishing boats are available for hire in Tahiti, Moorea, Raiatea, Bora Bora, Rangiroa, Huahine, and Manihi. The Haura Club in Papeete, an affiliate of the International Game Fish Association, can provide further fishing information; write them at P.O. Box 582, Papeete. Visiting fishermen may use the club's scales and the service of the weighmaster. The club is located on Route de l'Ouest.

Trout fishermen can fish in mountain streams for Tahitian trout, called *nato*. You also might want to seek out a Tahitian for a lesson in night lagoon fishing.

Scuba diving. Warm waters, fantastic coral formations, and an abundance of colorful tropical fish lure many divers to French Polynesia. Good diving locations exist off Tahiti, Huahine, Raiatea, Bora Bora, and Rangiroa. Although diving is possible all year, conditions are best between June and September.

Many resort hotels have diving equipment and boats available for hire. You can also rent diving equipment through two sports operators in Papeete—Marine Corail at Fare Ute and Tahiti Actinautic at the Tahiti Beachcomber.

Swimming and surfing. In addition to your hotel pool, you can swim in quiet lagoons or beautiful mountain rivers and pools. Papeete's municipal, olympic-size, swimming pool is just a 10-minute walk south from town center along the waterfront.

Surfing is as popular a sport today as it was when Captain Cook landed in the 1700s. Good surfing spots on Tahiti include the north coast near Arue, the beaches in the Papenoo district, and the west coast around Paea and Papara.

Hiking. Hikers learn early that the islands' mountainous interiors are rugged (however beguiling they may appear) and warrant the help of a guide. Inquire at your hotel for guide information. For details on mountain climbing, write Club Alpin, B.P. 65, Papeete.

Horseback riding. Rent a horse to journey into the island valleys or to gallop along a deserted beach. There are stables near Papeete at the race course in Pirae. Horses are also available for hire on Moorea outside the Club-Mediterranée and near the Hotel Moorea Lagoon, and in the Marquesas.

Tennis. On Tahiti, tennis players will find courts at the Fautaua Stadium, 2 km/1 mile northeast of Papeete, and at the Hotel Tahara'a, Holiday Inn, Maeva Beach Hotel, and Tahiti Beachcomber Hotel. On Moorea, there are tennis courts at the Club-Mediterranée, Hotel Bali Hai Moorea, and Hotel Moorea Village. Hotel Bali Hai on Huahine also has tennis courts. Rackets are sometimes hard to come by, so it's best to bring your own.

Golf. Atimaono Golf Course, 45 km/28 miles southeast of Papeete, is the country's only 18-hole course. Nine-hole pitch-and-putt courses are located on Tahiti at the Hotel Tahara'a and Tahiti Beachcomber.

Tahiti, the Main Island

Tahiti—French Polynesia's principal island—covers 1,041 square km/402 square miles. Figure 8 in shape, it somewhat resembles a floating sea turtle with a protruding head. The larger part is called Tahiti-Nui, the smaller section Tahiti-Iti.

About 70 percent of French Polynesia's 136,000 people live on Tahiti, either in Papeete (the country's capital) or along the island's narrow coastal shelf. The interior of the island—practically uninhabited—is an area of jagged peaks and deep gorges. Tahiti's highest peak is 2,231-meter/7,321-foot Mount Orohena.

A fringe of foam marks the coral reef encircling the island. The reef protects the lagoons and beaches; it strikes a dividing line between the indigo of the deep ocean and the lighter shades of blue and green in the lagoons. Occasional breaks in the reef allow boats and ships to sail through.

Tahiti is the visitor's main gateway to French Polynesia. Here, you experience the bustle of Papeete with its numerous restaurants and comfortable hotels. You can visit a colorful public market or ride into the countryside to see a *marae* (ancient temple) or a museum devoted to Gauguin. If you prefer, you can spend the day lying on a beach or beside your pool.

Getting acquainted with Papeete

Papeete, French Polynesia's capital and only city (56,000 population), lies on a busy, crescent-shaped harbor on the northwest coast of Tahiti. Arriving in

Bora Bora woman *weaves mat of dried palm fronds. Local shops display array of woven hats, mats, baskets.*

Sleepy *South Seas atmosphere pervades Uturoa, largest town on Raiatea. Lush greenery rises behind rusting corrugated iron roofs.*

the country by either air or sea, you will stop first in Papeete.

The town's business district—a conglomeration of modern concrete structures and brightly painted wooden buildings—rambles along the waterfront in a several block strip. Narrow streets dotted with iron-roofed houses drift back from this central district. Where these side streets end, lush green foothills rise toward jagged mountain peaks half hidden in the clouds.

Like many towns suffering growing pains, Papeete has a traffic problem. It seems as though nearly everyone in Papeete owns either a car, motorbike, motorscooter, or truck. During morning and evening rush hours, they converge on Papeete's narrow streets, creating one noisy traffic jam.

You'll see Papeete best on foot, beginning at the waterfront. Most town activity centers on or near the street rimming the harbor. This street, Boulevard Pomaré, is really a series of *quais*, starting on the southwest with Quai de l'Uranie, merging into Quai Bir-Hakeim, then Quai du Commerce, and lastly Quai Gallieni.

Papeete's waterfront has changed in recent years. The rim road, once a hodgepodge of old shacks and souvenir shops, is now a wide and attractive boulevard, divided by a grass strip and edged with sidewalks. Where old warehouses once stood, handsome new buildings have been built. The once-celebrated Quinn's—most famous bar in the South Pacific—has been replaced by a new shopping center. The area known as "Quinn's block" disappeared in December 1975, when a fire destroyed most of it.

An important part of waterfront color still remains. On Quai Bir-Hakeim, you can stroll by the yachts that tie up at the edge of the sidewalk. On their sterns you see markers reading like a roll call of world ports. Nearby, large passenger liners from all over the world still dock at the wharf on Quai du Commerce.

On the land side of the quais, people gather at sidewalk cafes to sip coffee and observe the passing scene. Supermarkets, department stores, Chinese shops, and shipping and airline offices are sandwiched between these eating establishments. You'll find more stores a block or two inland from the quais.

As you stroll along the waterfront, stop at the Tahiti Tourist Development Board in the Fare Manihini building on Quai du Commerce (near the ships' passenger terminal), or the Syndicat d'Initiative in Vaima Shopping Center to pick up maps and brochures on sightseeing, shopping, hotels, and restaurants.

Marché Papeete. Just a block inland from Boulevard Pomaré on Rue Halles (between Rue Cardella and Rue du 22 Sept. 1914), you'll find Papeete's open-air, roofed municipal market. Visit this colorful marketplace early. Activity begins around 5 A.M. daily when the first busloads of Le Truck passengers arrive. Soon the market is alive with a babble of voices, a blending of Tahitian and French. Items for sale include neatly strung colorful fish; pyramids of papayas, watermelons, and mangoes; fragrant rows of flowers; baskets of tomatoes, onions, and long skinny cucumbers; buckets of clams and oysters; and rows of woven hats, baskets, mats, and shell jewelry.

One of the best times to visit the market is Sunday —the principal market day when many of Papeete's

housewives do their week's shopping. Tahitians come to town from villages all around the island to sell their products. They travel to Papeete on Saturday, sleep at the market overnight, and get up at dawn Sunday to sell their wares. The market closes at 8:30 A.M. on Sundays. During the week it stays open until 5:30 P.M.

Government Center. The French Polynesian government buildings are located a block off Boulevard Pomaré along Avenuc Bruat. Flanking the avenue are the executive and judicial offices of the Territory; to the east on a parklike expanse is the Territorial Assembly building. Behind the government buildings, you'll see the High Commissioner's residence with its interesting five-gabled roof.

Glass-bottomed boat ride. One way to see underwater life without getting wet is to take a tour of the lagoon in a glass-bottomed boat. The daily 2-hour trip departs from the Maeva Beach and Tahiti Beachcomber hotels.

Excursions to other islands. From Papeete you can take a 20-minute flight to the primitive atoll of Tetiaroa—the island owned by Marlon Brando. (In ancient times it was the summer residence of Tahitian royalty.) On a day tour, you will enjoy a picnic lunch, cruise in the lagoon, and have time for swimming and snorkeling. Overnight accommodations are also available.

Excursions to Moorea, Bora Bora, Huahine, Raiatea, Manihi, and Rangiroa are also available out of Papeete.

Lagoonarium de Tahiti. About 13 km/8 miles southwest of Papeete, near the Maeva Beach and Beachcomber hotels, you can see more of French Polynesia's underwater life at the Lagoonarium de Tahiti. This underwater observatory provides viewing windows where visitors see coral gardens and reef and ocean fish. The Lagoonarium's restaurant features regular performances by a Tahitian dance troupe who arrive by double-hulled canoe.

Musée de Tahiti. Near the Lagoonarium, you'll find the Museum of Tahiti and the Islands. Formerly located in downtown Papeete, this museum now occupies the site of a former *marae* (Tahitian temple) in Punaruu, 16 km/10 miles southwest of town. Operated by the Societé des Etudes Océaniennes (Society of Oceanic Studies), the museum contains many archeological and ethnological artifacts of Polynesia as well as a display of the area's flora and fauna. The museum library features historical information about missionary times in Polynesia.

Where to stay. In the Papeete area you'll find comfortable hotels both downtown and along the beachfront within an 8-km/5-mile radius northeast and southwest of town.

Downtown hotels include the Hotel KonTiki, Hotel Mahina-Tea, Hotel Tahiti, Holiday Inn of Papeete, and the Royal Papeete Hotel. Northeast of town you can stay at several beach resorts—Hotel Royal Tahitien, Princesse Heiata, and Hotel Tahara'a. Beach resorts southwest of Papeete include the Tahiti Beachcomber, Te Puna Bel Air, and Maeva Beach Hotel.

After the sun goes down. Nearly every hotel in the Papeete area has a nightclub with nightly dancing. Tahitian entertainment is presented at least once a week by many of the larger hotels.

The Royal Papeete, Tahiti Beachcomber, and Maeva

LE TRUCK
It's Fun and Inexpensive

You might glimpse Le Truck for the first time as it bounces along the main road past your Tahiti hotel. Or perhaps you'll notice one parked in front of Papeete's municipal market. These brightly painted, open-sided, covered buses—the islanders' basic form of public transportation—can also be the answer to your transportation needs on Tahiti. You'll find a few Les Trucks on some of the outer islands. They offer an inexpensive way of touring.

To catch Le Truck, flag it down on the main road in front of your hotel. On Tahiti, you can board one at Papeete's municipal market, the start and finish for Le Truck service on the main island. Make sure the vehicle is heading in the direction you want to go.

Your fellow passengers include young Tahitian girls in brightly colored dresses, wide-eyed school children, housewives with baskets of vegetables and squawking chickens, and an occasional fisherman who ties his strings of fish on the ladder at the back. Teetering atop your vehicle in the baggage rack might be a dented milk can, a wash tub, and baskets of produce.

On your trip you'll soon learn that there is no set schedule. Your bus might detour down a narrow road to drop someone off in front of his house. Perhaps a guitar-playing youth will strike a chord, and soon everyone in the bus will be singing. Or if everyone becomes thirsty, the trip will be interrupted for a refreshment stop.

You experience Tahitian life first-hand on Le Truck. It's fun to try—even if you only have time for a short trip.

Beach hotels all have discos. Papeete travel agencies offer after-dark tours stopping at some of the town's lively nightspots.

Touring Tahiti

To discover Tahiti's quiet, tropical charms, take a trip along the 116-km/72-mile Route de Ceinture—the Belt Road. This paved route circles Tahiti-Nui, the larger portion of the island. Side roads branch off Belt Road to wind down the north and south coasts of Tahiti-Iti, the smaller portion of the island.

Driving along the coast, you'll pass black sand beaches, outcrops of lava rock, mountains that soar into the clouds, and deep valleys with plummeting waterfalls. Of note are the three waterfalls in Faaruumai Valley (just south of Arahoho Blowhole); the Cascade de Vaiharuru on the Faatautia River (south of Hitiaa); and Vaipahi Falls (west of Papeari).

Every few kilometers, you see a native village with

churches, a school, and charming houses painted in bright pastel colors. You'll be constantly reminded of Tahiti's lush, flowering beauty. Flamboyant trees display limbs laden with red color; gigantic blooms in reds, oranges, and pinks decorate towering hibiscus; and pink cassia send down showers of pale pink petals. Malay apple trees mix with banana, papaya, avocado, and breadfruit trees.

If you leave no later than 9 A.M. from Papeete, you can make the journey around Tahiti-Nui in a day. This will give you plenty of time to stop at points of interest, go for a swim, and have a picnic or long lunch at a pleasant restaurant such as the Restaurant Musée Gauguin near the museum.

If you wish to see some of Tahiti-Iti as well, try to allow at least 2 days for a leisurely trip. You can stay in a bungalow at Te Anuanua Hotel in Pueu, 66 km/ 41 miles from Papeete on Tahiti-Iti's north coast.

You can make the trip independently by rental car or motorbike, or by Le Truck. Guided tours travel around Tahiti-Nui daily from Papeete, or you can hire a car and guide-driver for a personal tour.

Try to avoid making your island trip on Sunday. On this day, many local inhabitants take to the road in sports cars, minibuses, Les Trucks, motorbikes, and bicycles.

Following the island road eastward from Papeete, you'll pass the following points of interest.

Tomb of Pomare V. Tahiti's last monarch is buried at Arue, 4 km/2 miles from Papeete. The tomb, constructed of coral from a nearby lagoon, is topped by an unusually shaped urn similar to a Grecian funeral urn. Some people feel that it resembles a bottle of Benedictine, one of the king's favorite alcoholic beverages.

Point Venus. A lighthouse now stands on the headland where Lieutenant James Cook and his expedition observed the transit of Venus in 1769. Nearby, a monument honors the 18th century European explorers who anchored in Matavai Bay and came ashore here— Samuel Wallis, Louis Antoine de Bougainville, and James Cook. In the Musée de la Découverte (Museum of Discovery), you'll see lifelike wax figures of the three explorers and the Tahitian monarchs who greeted them. The museum also houses a fine collection of artifacts, engravings, maps, and other memorabilia.

Point Venus is about 13 km/8 miles from Papeete. A sign marks the side road leading to the point.

Blowhole of Arahoho. About 22 km/14 miles northeast of Papeete, you'll come to this geologic phenomenon. Ocean waves surge through a natural formation in basalt rock, sending up jets of water that sometimes splash onto the road.

Monument to Bougainville. In Hitiaa, 39 km/24 miles from Papeete, a bronze sign marks the bay where Louis Antoine de Bougainville first anchored upon his arrival in 1768.

Side trip to Tahiti-Iti. In the Taravao area, you can branch off Belt Road for a trip to villages along Tahiti-Iti's north or south coast. Roads wind along each coast for about 18 km/11 miles. From the north coast route, a side road leads to a plateau view point over Tahiti-Nui.

Gauguin Museum. Back on the Belt Road near Papeari, you come to Musée Gauguin. Set in a spacious garden,

Tahitian youths *prepare vegetables for a* tamaaraa, *a traditional feast. Guests eat meal with fingers, then watch native entertainers perform traditional songs and dances.*

this museum is a series of rooms open to the tropical breezes. Only two original Gauguin paintings hang in this museum—a memorial to Gauguin and his work. Most of his paintings now belong to art collectors around the world.

Instead, the museum recreates the triumphs and tragedy of this great artist through the use of photographs, maps, reproductions, and other graphic devices. The museum is open daily from 9 A.M. to 5 P.M.

Gauguin arrived in Tahiti in 1891 at the age of 42. For 2 years he lived in Mataiea on Tahiti-Nui's southern coast. After a sojourn in France, he returned to French

Polynesia, settling first at Punaauia on Tahiti's west coast, then moving to Atuona in the Marquesas where he spent the last 8 years of his life. He died at the age of 54, penniless and unrecognized. Today much of the world knows Gauguin's work. He used bold colors to vividly depict the Tahitian people and their land.

Botanical Garden. Adjacent to the museum is a botanical preserve created by American botanist Harrison Smith. In this garden, you'll discover an impressive collection of trees, shrubs, and flowers representing nonindigenous tropical vegetation of French Polynesia. Meandering paths lead past towering trees, stands of bamboo, and lovely flower beds. A couple of tortoises in the garden love to have their heads scratched.

The gardens are open daily from 10 A.M. to 5 P.M.

Maraes. You'll find two *maraes* on Tahiti-Nui's west coast southwest of Papeete—Marae Mahaiatea (35 km/ 22 miles from town) and Marae Arahurahu in Paea (19 km/12 miles from Papeete). During ancient times *maraes* were Polynesian open-air temples of worship. Constructed of several tiers of stone or coral, the temple stood at one end of a rectangular courtyard.

Marae Arahurahu has been restored by the Society of Oceanic Studies. Marae Mahaiatea lies in ruin.

Maraa cave. The largest cave on the island is located on the coast between Marae Mahaiatea and Marae Arahurahu. Water drips constantly from the ceiling of the fern-covered grotto into a dark, cold lake. A short trail (marked by a sign) leads from the road to the mouth of the cave.

Exploring the Outer Islands

To discover the Polynesia of your dreams, you must travel to the outer islands. Here you'll see rugged, emerald green mountains towering above unbelievably clear lagoons; fishermen paddling outrigger canoes and pareu-wrapped women strolling along the road (scenes reminiscent of the Polynesia depicted by Melville, Gauguin, and Michener).

Luring travelers to the outer islands are beautiful beaches, lagoons ideal for snorkeling, and a pace of life that needs no clock.

Moorea, for a slower pace

As you gaze across the bay from Papeete at sunset, the jagged peaks of Moorea—silhouetted against a brilliant red-orange sky—will beckon you. Heed the call and take a short 17-km/11-mile trip to Moorea's shores. You'll be rewarded with tranquil beauty and a pace of life much slower than Papeete's.

By air, it's only a 7-minute flight from Papeete's Faaa Airport to Moorea's airport near Temae, on the northeast side of the island. Numerous flights operate daily during daylight hours. From Papeete's waterfront, launches make the 1½ hour trip daily to Moorea. (To enjoy the scenery, take the boat trip at least one way.

Morning—before the seas get rough—is the best time for boat trips.)

If you prefer, you can travel to Moorea with a group. Local operators offer 1 to 3-day trips from Papeete. (Day tours to Moorea go one way by air, the other by boat.)

Island tour. One of the best ways to see tiny Moorea —only 220 square km/85 square miles—is to travel along the coast road that circles the island. Most of Moorea's 6,000 people live in villages along the narrow coastal shelf. Behind their tin-roofed, wooden houses, mountains covered in lush vegetation soar skyward.

On this route, you'll catch glimpses of Polynesian life—children fishing from a bridge, women in bright-colored pareus riding bicycles or motorscooters, and skinny loaves of French bread sticking out of wooden mailboxes. In the villages, fascinating Chinese stores carry everything from pareo prints to fresh fruits, canned vegetables, plastic dishpans, and bicycle tires.

If you don't have the time for the entire 53-km/33-mile circuit, take a shorter journey along the north coast. Here you'll find a good sampling of interesting villages, spectacular volcanic peaks, beautiful beaches, and two fiordlike bays—Opunohu and Cook's.

In Papetoai, on the north coast near the western shore of Opunohu Bay, you'll discover an octagonal church. Built in 1829 by missionaries, it is the oldest European structure still being used in the South Pacific. You also may want to see the Catholic church in Paopao on Cook's Bay; an impressive mural by Pierre Heyman decorates the area above the altar.

At the head of Opunohu Bay, a winding side road leaves the shore route and climbs into the hills. In Opunohu Valley, you see several *maraes* (ancient Polynesian temples) that have been restored under the guidance of archeologists from Hawaii's Bishop Museum. From the Belvédère lookout point, you'll see both Opunohu and Cook's bays cutting into the north coast.

You can travel the island by rental car, jeep, motorbike, or bicycle. Bus tours and lagoon excursions are available. Even if you're traveling with a group, spend a little time exploring at your own leisurely pace. Relax and enjoy a beach picnic or visit one of the local villages.

The island also has taxis, irregular Le Truck service, and limited airport shuttle service from hotels.

Where to stay. Most of Moorea's hotels—built as thatch-roofed bungalows—are located facing the beach along the island's west and north coasts. You can choose from Club-Mediterranée Moorea, Hibiscus Hotel, Les Tipaniers, Moorea Village, and Captain Cook Beach Hotel (all on the west coast); Moorea Lagoon (on the peninsula between Opunohu and Cook's bays); Aimeo Hotel (on Cook's Bay); Hotel Bali Hai Moorea (just east of Cook's Bay); and Kia Ora Moorea (on the east coast).

After the sun goes down. Several of Moorea's hotels feature Tahitian music nightly. The Hotel Aimeo and Bali Hai hold *tamaaraas* (Tahitian feasts and dancing) on a weekly basis. Among interesting nightspots on the island are the Kia Ora's disco on a converted copra schooner and the One Chicken Inn in Paopao. At the inn, you experience a real raucous Polynesian Saturday night party with the locals.

All the major hotels have restaurants. In addition, visitors enjoy the Manava on Cook's Bay, Chez Michou near the Bali Hai, and Temae at the airport.

Bora Bora, the "most beautiful" island

Perhaps the most acclaimed of the French Polynesian isles, Bora Bora has long been known for its beauty. For some travelers, including writer James Michener, it's the most beautiful island in the world.

To find out if you agree, go and see for yourself. From Papeete, nonstop daily flights take only 50 minutes. (Schooners sail weekly from Papeete to Bora Bora.)

A relatively small island, Bora Bora is home to about 2,600 people. Its topography is dominated by craggy mountains that loom dramatically above the turquoise green lagoon surrounding the island. One of the loveliest lagoons in French Polynesia, it is nearly enclosed by a barrier reef dotted with tiny *motus* (islets). Bora Bora's airstrip sits on one of these islets—Motu Mute. A launch ferries passengers across the shimmering lagoon to the main island.

You can make the round trip to Bora Bora from Papeete in one day if you don't mind crowding in several hours of travel. Or you can relax on Bora Bora for several days, enjoying the island's beauty and leisurely pace. Local operators offer 1, 2, and 3-day tours from Papeete.

Touring the island. A 27-km/17-mile unpaved road circles the island. You can take a bus tour or make the trip by taxi, rental car or jeep, motorbike, or bicycle. There's also irregular Le Truck service.

Traveling along the lagoon's edge, you'll pass groves of coconut palms and tiny villages hugging the shoreline. You might also see the ruins of *maraes*—the island has about 40 of them.

Vaitape contains the tomb of French navigator Alain Gerbault, who circled the globe alone in a small boat in the 1920s. Vaitape is the administrative center for the island.

After you've toured the island, you can take an excursion in an outrigger canoe, picnic on a motu, join a round-the-island boat trip, or view the lagoon's coral gardens and fascinating marine life from a glass-bottomed boat. Your hotel can provide information on these activities.

Where to stay. Five Bora Bora hotels offer guests comfortable bungalow-style accommodations—Hotel Bora Bora, Club-Mediterranée-Noa Noa (an extension of Club Med Moorea), Hotel Marara, Oa Oa Yacht Sport Hotel, and Altex Bungalows.

Several hotels feature Tahitian music on a regular basis.

Huahine, two islands at high tide

Growing in popularity as a tourist destination is Huahine, 177 km/110 miles northwest of Papeete. Fourteen 50-minute flights weekly link Papeete with the Huahine airport on the western edge of Lake Fauna Nui. A schooner also travels weekly to Huahine.

At high water, Huahine is really two islands— Huahine-Nui in the north and Huahine-Iti in the south —divided by a strait connected by a bridge. Each island has a mountain—710 meter/2,331 foot Mount Turi on Huahine-Nui and 456 meter/1,495 foot Mount Moufene on Huahine-Iti. A barrier reef protects the island sections.

Nor far from the airport on Huahine-Nui, you can visit Maeva Village, built at a point where Lake Fauna Nui joins a lagoon. Maeva's houses sit on stilts over the water. A century-old system of fish traps is still used near the village. (The island's people make their living by fishing and farming.)

You'll find numerous ancient maraes in the Lake Fauna Nui district. At one time, all district chiefs lived side by side in this area and worshiped in their own maraes. Recent archeological discoveries indicate that Huahine has been populated for at least 1,100 years.

The island's principal town is Fare on Huahine-Nui's west coast. Reminiscent of a frontier town, Fare has aging colonial-style wooden buildings lining its tree-shaded waterfront street.

The unpaved main road connects villages on Huahine-Nui with villages on Huahine-Iti. Island transportation for visitors includes rental cars, rental bicycles, and taxis. Le Truck service is irregular. Visitors can also join island tours by taxi and bus or go sightseeing in a native canoe or motorboat.

The Hotel Bali Hai Huahine, just a 5-minute walk from Fare, is the island's only tourist-type hotel. You can also stay in one of several small hotels with modest rooms, or arrange to stay with a local family.

Raiatea, the second largest island

Second only in size to Tahiti (288 square km/179 square miles), the large island of Raiatea lies 220 km/137 miles northwest of Papeete. About 9,900 people live on Raiatea. To the north, the neighboring island of Tahaa shares a barrier reef and lagoon with Raiatea. A narrow 3-km/2-mile-wide channel separates the two islands.

Raiatea is thought to be the site of one of the first ancient Polynesian settlements. From here Polynesians sailed northward to populate the Hawaiian Islands and southwest to form the Maori colonies in New Zealand.

From Papeete, planes fly daily to the Raiatea airport near Uturoa. The flight takes about 45 minutes. Schooners sail weekly from Papeete to Raiatea. To reach Tahaa, you must travel from Raiatea by boat.

On Raiatea you can explore by car, bicycle, or taxi. Local bus and boat tours are available, and there is some Le Truck service. A road follows the shoreline from Opoa on the east coast northward around the island to Fetuna on the southwest coast.

Uturoa. This main village sits on Raiatea's northeast tip. With a population of 2,500, Uturoa is French Polynesia's second largest town. Several interesting Chinese stores on the main street are crowded with merchandise —pareo prints, handmade baskets, native carvings, and island necessities such as groceries and motorbikes.

If you come to Uturoa on Wednesday, Friday, or Sunday, be sure to visit the lively public market near the pier. People from Raiatea and Tahaa travel by boat and Le Truck to sell their produce. Fish, fruit, vegetables, pigs, ducks, and chickens are all for sale in the marketplace.

Opoa. On the east coast about 30 km/19 miles south of Uturoa, Opoa was the religious center of the Society Islands in pre-European times. On a point of land east of the village, you'll find Marae Taputapuatea. Restored in 1968, this temple was once one of the most important maraes in the South Pacific—the ancient seat of knowledge and religion.

Faaroa River. Be sure to take a boat tour up the Faaroa River while you're on Raiatea. (The river is 13 km/8 miles northwest of Opoa.) From this river, the original Maoris sailed for New Zealand. The ancient homeland of the Maoris is now overgrown with tropical vegetation.

Trip to Tahaa. Tours to Tahaa depart from the Hotel Bali Hai Raiatea, located southeast of Uturoa. The boat trip to the island takes about 40 minutes. The first stop is Tiva, a small village, where passengers visit Chief Tavana's home. The chief has a shark aquarium, a turtle pool, and a museum of sea relics.

Firewalking. The ceremony of firewalking, *Umu-ti,* on Raiatea dates from early times. Today, it is performed on the grounds of the Hotel Bali Hai Raiatea. Villagers from Apoiti re-create the ancient rite of walking barefoot across white-hot stones.

Where to stay. Raiatea's only tourist-style hotel is the Bali Hai Raiatea, less than 2 km/1 mile southeast of Uturoa. There are also several small hotels with modest rooms on Raiatea and Tahaa.

Remote Polynesian retreats

Several islands in the more remote areas of French Polynesia—such as the Tuamotus, Marquesas, Australs, and Gambiers—can be reached by plane or boat from Papeete. However, most of these islands remain basically undeveloped without hotels. Accommodations can be arranged with island families.

Two islands in the Tuamotu group, northeast of Tahiti, offer tourist hotels—the Kia Ora Village on Rangiroa and Kaina Village on Manihi. Both of these islands are atolls—thin strips of sand dotted with coconut palms. On one side of the narrow beach is the pounding surf, on the other a quiet lagoon. These islands offer peaceful surroundings, miles of beach, and your choice of water activities.

Know Before You Go

The following practical information can help you plan your trip to French Polynesia.

Entry/exit procedures. For stays of less than 30 days, you will need a valid passport and an onward travel ticket. Longer stays require a visa.

Visitors coming from Fiji and the Samoas must have all baggage (except hand luggage) fumigated upon arrival. Taking about 2 hours, the fumigation is required to protect French Polynesia's coconut trees from pests found on other South Pacific islands. Visitors may wish to carry clothing and toilet articles for the first night's stay in hand luggage.

All visitors need smallpox vaccinations. Travelers arriving from an infected area need vaccinations against yellow fever and cholera.

There is no airport departure tax.

Customs. In addition to personal belongings, you can bring in 400 cigarettes, 50 cigars, or 500 grams/1 pound of tobacco; and 1 litre/quart of spirits. Amateur photographers are allowed 2 still cameras with 10 rolls of unexposed film, and 1 movie camera with 10 rolls of unexposed film.

Currency. The French Pacific Franc (CPF or FR). The recent exchange rate is approximately CPF 71.43 = US $1; CFP 62.11 = Australian $1; and CFP 65.53 = New Zealand $1.

Tipping. Tipping is not customary in French Polynesia. It is against the Tahitian idea of hospitality.

Time. French Polynesia is GMT (Greenwich mean time) −10. For example, when it is 1 P.M. Saturday in Papeete, it is 3 P.M. Saturday in San Francisco; 11 A.M. Sunday in Auckland; and 9 A.M. Sunday in Sydney.

Weather and what to wear. French Polynesia has a tropical climate cooled by trade winds. Travelers who visit during the cool, dry season from March through November, enjoy temperatures averaging 23°C/73°F. During the warm moist season— December through February—you can expect 13 to 18 days of rain a month, and temperatures can reach 30°C/86°F.

Casual lightweight attire is the key to proper dress in French Polynesia. Even in the evening, men can wear just slacks and a shirt. Ties and jackets aren't required in restaurants. Women often wear casual, long dresses to dinner.

Other items you'll want to pack include an umbrella or plastic raincoat, a sweater or jacket for cool evenings, sunglasses and suntan lotion, mosquito repellent, and tennis shoes or plastic beach shoes for coral reef exploring.

For more information. For further information on French Polynesia, write to the Tahiti Tourist Board, B.P. 65, Papeete. Transportation Consultants International represents the Tahiti Tourist Board in North America; contact them at 700 South Flower St., Suite 1704, Los Angeles, CA 90017.

Residents of Australia and New Zealand can write the Tahiti Tourist Board at 23 Hunter Street, Currency House, Sydney, Australia. In Great Britain contact the French Government Tourist Office in London.

THE SAMOAS

The Samoas—American and Western—are considered the heart of Polynesia. Early Polynesians sailed from here to populate other Pacific islands.

Today, these two politically separate countries share the world's largest full-blooded Polynesian population and a strong belief in tradition. After a short time in the Samoas, you'll learn how much *fa'a Samoa*—the Samoan Way—is valued.

Much of the charm of the Samoas lies in the simple village life and the friendly people. Passing thatch-roofed *fales* (open-air dwellings), you see village chiefs sitting cross-legged on woven grass mats, solving problems unhurriedly and with great dignity. The women sit placidly stringing shells on fishline for *ulasisis* (shell leis) and weaving baskets made of pandanus leaves. Smiling children come running to meet you, and villagers welcome you with the cheery Samoan greeting, "*Talofa*." Hospitality is an important part of fa'a Samoa.

In addition to the friendly Samoan people, you'll find a striking landscape—soaring volcanic mountain peaks, rugged coastlines, calm lagoons and white sandy beaches, and tropical rain forests rich in flowering plants.

The Heart of Polynesia

The 16 islands of the Samoan group cluster near the heart of Polynesia. (Western Samoa is about 4,205 km/2,613 miles southwest of Hawaii and 2,897 km/1,800 miles northeast of New Zealand.) Stretching some 402 km/250 miles across the South Pacific, this chain of islands is divided into two political units—the U.S. Territory of American Samoa and the independent country of Western Samoa.

At the eastern end of the Samoan chain, the seven islands of American Samoa cover a land area of 197 square km/76 square miles. The country's capital, Pago Pago, is located on the main island of Tutuila. Other islands include Aunu'u, the Manu'a group (Ta'u, Olosega, and Ofu), Swains, and Rose. Uninhabited Rose Island is a wildlife sanctuary.

Western Samoa lies about 129 km/80 miles northwest of American Samoa. Its nine islands comprise a land area of 3,031 square km/1,100 square miles. A narrow strait separates the country's two main islands—Savai'i and Upolu. Savai'i is the westernmost and largest island in the Samoan group. Western Samoa's capital, Apia, is located on Upolu. The country's other islands include Manono and Apolima, located in the strait between Upolu and Savai'i, and five uninhabited islands within or near the reef surrounding Upolu.

Lush, volcanic isles

Most of the islands in both American and Western Samoa are high islands of volcanic origin. Jungle-clad mountains rise abruptly from the sea, jagged peaks stretch toward the sky, and fiordlike bays cut deeply into narrow valleys. Rivers cut through the dense forests, plunging down steep cliffs into inviting pools. Along the narrow coastline, beaches rim blue-green lagoons protected by coral reefs.

Island flora. Tropical plants thrive in the volcanic soil. Rain forests rich in banyan trees, ferns, and vine creepers cover much of the islands. Blossoming hibiscus, ginger, frangipani, gardenias, and orchids add splashes of color to the dark greenery.

Wildlife. Over 50 species of birds inhabit the Samoas. They include tooth-billed pigeons, Samoan fantails, Samoan broadbills, reef herons, and fruit doves. Field rats, lizards, and flying foxes (a type of bat) also roam the islands. Domesticated animals include beef and dairy cattle, pigs, and poultry.

Cradle of Polynesia

Scientists say the first Polynesians migrated from Southeast Asia to Samoa long before the birth of Christ. From Savai'i, the cradle of Polynesia, the race spread to other islands in the Pacific.

Dutch navigator Jacob Roggeveen was the first European to sight the islands in 1722. More than 40 years later, Louis Antoine de Bougainville visited the Samoas, which he named the Navigator Islands. Next came La Perouse in 1787. Little information about the Samoas reached the outside world until 1830, when John Williams of the London Missionary Society arrived.

By the mid-19th century Britain, Germany, and the United States began to show commercial interest in the Samoas and sent representative consuls to the islands. Augmenting the Samoan tribal strife already existing during this period, fierce rivalry developed between the competing countries. This power struggle almost resulted in war.

Finally, in 1899 a treaty was drawn up giving the Eastern Samoan islands to the United States and the Western Samoas to Germany. Britain withdrew, having territorial rights elsewhere in the Pacific.

As a territory, American Samoa was administered by the U.S. Navy for the first half of the 20th century. When the naval base was closed in 1951, administration was transferred to the U.S. Department of the Interior.

After World War I, the League of Nations mandated Western Samoa to New Zealand. Following World War II, the country became a Trusteeship Territory, still administered by New Zealand. After a period of self-

(Continued on page 33)

Cruise ship *anchors in deep water of Pago Pago Bay. Steep, forested mountains rim fiordlike harbor, considered one of the Pacific's most spectacular. Tramway offers 6-minute ride above port to summit of Mount Alava.*

Dressed *in bright red* lava-lavas, *men join in tug of war during holiday festivities in American Samoa.*

PACIFIC ARCHITECTURE
It's Eclectic

FIJIAN BURE

SAMOAN FALE

PALAU MEN'S HOUSE

NEW CALEDONIA HUT

Take heavy lengths of timber cut from a coconut tree and lash them together to make a sturdy frame. Add walls made of woven niaouli bark or bamboo. Top it all off with a high-pitched roof of palm leaves or grass thatch, and you've created a traditional Pacific island home.

Built from the materials of the earth, it's a simple abode, designed mainly to protect its inhabitants from sun and rain. The steeply pitched roof allows warm air to rise, providing natural air conditioning. Most activities take place outside in the balmy tropical breezes.

Many of today's Pacific islanders choose to live in modern houses built of concrete blocks or wood topped by corrugated metal roofs. But traveling through the countryside, you'll still see traditional homes.

The architecture of these huts may vary from country to country and even from region to region. In the Samoas for example, the thatch-roofed homes are round with open sides that allow for maximum natural air conditioning. Although some of the huts in New Caledonia and Papua New Guinea are also round, they have low sides and more steeply pitched conical roofs.

Europeans introduced the rectangular shape to Pacific island architecture; you'll find examples of this type in Fiji. A-frame architecture is used in the men's council houses of Palau and Yap and in the *haus tambaran* (spirit house) style of Papua New Guinea.

The variety of hut shapes and construction materials adds an interesting facet to your Pacific island explorations.

government in the 1950s, Western Samoa finally achieved independence on January 1, 1962.

American Samoa's government today. American Samoa is an unincorporated territory of the United States administered by the Department of the Interior. American Samoans have free access to the United States but are not U.S. citizens.

Until recently, the territory's governor was appointed by the Department of the Interior, but he is now elected by the people. The territory has a bicameral legislature, the *Fono,* consisting of a House of Representatives elected by universal adult suffrage and a Senate elected by the *matais* (chiefs) in accordance with Samoan custom.

Government in Western Samoa today. Western Samoa is a constitutional monarchy. The country's constitution—its supreme law—provides for a head of state, prime minister, legislature, and judiciary.

The present head of state, Malietoa Tanumafili II, will rule for life. Succeeding heads of state will be elected every 5 years by the Legislative Assembly. According to tradition, the monarch is chosen from the Four Royal Sons or families.

The matais of Western Samoa, numbering over 10,000, elect 45 members of the Legislative Assembly. Two other members are elected by universal adult suffrage.

Executive governmental matters are carried out by a prime minister, elected by the Legislative Assembly with the approval of the head of state.

The Samoan People

The world's largest full-blooded Polynesian population resides in the Samoas. Nearly 90 percent of the Samoas' 185,000 people are Polynesian. The other 10 percent include Asians, Americans, Europeans, Australians, and New Zealanders.

Western Samoa's population numbers 155,000, most of whom live on Upolu. The majority of American Samoa's 30,000 residents call Tutuila home.

Fa'a Samoa, the Samoan Way

The Samoans are friendly, generous, modest, and fun-loving. Proud of their heritage and customs, they work to preserve them. In Samoan conversation you'll often hear the expression *fa'a Samoa*—the Samoan Way. Adhering to tradition, the people have managed to withstand many outside influences, at the same time adapting foreign ideas to their way of life.

Extended family. Despite western influences, the basic unit of the village community remains the *aiga* (extended family), a group consisting of blood relatives, in-laws, and adopted members. Traditionally, people must place the extended family before themselves; and no family member should go in need.

Chiefs. The family members of each aiga elect a *matai* (chief) as head of the family. In return for services rendered and money contributed by family members, he represents them in village affairs, takes responsibility for their protection and well-being, and acts as trustee for family lands and property.

Above the family chiefs is a hierarchy of chiefs. Each of these chiefs has his own talking chiefs who act as his orators. Custom requires that frequent speeches be made. The talking chiefs know the correct language and the ranks and titles of people being addressed.

In the Samoas, titles are hereditary only to a degree. Every energetic and capable young man can aspire to a title someday. At present there are more than 8,000 Samoan chiefs of varying ranks.

Life in the Samoas

Most Samoans reside in villages. Western Samoans remain relatively traditional in their life styles, whereas American Samoans have adopted some new ideas. Traditional customs still exist in both countries.

Many Western Samoans still live in traditional *fales*—elliptical, open-sided houses set in a semicircle around a grassy village green. Topping each fale is a thatch (or corrugated metal) roof supported by a circle of pillars. Woven mat blinds are lowered for protection against rain and wind. On the floor of the fale is a raised platform of coral, topped with smooth pebbles and covered by mats. Modern fales contain some furniture.

American Samoans have adopted western-style fales, rectangular in shape and built of concrete blocks with corrugated metal roofs. The dwellings have pastel-colored walls and large, louvered windows. You also see some traditional fales.

Dress. Samoan men prefer *lava-lavas*—bright, knee-length wraparound skirts—worn with or without shirts. Samoan women wear dresses, skirts and blouses, or the more traditional *puletasi* (tunic and long skirt).

Religion. In both American and Western Samoa, religion plays an important role in the lives of the people. You'll see numerous imposing, elaborately designed churches here. Every village, no matter how small, has at least one steepled church.

In addition to two Sunday services, families gather in their homes early each evening for 10 to 15 minutes of prayer. Visitors should not walk through a village or enter a fale during this prayer time.

Most Samoans are Protestant, though there are some Roman Catholics and Mormons.

Language. English is the official business language of the Samoas. You'll find Samoan spoken widely in both countries.

The Samoan language is closely related to other Polynesian tongues. In pronouncing words, note that the Samoan "g" is equivalent to the English "ng." For example, Pago Pago is pronounced "Pango Pango."

Economic mainstays

Unlike many South Pacific countries, American Samoa does not rely mainly on copra for economic support. The country's thriving fish industry produces such items as canned fish, pet food, and fish meal. Economic development in American Samoa is encouraged through U.S. federal appropriations.

In contrast, Western Samoa's economy depends on

FESTIVAL TIME

Both American and Western Samoa offer a variety of special events that visitors can enjoy.

January—April

Cricket season. In both American and Western Samoa, cricket season runs from January to April. You can see matches in Pago Pago and Apia.

Rugby season. March through June you can enjoy rugby matches in Apia and in the villages of Western Samoa.

Flag Day. American Samoa's biggest holiday is Flag Day, April 17. Parades, singing, dancing, longboat races, and numerous other events herald the first rais-ing of the American flag in the territory.

Anzac Day. On April 25 Western Samoa observes this day in commemoration of the casualties of war.

May—August

Independence Day. Western Samoa's biggest event is Independence Day, celebrated from Saturday through Wednesday the first week in June. You'll see dance performances, sports events, feasting, and longboat and horse races in Apia.

Samoa International Golf Tournament. Western Samoa holds this annual tournament in August at the Royal Samoa Golf Club in Fagali'i.

September—December

White Sunday. On the second Sunday in October, American and Western Samoan children are honored. Special plays are presented at churches, and children dressed in new Sunday whites take the honored seats at family feasts.

Palolo scooping. Sometime between October and early November the coral worms, called *palolo*, float up from the reefs in both Samoas. Thousands of islanders wade out and enthusiastically scoop up the "caviar of the Pacific."

---

three agricultural crops—coconuts, cocoa, and bananas. Other exports include lumber, fruits, and vegetables.

Tourism is becoming an important industry in both countries.

Cricket, Samoan-style

The most popular sport in both American and Western Samoa is cricket—Samoan-style. Throughout the year Samoans play the game on village greens. Unlike traditional British cricket which has 11 team members, Samoan cricket can include the whole community— 50 to 100 men, women, and children. Children too young to play practice by using coconut fronds instead of wooden bats.

Other competitive sports enjoyed by the Samoans include boxing, rugby, American football, basketball, volleyball, and tennis. You can watch lawn bowling throughout the year at the Apia Bowling Club, next door to the Tusitala Hotel in Apia.

Planning Your Trip

The islands of American and Western Samoa lie south of the equator and east of the International Dateline.

Neighboring countries include both Fiji and Tonga.

Both American and Western Samoa are easily reached by air. International flights land in American Samoa at Pago Pago's Tafuna Airport (11 km/7 miles southwest of town center) and at Western Samoa's Faleolo Airport (37 km/23 miles west of Apia). Buses and taxis provide transportation into town from both airports.

Two local carriers—Polynesian Airlines and South Pacific Island Airways—provide daily service linking Pago Pago and Apia. The flight takes about 30 minutes.

Pago Pago and Apia are ports of call for a number of passenger and passenger/cargo lines sailing the South Pacific. In American Samoa passengers disembark at the main dock in the central part of busy Fagatogo, just southeast of Pago Pago. Ships arriving at Apia, Western Samoa, dock directly across the waterfront road from Aggie Grey's Hotel.

For information on local transportation, see page 37 (American Samoa) and page 40 (Western Samoa).

Where to stay

In the Samoas, you can choose to stay in a large, modern hotel, a simple bungalow or small motel, or a tent. Most of the hotels and motels have dining rooms, cocktail lounges, and coffee and tea making facilities.

American Samoa has only one large hotel—the Pago Pago Rainmaker. Western Samoa's major hotels are Aggie Grey's, a South Pacific landmark, and the Tusitala.

For more information on accommodations in American Samoa, see page 37; Western Samoa information will be found on page 40.

Flanked by village elders, *Samoan chief's daughter solemnly prepares*
kava in large wooden bowl for guests. During welcoming ceremony,
guests sit cross-legged on mats, each drinking a cup of kava in single gulp.

Fia fia, the Samoan feast

One of the best ways to experience both traditional
Samoan food and entertainment is to attend a *fia fia* —
a Samoan feast. In both American and Western Samoa,
the fia fia is an important part of island life; no special
occasion passes without a feast to honor it.

The fare. Fia fia means food in Samoan, and you'll find
an exotic array at a Samoan feast. Many of the items
are baked in an *umu* (Samoan underground oven),
where food wrapped in banana leaves cooks slowly over
hot stones. From these ovens come fish, chicken, and a
variety of fruits and vegetables.

Other island specialties include suckling pig (cooked
on a spit or in an umu), barbecued chicken, pigeon, crab,
masi (biscuits made from grated, fermented breadfruit),
and *ota* (raw fish marinated with chili, pepper, or garlic).

If you are in the Samoas in October or early November,
you can sample the South Seas version of caviar —*palolo.*
These coral worms —considered a local delicacy —wiggle
out of the reef just once a year.

Kava ceremony. While the food is cooking, you might
be fortunate enough to participate in a kava ceremony.
At a village fia fia, this is performed by the village chiefs
in the guest fale where you sit cross-legged (Samoan-
style) on a matted floor. The kava—made from dried,
pulverized pepper plant root mixed with water—will be
solemnly prepared before you in a large wooden bowl,
usually by a chief's daughter. One by one each guest is
handed a cup of kava, which should be drunk in a single
gulp. The kava ceremony is an important ritual of Samoan hospitality.

The entertainment. Following the kava ceremony and
before the meal, Samoans in traditional dress perform
ancient songs and dances.

Etiquette, Samoan-style. If you participate in a village fia fia, you should follow certain Samoan rules of
etiquette.
• Before drinking a cup of kava, first tip a little liquid
from the cup onto the ground immediately in front of
you, at the same time saying *"Manuia."*
• Don't walk across the mats in the fale; instead, circle
around the edge of them as you approach your host.
Never speak to anyone seated in the fale while you are
standing. Address the chief from a sitting position.
• When you sit, cross your legs in front of you, or fold
them behind you. It is considered rude to stretch out
your legs and feet in front of you.
• Before eating, wait for grace to be said.

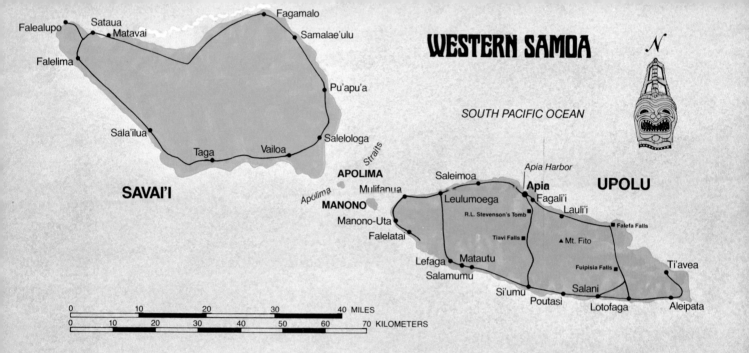

Shopping for Samoan specialties

Travelers can shop for interesting handicrafts in both American and Western Samoa. Many visitors select attractive Samoan woven products such as double-woven floor mats, plaited place mats, baskets, and woven purses. Samoan women are highly skilled in weaving.

Other local craft items include hand-painted fabric, tapa cloth, lava-lavas and puletasis, woodcarvings, and shell jewelry.

Most stores in American Samoa are open Monday to Friday from 8 A.M. to 5 P.M. and on Saturday from 8 to 1. In Western Samoa, you can shop from 8 A.M. to 4 P.M. weekdays and from 8 to 12:30 on Saturday. During the week, stores are closed at lunch (noon to 1:30 P.M.). In both countries most stores are closed on Sundays and public holidays.

Recreational opportunities

As in many areas of the South Pacific, the climate and waters of the Samoas encourage water sport activities. Both countries have a number of good beaches where you can go swimming or surfing.

Scuba and skin diving. Scuba and skin divers will be delighted with the clear waters around American Samoa, where visibility averages 30 meters/100 feet. Good diving spots include Taema Banks about 3 km/ 2 miles outside of Pago Pago Bay and Nafuna Bank 2 km/1 mile off Aunu'u Island. For information on diving and snorkeling in American Samoa, inquire at your hotel or at the Office of Tourism in Pago Pago.

In Western Samoan waters, scuba and skin divers report visibility up to 152 meters/500 feet. Good diving spots on Upolu include the lagoons at Lauli'i and Luatuanu'u. You can rent snorkeling and diving equipment at Aggie Grey's Hotel, the Hotel Tusitala, and Seafari Samoa, Ltd., all in Apia.

Fishing. In the waters off American and Western Samoa, fishing prospects are topnotch. Catches include marlin, tuna, wahoo, mahi mahi, sailfish, and broadbill. For more information, check with your hotel.

Golf. In American Samoa golfers enjoy the 9-hole course near Pago Pago's Tafuna Airport. Western Samoa visitors can play the Royal Samoa Golf Club's 9-hole course at Fagali'i, about 5 km/3 miles east of Apia on Upolu. Visitors can make arrangements to play through the club secretary.

Tennis. If tennis is your game, you can wield your racket in American Samoa at a number of courts in and around Pago Pago. You'll find courts in Pago Pago Park and Utulei and Fagatogo villages (within walking distance of the Pago Pago Rainmaker Hotel).

In Western Samoa you can play tennis on grass, asphalt, and concrete courts in and around Apia.

First Stop, American Samoa

For many visitors, the first stop will be Tutuila—American Samoa's major island. Here, cloud-topped mountains rise steeply from placid lagoons; row after straight row of coconut palms wave in the breeze; and tiny villages cluster on white sand beaches.

Near the island's center, Pago Pago Bay thrusts a fiordlike arm deep into the land, nearly bisecting 10-km/

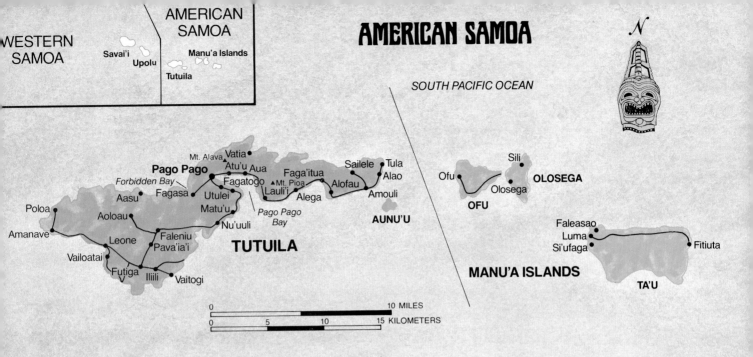

6-mile wide, 29-km/18-mile long Tutuila. One of the world's most spectacular tropical island harbors, Pago Pago Bay was formed centuries ago when the seaward wall of a great crater collapsed, allowing water to enter the steep-sided, lushly green volcano.

Getting around American Samoa

Visitors usually spend most of their time exploring the shore of Pago Pago Bay and touring the rest of Tutuila Island. Nearly 80 km/50 miles of paved road curve along the island's south shore. Some north shore villages are reached by side roads branching off this main road.

Taxis are plentiful on Tutuila; they come in all shapes, sizes, and colors. If you want to rent a car, bring along a current driver's license. Traffic keeps to the right.

An inexpensive method of local transportation is the open-air bus. Passengers can travel from one end of Tutuila to the other for less than a dollar. Although buses run frequently to the villages east and west of Pago Pago, they don't follow a precise timetable or a prescribed route but go where the passengers want them to go. Don't expect specified bus stops. When you want to board a bus, flag it down and tell the driver where you want to be let off. There is no bus service after 5 P.M. or on Sundays or holidays.

Boat service. Adventurous travelers can explore the islands by cargo boat. Used primarily to transport freight between the islands, they also carry passengers.

Cargo boats make the 129-km/80-mile trip from Pago Pago to Apia, Western Samoa, several times a week. There's also once-a-week boat service to the Manu'a group from Pago Pago.

Twice weekly, a government boat makes a full-day trip around Tutuila from Pago Pago, dropping off school supplies. Stops include the small, offshore island of Aunu'u and villages along the north shore.

Air travel. In addition to regular daily air service between Pago Pago and Apia, daily flights on South Pacific Island Airways also serve the Manu'a Islands.

Island tours. Local operators offer a variety of tours around Pago Pago, to other villages on Tutuila, and to the Manu'a group.

Accommodations are limited

American Samoa has only one large hotel—the 188-room Pago Pago Rainmaker, located on a peninsula jutting into Pago Pago Bay. With buildings designed to resemble traditional Samoan fales, the hotel sits on the site of the old Navy Goat Island Club. It was named after the old Rainmaker Hotel made famous in Somerset Maugham's short story, "Rain."

The Motel Pago Pago (Herb and Sia's), situated in the downtown area, provides a family-type atmosphere in its 8-room establishment.

The government has recently opened a campground at Aoa on Tutuila's northeast coast. Here, vacationers can stay in a tent or Samoan-style fale. A Samoan guest fale is also under construction on Ta'u in the Manu'a group.

Dining in American Samoa

Hungry travelers find variety ranging from authentic Samoan foods to American hamburgers at the Pago Pago Rainmaker Hotel. At least once a week the hotel offers a Mongolian barbecue, where guests select desired meat, vegetables, and sauces which the chef cooks.

For a special treat attend a fia fia, a Samoan feast. The feasts are presented regularly at the Rainmaker Hotel and Motel Pago Pago. Local tour operators also sponsor group trips to fia fias in nearby villages.

Soli's Restaurant has a Polynesian floor show several nights a week. Nightclub tours are available.

Samoan girls *splash in pool at waterfall's base near Apia. Visitors traveling Upolu's coastal or cross-island roads discover numerous inviting spots to picnic or swim.*

South Pacific landmark, *Aggie Grey's gained fame as World War II gathering place for Seabees and sailors. Aggie still presides at Apia hotel, which attracts a cosmopolitan crowd.*

Exploring the Pago Pago area

Pago Pago (pronounced "Pango Pango") is one of several small villages situated along the narrow shore of beautiful Pago Pago Bay. Here you'll find most of the shops, ship docks, and business and government buildings of American Samoa. At the southwest edge are the Pago Pago Rainmaker Hotel and the adjacent villages of Fagatogo (pronounced "Fangatongo") and Utulei. In fact, Fagatogo is really the capital of American Samoa. However, because of the fame of Pago Pago Bay, Pago Pago is used collectively to refer to several villages.

Jagged, bush-covered mountains ring the harbor, ascending abruptly from the coast. Across the harbor from the Pago Pago district, Mount Pioa looms from a height of 524 meters/1,718 feet. Called "The Rainmaker" by the Samoans, this massive bulk of volcanic rock attracts moisture-filled clouds around its summit, bringing Pago Pago more than its fair share of rain.

Visitors find the Pago Pago area an unhurried, restful place to visit. Shops offering a miscellany of merchandise line the main streets. Residential sections sprawl up the hills, and footpaths continue from dead-end roads to the entrances of houses. Almost every block has its place of worship.

Below are some of the sights to visit in the Pago Pago area.

Tramway ride. One of the first things most visitors enjoy is the 6-minute aerial tramway ride to the top of Mount Alava. It operates daily from 8 A.M. to 4 P.M. except during strong winds. The best times to take the ride are early morning and late afternoon.

Boarding the tram car at Solo Hill (a short distance from the Pago Pago Rainmaker Hotel), you'll cross the harbor and ascend 488 meters/1,600 feet to the mountaintop.

On a clear day, you can see Pago Pago township, the harbor, Western Samoa's islands to the northwest, and the Manu'a group to the east. The tramway was built in 1965 to transport personnel and heavy equipment during construction of a television transmitting tower on Mount Alava.

Government House. As you leave Solo Hill on your tram ride, you pass over the rooftop of Government House. For more than 70 years, this two-story white, wooden mansion has served as the home of the territory's chief executives.

Television Center. In Utulei, across the road from the Pago Pago Rainmaker, visitors can tour the Michael J. Kirwan Educational Television Center. Heart of the educational television system established by former Governor H. Rex Lee, the center produces lessons for American Samoa's elementary and secondary school students. In the evenings, station programs educate and entertain adults.

Guided tours are held Monday to Friday between 2 and 5 P.M.

Jean M. Haydon Museum. Named after the wife of former Governor John M. Haydon, this museum contains an impressive assortment of Samoan artifacts and ancient handicraft items.

Located in downtown Fagatogo next to the fire station, the museum is housed in the old post office—an early 20th-century building dating from the U.S.

Navy years. You can visit the museum weekdays from 10 A.M. to 4 P.M. and Saturdays between 10 and noon.

Sadie Thompson territory. If you've read Somerset Maugham's story, "Rain," you'll want to see the site where the author reputedly gathered material for his famous tale. The former boarding house, now the Max Haleck Store #3, is located on Fagatogo's main road past the marketplace.

Other sights. Another Fagatogo point of interest is the Fono building, home of the territory's legislature. Its architecture combines traditional fale construction and modern materials. In front of the Fono building is the *malae* (village green), where traditional games, singing, and dancing take place on special occasions.

West of the malae, the town market attracts villagers from outlying areas who come to sell taros, yams, bananas, and vegetables. Across the street from the market, you'll see the High Court, a stately, two-story white building reminiscent of a southern U.S. mansion. It has been designated a historical monument.

Touring Tutuila

Outside of Pago Pago, the island offers green tropical forests, waterfalls, rivers, beautiful coastal and mountain scenery, charming villages, and friendly villagers.

You can see much of the island by taking the main road west or east from Pago Pago, skirting the island's inhabited southern and western coasts. Tutuila's rugged northern coast has few villages.

To the west. West of Pago Pago you'll find a number of interesting villages and some beautiful scenery.

Along the coast near Vailoatai you'll discover black lava cliffs and spectacular blowholes. Farther west, stop at Leone—American Samoa's second largest town and former capital.

You can observe the making of Samoan handicrafts at several villages along the way. Inland at Aoloau, see how Samoan plants are used for food, traditional medicines, housing, and utensils. In Amanave, near Tutuila's western tip, villagers demonstrate weaving and woodcarving.

To the east. East from Pago Pago, the road winds along the rocky coastline past thatch fales, pastel western-style houses, churches, and wrecks of old fishing vessels half sunk in the surf. The road ends 26 km/16 miles east of Pago Pago at Tula village.

The north coast. From central Pago Pago, travelers reach the north coast on a road that cuts snakelike across Fagasa Pass to the north side of Tutuila. From a roadside lookout point, you see Pago Pago Valley in one direction and Forbidden Bay in the other.

American Samoa's other islands

Visitors who seek a glimpse of untouched American Samoa can visit islands in the Manu'a group (Ta'u, Olosega, and Ofu). Located about 129 km/80 miles north of Tutuila, they can be reached by daily flights, weekly Inter-Island Transport boat service, and day or overnight tours. It was on the island of Ta'u that anthropologist Margaret Mead in 1925 gathered material for her classic book, *Coming of Age in Samoa*.

Visiting Western Samoa

The charm of Western Samoa lies in its relative lack of development. Your first exposure comes on the 32-km/20-mile drive from Upolu's Faleolo Airport into Apia. Considered one of the most beautiful routes in the South Pacific, it passes lagoons bordered by leaning palm trees and numerous villages with impressive churches and traditional thatch-roofed fales.

Most of the country's residents live in small villages on the main islands of Upolu and Savai'i, and on the smaller islands of Manono and Apolima. Only 20 percent of the country's people live in Apia, the capital.

Getting around Western Samoa

You can explore Upolu on your own or join an organized tour. Roads follow the island shore and cross it to link major points of interest.

Numerous taxis are available at moderate rates for exploration around town. Local, wooden-seated buses offer an inexpensive way to see the island. You can pick up a bus timetable at the Transport Board office located near the police station in Apia.

If you choose to tour the island independently, you can rent a car in Apia from several different firms. Motor-scooters are also available for hire. On presentation of your driver's license at the police department, you will be issued a Western Samoa license for a fee of one *tala* (the Western Samoa dollar). The local license is required by law before you can rent a vehicle.

Transportation on Savai'i is limited to coastal village bus service. The island has no rental cars or taxis. Tour operators in Apia offer both sea and air tours to Savai'i and a boat tour to tiny Manono.

Boat travel. The *Limulimutau*, a passenger/vehicle ferry, sails daily at 7 A.M. from the Mulifanua Wharf on western Upolu. After unloading at the Salelologa Wharf on Savai'i, the boat returns across the channel at 10 A.M. Taking about 1½ hours each way, the trip provides a good view of Upolu, Savai'i, and the smaller islands of Manono and Apolima.

Local flights. Polynesian Airlines provides regular service from Apia's Faleolo Airport on Upolu to Savai'i. Daily flights connect Apia with Pago Pago in American Samoa.

Hotel with a history

Most famous of Western Samoa's hotels is Aggie Grey's —a South Pacific landmark frequented over the years by countless writers, film stars, poets, and adventurers.

Aggie, the energetic owner-founder of the hotel, is believed to be the model for the character of Bloody Mary in James Michener's book, *Tales of the South Pacific*. She began her business career in 1919 by opening a bar called the Cosmopolitan Club on the site of the current hotel.

With 115 modern rooms, the hotel today sits in a tropical garden setting just across the road from the ocean, a short distance from downtown Apia.

Samoan architecture has been adapted in the design of Apia's only other large hotel—the 96-room Tusitala. The hotel is situated across the road from the harbor within walking distance of town center.

Small hotels in downtown Apia include the Tiafau Hotel and the Apian Way Inn (run by Aggie's sister Mary Croudace). You'll find tiny Paradise of Entertainment Bungalows (9 rooms) on Vaiusu Bay about 5 km/3 miles from downtown Apia. The bungalows of Samoan Hideaway Beach Resort overlook the water 26 km/16 miles from town on Upolu's southern coast.

On the island of Savai'i, visitors stay at the Savai'ian Guest Fales to experience traditional, open-air Samoan living. Tour operators can arrange for an overnight stay on Savai'i.

Dining in Western Samoa

In Apia the Apian Way Hotel is noted for excellent seafood; Aggie Grey's offers a weekly barbecue; and the Tiafau Hotel has a steak and lobster night. For Chinese food try Pinati's or Leung Wai's.

Fia fias (Samoan feasts) are held regularly at Aggie Grey's Hotel, Hotel Tusitala, Tiafau Hotel, and the Samoan Hideaway Beach Resort. Local operators also sponsor group trips to nearby village fia fias.

Apia, the capital

Perched on the north coast of Upolu, Apia is reminiscent of an old South Seas port during early trading days. Colonial-style wooden buildings and churches straggle along the tree-shaded main street—Beach Road—that curves around the harbor.

From Apia, you can visit several nearby sights.

Mulinu'u. Just a 5-minute drive around Apia Harbor to its western tip brings you to Mulinu'u, the location of *Fale Fono* (Parliament House); the *malae* (village green) where national celebrations are held; Land and Title Courts; and Independence Monument. You'll also see Tiafau, traditional burial ground of Samoan royalty.

Vailima. Located 5 km/3 miles inland from Apia, the former home of Robert Louis Stevenson is the current residence of Western Samoa's head of state. The gracious, serene-looking house is approached by the famous Road of Loving Hearts. Flanked on both sides by handsome old teak trees, this road was built by the Samoan people for Stevenson, their beloved "Tusitala" (teller of tales). The grounds are open to the public, but visitors aren't permitted inside the house.

Directly above Vailima is Mount Vaea. At its summit is Stevenson's tomb with the words of his immortal "Requiem" carved on it. A rugged switchback trail ascends 152 meters/500 feet to the top. This hike—recommended only for the fit—is best made early in the day before temperatures get too hot.

Upolu, miles of unspoiled scenery

Any trip on the island of Upolu passes through mile after mile of unspoiled landscape. You can travel around the island skirting the north and south coasts or cut across the island on several roads. Pause, if you like, at villages and plantations (coconut, cocoa, and coffee); and stop for a swim or picnic at inviting waterfalls, pools, and beaches.

Waterfalls. Traveling 29 km/18 miles east of Apia, you'll come to Falefa Falls tumbling into a deep, verdant valley. Turning south, the road climbs to Mafa Pass where you'll enjoy a breathtaking view of the shoreline. Descending past Fuipisia Falls, you enter the Aleipata district on the southeast coast, an area known for sandy beaches and quiet lagoons.

Lefaga. If you take the road leading south from Apia, you'll cut across the central part of the island past Tiavi Falls. At Si'umu turn west along the coast. Stop at Salamumu—considered one of the most attractive collections of thatch fales in Western Samoa—then continue on to Lefaga. The American movie *Return to Paradise* was filmed here in 1952.

Western Samoa's other islands

Across the narrow Apolima Strait from Upolu, you can visit Savai'i. From here, Polynesians sailed the ocean to colonize other Pacific islands.

The largest island in the Samoas, Savai'i is even less westernized than Upolu. Visitors stay in open-air guest fales. The island can be reached by regular air and ferry service. You can also take a tour to the island.

A 30-minute boat trip from Manono-Uta on the western end of Upolu transports passengers to Manono Island in the Apolima Straits. Since there are no cars on the island, you can stroll at a leisurely pace enjoying white sandy beaches and coconut palms.

Know Before You Go

The following practical information will help you plan your trip to the Samoas.

Entry/exit procedures. If you are a United States citizen entering American Samoa, you will need only proof of citizenship. Non-U.S. citizens need passports, and visas for stays longer than 30 days.

Visitors to Western Samoa will need valid passports, but no visas for stays up to 30 days. Visitors planning longer stays can obtain visas from New Zealand and British consular offices or from the Immigration Division of the Prime Minister's Department in Apia.

Both Samoas require smallpox and yellow fever inoculations for travelers arriving from an infected area. (Note: Since health requirements change from time to time, check with your local public health department before leaving on your trip.)

American Samoa has no airport departure tax. In Western Samoa you will pay WS $2 when you depart by air.

Customs. Visitors to both countries must make a written declaration upon arrival. You may bring in duty free 1 bottle of liquor and 200 cigarettes.

Currency. In American Samoa, you use the U.S. dollar. The recent exchange rate is about U.S. $1 = Australian $.87, and New Zealand $.92.

Western Samoan currency is the tala (for dollar). The recent exchange rate is about WS $1 = U.S. $1.20, Australian $1.04, and New Zealand $1.10.

Tipping. Tipping is neither customary nor expected in either American or Western Samoa.

Time. Both American and Western Samoa are GMT (Greenwich mean time) −11. For example, when it is 1 P.M. Saturday in the Samoas it's 4 P.M. Saturday in San Francisco; noon Sunday in Auckland; and 10 A.M. Sunday in Sydney.

Weather and what to wear. American and Western Samoa enjoy a tropical climate. American Samoa gets more rain than its neighbor, with over 500 cm/200 inches per year in Pago Pago. Western Samoa's average is 282.5 cm/113 inches.

The best time to visit either country is winter—June through October. During the Samoan summer months, downpours can last days at a time. Humidity stays at about 85 percent all year, but the trade winds cool the air between May and November. The average temperature is around 27°C/80°F.

Lightweight, informal attire is appropriate all year in the Samoas. However, women should not wear shorts in town, at church services, or at village feasts. Useful items to pack include sunglasses, suntan lotion, a rain hat, and rubber soled beach shoes.

For more information. For further information on the Samoas, write to the Department of Economic Development, Government of Western Samoa, Apia, Western Samoa; and the Director of Tourism, P.O. Box 1147, Pago Pago, American Samoa 96799. The Pacific Islands Tourism Development Council, represented in North America by Transportation Consultants International (700 S. Flower St., Los Angeles, California 90017), can also provide information.

TONGA

Tonga, situated just west of the International Date Line, is the first country to greet each new day.

At first glance, Tonga may seem similar to other South Pacific island groups, but it has one unique difference: Tonga is a constitutional monarchy—the last remaining Polynesian kingdom. In past centuries, many Pacific islands—including Tahiti, the Samoas, and the Cooks—were ruled by royalty. Today, the only remaining South Pacific monarch is Tonga's King Taufa'ahau Tupou IV.

Tonga's attractions feature the South Pacific charms of coral reefs, clear blue skies, and inviting atolls. Its gentle people maintain a traditional way of life that has changed little in more than 10 centuries.

As you travel in Tonga, you'll get to know these people. You'll watch them gracefully perform traditional dances, admire their handicraft skills used in making tapa and woven mats, enjoy their foods at bounteous Tongan feasts, and mingle with them in villages and public markets. You'll soon understand why Captain Cook called Tonga "The Friendly Islands."

Many Islands, Little Land

Tonga's 150 islands lie in a 426-km/265-mile-long archipelago just west of the International Date Line. Nuku'alofa, the country's capital, is a 2-hour flight southeast of Suva, Fiji, and a 1½-hour flight southwest of Apia, Western Samoa. Tonga lies 3,219 km/2,000 miles northeast of Sydney, Australia, and 1,770 km/1,100 miles northeast of Auckland.

The islands divide naturally into three groups—Tongatapu in the south, Ha'apai in the center, and Vava'u in the north. Tonga's land area totals only 697 square km/269 square miles. Only 45 of Tonga's islands are inhabited; more than 75 percent of the population lives on Tongatapu, the main island.

High and low islands

Tonga is a contrast of hilly volcanic islands and nearly flat coral formations. Highest point is the 1,125-meter/

3,690-foot extinct volcanic cone on the island of Kao, in the western part of the Ha'apai Group. The neighboring island of Tofua has an active volcano. Nearly all the other islands in the Ha'apai Group are flat.

Tongatapu—only 82 meters/270 feet above sea level—possesses no distinctive hills and no running streams. In contrast, rolling hills mark the neighboring island of Eua. The northern Vava'u Group is also hilly and forested.

Discovered by the Dutch

Two Dutch navigators, Willem Schouten and Jakob Lemaire, were the first Europeans to visit Tonga in 1616, followed by Abel Tasman, who arrived in the islands in 1643. Others followed—Captain Samuel Wallis in 1767; Captain James Cook in 1773, 1774, and 1777; and Captain William Bligh in 1789. (The famous mutiny on the *Bounty* occurred in Tongan waters.)

Missionaries from the London Missionary Society arrived in Tonga in 1797, but things didn't go favorably for them. Two years later several were killed in a civil war, and others fled to Sydney. More missionaries arrived in the 1820s and by midcentury, despite continuing civil war, they had converted most Tongans to Christianity.

The warfare that had wracked the country for a half century finally ended in 1845 when the victor, George Tupou I, became king. He introduced a constitutional form of government and land reforms that are still in effect. Political and social stability exists largely because of his decisions.

Today, the kingdom of Tonga is ruled by a direct descendant of King George, King Taufa'ahau Tupou IV, who became king in 1965 following the death of Queen Salote Tupou. The royal family traces its descent from ancient ruling chiefs whose names are preserved in Tongan art and legends.

For 70 years—from 1900 to 1970—Tonga operated under the protection of Great Britain as a British Protected State. The country became fully independent in 1970.

Tonga's People

According to archeologists, the Tongan islands have been inhabited since the 5th century B.C. Most of Tonga's 90,000 people are Polynesian, descendants of the first inhabitants. (There are also a few other Pacific Islanders and Europeans.)

You'll find the people of Tonga warmhearted, friendly, and eager to show you their country. Though Tongan is the official language, many people also speak English.

A simple life style

For the most part Tongans live a simple existence, taking what they need from the land and the sea. Congregating in scattered seashore villages of several hundred people, they live in traditional oval-ended, thatch-roofed fales

Tongan flag *flies atop red-roofed cupola of Royal Palace in Nuku'alofa. Victorian decoration and second-story veranda enhance white wood home of Tonga's monarch. Well-kept grounds surround palace.*

Copra, *mainstay of island economy, dries on mats in sun. Dried meat is shipped to crushing mill where oil is extracted. Village dwelling combines thatch roof with wood walls and louvered windows.*

or houses built of local timber or concrete block. Some of these modern structures have thatch roofs while others are topped with corrugated iron.

Bound to the traditions of their ancestors, the people have preserved customs, legends, and archeological treasures. Royal traditions still triumph, for the king symbolizes Tonga's proud independence. Tongans have great respect for their king, his nobles, and the great hereditary chain of chiefs existing within the country's social structure.

Dress. Tongan respect for customs is reflected in their attire. Most Tongans dress in traditional wraparound *valas* (skirts)—long for women, short for men.

Finely woven mats, called *ta'ovala*, are worn over these around the waist. (Women sometimes wear a *kiekie*, a highly decorative waistband, instead of the mat.) These mats—held on by a *kafa* (belt) of woven coconut fiber—indicate respect for elders and the royal family. No well-dressed Tongan would consider attending an important occasion without wearing a ta'ovala. Though some mats are tattered beyond belief, the treasured heirlooms are still worn for very special functions.

As you travel in Tonga, you'll see many people dressed in black. Tongans believe that the black of mourning should be worn for many months after a relative's death, and Tongan families are very large.

Land. In Tonga, all land is the property of the crown. The system of land distribution designed by King George Tupou I is unique. At age 16, each male Tongan may request a parcel of farmland (called an *'api*) and a village site on which to build a house.

Economy. Agriculture dominates the Tongan economy. Major exports are bananas, copra, and desiccated coconuts. Other crops—harvested primarily for local consumption—include pineapples, watermelons, tomatoes, taro, and yams. Tongans catch fish for their dinner tables and raise a few cows, some poultry, and a large number of pigs. These pigs are in great demand for festive occasions. As many as 8,000 pigs have been roasted for a single feast attended by thousands of people.

Between July and October some Tongans supplement their income by whale hunting. Tonga is one of the few places in the world where men still hunt the humpback whale using small boats and harpoons. Although the number of whales killed is small, the profit for the whaler can be great. Almost every morsel of whale—including the skin and blubber—is sold as food.

Religion. Tongans devote Sundays to church going and relaxation. Observance of the Sabbath is even written into Tonga's constitution: "The Sabbath Day shall be sacred in Tonga forever and it shall not be lawful to do work or play games or trade on the Sabbath. Any agreement made or documents witnessed on this day shall be counted void and not recognized by the Government." Anyone who disobeys this law can be fined T\$10 or be sentenced to up to 3 months of hard labor for nonpayment of the fine.

In recent decades this law has been stretched enough so that taxi drivers can transport passengers to and from ships and planes, and hotels can be operated.

Many Tongans belong to the State Church (a Tongan version of the Wesleyan Methodist). Other local denominations include the Free Church of Tonga, Roman Catholic Church, Mormon Church, Seventh-Day Adventist Church, and Anglican Church. If you're in Tonga on a Sunday, you may enjoy attending a church service where you'll be rewarded with harmonized hymn singing. Afterwards, you might be invited to join a Sunday feast.

Love for sports

Tongans share a boundless enthusiasm for sports—so much so, in fact, that at one time when cricket was

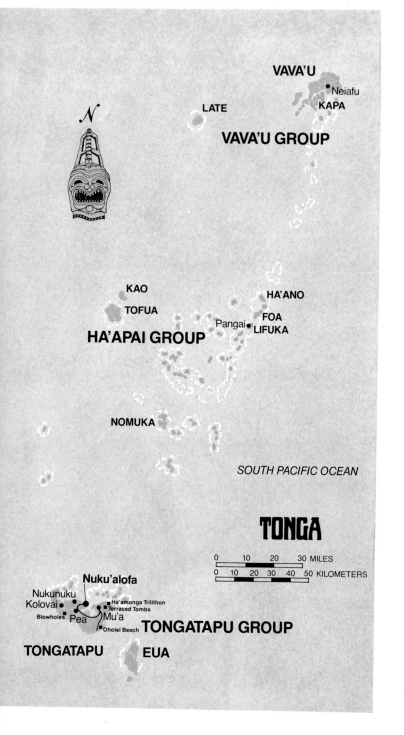

popular, the government put a curb on it by issuing a regulation prohibiting play except at certain hours on designated days. Rugby union and soccer matches also generate a lot of interest. Other popular spectator sports include basketball, tennis, track and field events, boxing, and sumo wrestling. Major sports events are held at the sports grounds in Nuku'alofa.

Tongans also enjoy several indigenous games. One game, *lafo,* is similar to bowls except that it is played with round wooden disks made from coconut shells instead of bowls. Another favorite is a juggling game called *hiko.* Young girls juggle up to six candlenuts or oranges at one time while singing or reciting special rhymes in archaic words.

Planning Your Trip

Tonga's proximity to Fiji and the Samoas makes it feasible to combine a visit to Tonga with travel to these other South Pacific islands.

Regularly scheduled direct flights link Tonga with Fiji, Western Samoa, American Samoa, and New Zealand. Planes land at Fua'amotu Airport on Tongatapu, the country's main island. Taxis and buses transport passengers on the 21-km/13-mile trip into Nuku'alofa, the capital.

Cruise ships and cargo/passenger liners call at Tongan ports on South Pacific excursions. At Nuku'alofa, ships dock within a few blocks of the business district. Some ships also stop at Neiafu on Vava'u.

Traveling around Tonga

Nuku'alofa visitors can choose from several forms of transport. Most interesting, perhaps, is the *ve'etolu*—a colorful three-wheeled, open-sided taxi. Regular taxis are also plentiful. Taxi fares should be agreed upon in advance. If you and a friend would like to explore the town aboard a two seat, three-wheeled bicycle, you can rent one at the International Dateline Hotel.

A rental car offers a good way to see the island of Tongatapu independently. Visiting drivers need a Tongan driver's license, obtained by showing a current domestic license and paying a small fee at the Police Traffic Department in Nuku'alofa. Traffic keeps to the left in Tonga. Outside Nuku'alofa, pigs and other livestock are occasional road hazards.

Tongatapu also has public bus service. On Sundays public transportation is limited to vehicles taking visitors to and from the airport or wharf.

Outer island transportation is limited.

Air service. South Pacific Island Airways and Tonga Air provide regularly scheduled air service linking Tongatapu with Eua, the Ha'apai Group, and Vava'u.

Boat service. To sail from Nuku'alofa to Ha'apai and Vava'u, you can board an interisland boat. A shorter trip—just 3½ hours—goes south to Eua, second largest island in the Tongatapu group. Check boat schedules carefully—they can change on short notice because of

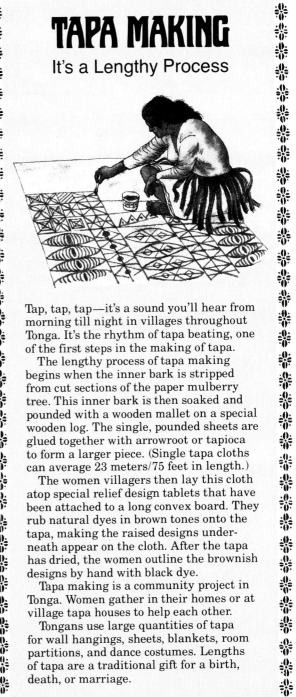

TAPA MAKING
It's a Lengthy Process

Tap, tap, tap—it's a sound you'll hear from morning till night in villages throughout Tonga. It's the rhythm of tapa beating, one of the first steps in the making of tapa.

The lengthy process of tapa making begins when the inner bark is stripped from cut sections of the paper mulberry tree. This inner bark is then soaked and pounded with a wooden mallet on a special wooden log. The single, pounded sheets are glued together with arrowroot or tapioca to form a larger piece. (Single tapa cloths can average 23 meters/75 feet in length.)

The women villagers then lay this cloth atop special relief design tablets that have been attached to a long convex board. They rub natural dyes in brown tones onto the tapa, making the raised designs underneath appear on the cloth. After the tapa has dried, the women outline the brownish designs by hand with black dye.

Tapa making is a community project in Tonga. Women gather in their homes or at village tapa houses to help each other.

Tongans use large quantities of tapa for wall hangings, sheets, blankets, room partitions, and dance costumes. Lengths of tapa are a traditional gift for a birth, death, or marriage.

weather or local commitments. No boats operate on Sundays.

Tours. Tongatapu excursions explore Nuku'alofa and the island of Tongatapu. Other tours feature glass-bottomed boat rides, evening feasts on the beach, and picnic excursions to nearby islets. Visitors can also travel to both Eua and Vava'u.

Varied accommodations

In Tonga accommodations range from resort hotels to simple guest houses. Most have dining rooms.

On Tongatapu most accommodations are located in or near Nuku'alofa. Largest (75 rooms) is the first class International Dateline Hotel, located near town center facing the harbor. Travelers who prefer a smaller hotel can choose among several attractive possibilities, including the Polynesian-style Moana Hotel, just opposite the Nuku'alofa fishing harbor; The Beach House, a large colonial-style wooden house on the waterfront; The Way In Motel, a 10-minute walk from town center; and Joe's Hotel, downtown facing the harbor.

Tonga's only other first class hotel is the Port of Refuge International in Neiafu on Vava'u. With 30 Tongan-style thatched bungalows, this resort hotel overlooks the harbor. Another small hotel on Vava'u is Stowaway Village, designed like a Tongan village facing the harbor.

Eua has one small hotel—the Polynesian-style Taha-Kae-Afe Lodge. In the Ha'apai Group, visitors can arrange to stay in a village. Check with the Tonga Visitors Bureau in Nuku'alofa.

Feasting in Tonga

Tongans are known throughout the South Pacific for the amount and variety of foods offered at their feasts. *Polas*—long trays made from plaited coconut fronds—sag under the weight of some 30 different types of food including suckling pig, fish, crayfish, beef, octopus, vegetables, and fruits. Many of these delicacies are baked in an *umu*, an underground oven, while the suckling pig is roasted on a spit over an open fire.

Coconut cream is the basic sauce for many Tongan dishes. Favorite foods you might want to sample include *'ota iki'*—marinated raw fish in a coconut cream, lemon, onion, and herb marinade; and *lu pulu*—meat and onions marinated in coconut milk, wrapped in taro leaves, and baked in an umu.

Several tours on Tongatapu and some of the outer islands feature a Tongan feast. Check with your hotel for information.

After-dinner entertainment. Usually singing and dancing follow a Tongan feast. The dancing is both reserved and graceful. In contrast to Tahitian dancing, which emphasizes hip movements, Tongan dancing features hand and foot movements. The dancers relate the story in song as they perform, dressed in colorful costumes of tapa cloth and leaves, their bodies glistening with scented coconut oil.

In addition to feast entertainment, programs of Tongan dancing are presented regularly at several Tongatapu hotels, including the International Dateline Hotel, Samaritan, Joe's Hotel, and the Olata'ane Motel.

Other dining possibilities. You can also try various restaurants in the Nuku'alofa area including the restaurants at the International Dateline Hotel, The Beach House, and Joe's Hotel; and Tong-Hua Restaurant. You can buy snacks at Cafe Fakalato and John's Place, both near the center of Nuku'alofa.

Local brew. While in Tonga, try *otai*—a fresh fruit punch, and *kava*—a brew made from the root of a pepper plant. Besides performing kava ceremonies on all formal

Interisland boats *transport freight and passengers—and often domestic animals and livestock—between islands. Longer trips cruise across open sea.*

occasions, Tongans also gather informally to drink kava and exchange gossip.

Shopping for handicrafts

Tonga ranks as one of the best marketplaces in the South Pacific for well-made traditional handicrafts. Among the specialties are tapa cloth (see page 45) and finely woven mats and baskets. The giant woven Ali Baba baskets make excellent laundry containers. Other high quality goods include trays, fans, turtle shell ornaments, and woodcarvings.

FESTIVAL TIME

Parades, singing, elaborate feasts, and contests highlight many of Tonga's celebrations. Below are a few that might enrich your stay in Tonga.

January—April

Good Friday and Easter Sunday. You can hear magnificent choral singing in churches throughout Tonga during this time.

Anzac Day. On April 25, military parades are held by Tongans to honor the soldiers killed during war.

May—August

Birthday of H.R.H. Prince Tupouto'a. Military parades herald the birth of the crown prince on May 4.

Opening of Parliament. A colorful ceremony—including a 21-gun salute—marks the opening of Parliament in early June.

Emancipation Day. On June 4 Tongans celebrate their unity under one king (King George I) and their union with the Commonwealth in 1970.

Birthday of King Taufa'ahau Tupou IV. On July 4, parades,

religious ceremonies, and feasts celebrate the king's birthday.

September—December

Royal Agricultural Show. King Taufa'ahau Tupou IV visits all the island groups in September or October to attend shows displaying produce. Horse races, chariot races, and coconut tree climbing contests are added events.

Music Festival. In December instrumental groups, choirs, and soloists compete in Nuku'alofa.

King Tupou I Day. The king is honored on December 4.

Available in small shops throughout Nuku'alofa, handicraft items are also sold at the Langa Fonua Women's Institute on Taufa'ahua Road in Nuku'alofa and at the Talamahu Market. When cruise ships are in port, you can buy handicrafts in Fa'onelua Gardens next door to the Tonga Visitors Bureau. Langa Fonua also has a small shop in Neiafu on Vava'u.

If you have a stamp collector in the family, stop at the philatelic section of the Treasury Department on Vuna Road. Here you'll find Tonga's uniquely shaped stamps that rank among the most unusual in the world.

You can buy duty-free items such as cameras, radios, jewelry, and perfumes at the International Dateline Hotel and the Fua'amotu airport. The Tonga Broadcasting Commission's shop in Nuku'alofa sells a variety of radio and sound equipment.

Shops in Tonga are open Monday through Friday from 8:30 A.M. to 5 P.M., and on Saturday, 9 A.M. to noon. All stores are closed on Sunday.

Recreational activities

Tonga's abundant white sand beaches and reef-protected lagoons offer plentiful swimming and snorkeling opportunities. Tongatapu's best beaches include Oholei, Ha'amalo, Ha'atafu, Monotapu, Laulea, 'Utukehe, Fahefa, and Fua'amotu. Nearly all the beaches in the Ha'apai Group are good. On Vava'u favorites are Keitahi, Talau Fanga, and Toula.

Skin and scuba diving. Divers will enjoy Tonga's underwater delights including fan black coral, drop-offs, caves, deep reefs, and sunken ships. For diving information, contact the Tonga Dive Club through the Tonga Visitors Bureau. The club has its own compressor, boat, and a limited number of tanks.

Fishing. Your hotel can provide information on deep-sea fishing excursions. Charter boats are available for hire, and catches include barracuda, tuna, marlin, and sailfish.

Boating. You can hire a boat for an hour or a day to go water-skiing, diving, fishing, or cruising to an offshore islet for a picnic. Check with your hotel for boat rental information.

Other sports. Other recreational possibilities include horseback riding, bicycling, and hiking. Inquire at your hotel for information on equipment and destinations.

Tennis players find courts at the International Dateline Hotel on Tongatapu and the Port of Refuge International on Vava'u. There's a 9-hole golf course at Manamoui Racecourse, which is located 8 km/5 miles from Nuku'alofa.

Visiting Tongatapu

Located at the southern end of the Tongan archipelago, the Tongatapu Group consists of two large islands—Tongatapu and Eua—plus several smaller ones. Most heavily populated of the Tongan islands, Tongatapu is the largest island in the archipelago.

On Tongatapu's northern shore you'll find Nuku'alofa, the country's capital and major port of entry. After exploring the city, you can tour the island of Tongatapu, travel to nearby Eua island, and arrange to visit Tonga's other island groups to the north.

Nuku'alofa, the capital

Sprawling along the sea and backed by a lagoon, Nuku-'alofa is a commercial town of white-frame, picket-fenced houses.

Nuku'alofa's small size (30,000 people) makes it easy to explore on foot. Vuna Road, a wide thoroughfare skirting the waterfront, is the center of activity. At one end of the road you'll find the Royal Palace, at the other end, the Yacht Club. Along the road between these points are the public market, the town *malae* (meeting place), the Tonga Visitors Bureau, and numerous hotels. At a right angle to Vuna Road is Taufa'ahau Road where you'll find markets, small shops, general stores, pool-rooms, cinemas, transportation offices, government buildings, and churches.

The Royal Palace. Overlooking the sea and Nuku-'alofa's waterfront, the Royal Palace stands in immaculately kept grounds bright with tropical flowers and shrubs. Norfolk pines surround the two-story white-frame Victorian structure with its distinctive red roof, wide verandas, and stately cupola. Built in 1867, the palace remains unchanged except for the addition of the veranda in 1882.

Although it is not open to the public, you can view the palace easily over the surrounding low coral wall.

The Royal Chapel. The royal family worships in the chapel adjacent to the palace. Visitors may attend church services on Sunday evenings. The coronations of King George Tupou II, Queen Salote, and Tonga's present king took place here. All weddings and baptisms of royalty also occur in this chapel.

The chapel, prefabricated in New Zealand, was assembled here in 1882.

Royal Tombs. Elevated above the ground, the Royal Tombs are situated near the center of town on the estate of Tonga's first king, George Tupou I. He and Queen Salote are both entombed here.

Talamahu Market. Three blocks east of the Royal Palace, you can stroll around Tonga's major fruit and vegetable market. Farmers gather here to sell their produce—pineapples, watermelons, oranges, papayas, and a variety of vegetables. Handicraft items are also available for sale at the market.

Fa'onelua Tropical Gardens. Here you can see a model Tongan village and tour the gardens which feature more than 100 varieties of hibiscus as well as other flora indigenous to the South Pacific.

Touring the island

Heading east or west from Nuku'alofa, you drive through many Tongan villages, travel deep into banana and coconut plantations, and pass white sand beaches. In either direction, you'll find plenty of interesting places to explore.

To the east. One of your first stops east of Nuku'alofa will be Captain Cook's landing place just west of Mu'a. A monument marks the spot where Cook came ashore in 1773.

Northeast of Mu'a you'll come to the Langi—terraced tombs of ancient kings dating from around A.D. 1200.

Large blocks of coral stone about 4 meters/12 feet high face the 4-sided mounds.

Ten km/6 miles northeast of the tombs is a stone monument called the Ha'amonga Trilithon. Erected around A.D. 1200, it consists of two great uprights—5 meter/16-foot high coral slabs—topped by a horizontal connecting stone or lintel about 6 meters/19 feet long.

For years experts thought the trilithon was a gateway to a royal compound. However, recent observations by the present king have led to the theory that the trilithon probably was used as a seasonal calendar. Notches carved in the lintel point directly on the rising sun on the longest and shortest days of the year.

If you travel 19 km/12 miles southeast from Nuku-'alofa, you can see one of the island's most scenic spots—Hufangalupe, "The Pigeons' Doorway." This area, along the southern coast of Tongatapu, offers several dramatic features: sea churning through a natural bridge, cliffs towering above the shore, a beguiling beach lying at the base of the cliffs. To reach this beach, follow a steep trail carved into the cliffs.

To the west. On the western side of Tongatapu, you'll see several more interesting attractions.

At Houma, 14 km/9 miles southwest of Nuku'alofa, waves provide a spectacular show, especially at high tide. Along this area's rocky terraced shoreline, the ocean surges through holes in the coral rock, creating water spouts up to 18 meters/60 feet high. The Tongans call this stretch of coastline *Mapu'a Vaea*, the chief's whistle, for the whistling noise the waves make as they shoot up through the blowholes.

Hundreds of flying foxes (a type of fruit bat) hang chattering from tree branches in Kolovai, 18 km/11 miles northwest of Nuku'alofa. At night they leave to forage for food, returning at dawn to roost once more. Tongan legend claims the bats are descendants of bats presented as a gift from a Samoan princess to an ancient Tongan navigator. Sacred to the Tongans and protected by custom, these bats can be hunted only by members of the royal family.

You also can tour the Dessicated Coconut Factory at Havelu (3 km/2 miles south of Nuku'alofa) to see how the coconuts are husked and the meat processed.

Eua, a delightful contrast

The island of Eua, located just 40 km/25 miles southeast of Nuku'alofa, offers a delightful contrast to its larger island neighbor. Visitors can enjoy one day or several days exploring this 88 square km/34 square mile island of rolling hills, dense forests, and high cliffs.

Eua's attractions are many. You'll want to visit Hafu Pool, a small, crystal-clear pond surrounded by hibiscus bushes and other tropical plants. On a walk through the island's forests, you'll hear—and perhaps glimpse—the chattering and screeching blue-crowned lories and red-breasted musk parrots.

Journeying to the southern part of Eua, you'll come to Matalanga'a Maui, a natural bridge cut by the surging sea. A short distance away are the cliffs of Lakufa'anga, dropping 107 meters/350 feet to the shore. Often you can see turtles in the sea at the base of these cliffs.

Transportation on Eua is limited—you can travel by foot, horseback, or rental jeep.

Other Island Groups

North of Tongatapu, you can visit two strikingly different island groups. The Vava'u Group, at the northern tip of the Tongan Kingdom, is a group of hilly, verdant islands.

South of the Vava'u Group is the Ha'apai Group, a cluster of low islands that barely peak above the sea. The highest points on these islands are the palm trees lining sandy shores.

Seeing Vava'u

Located 274 km/170 miles north of Tongatapu, the 34 islands of the Vava'u Group cover a land area of about 117 square km/45 square miles. With a population of 15,000, Vava'u is the largest island in the group and the main tourist center. Many of the tiny, densely forested islands in the group remain uninhabited.

Neiafu, the group's capital, nestles into a hillside overlooking one of the most beautiful ports in the South Pacific—the Port of Refuge. Arriving by boat, you'll sail up a 13-km/8-mile channel to the fiordlike harbor entrance.

While in Neiafu, you'll want to take a short boat trip to Swallows' Cave. Sunlight streams through an opening in the cathedral-like chamber creating multicolored splendor. In autumn, the cave is a sanctuary for thousands of swallows.

Skin divers might enjoy a visit to Mariner's Cave. Legend relates that this drowned grotto provided refuge for a young chief and his beloved long ago when feuds rocked Tongan families.

Traveling to the Ha'apai Group

The line of islands in the Ha'apai Group lies 161 km/100 miles north of Nuku'alofa, midway between Tongatapu and Vava'u.

Few visitors journey to the Ha'apai Group, since accommodations are limited to villagers' homes (check with the Tonga Visitors Bureau in Nuku'alofa for information). Those travelers who do come here discover islands blessed with deserted beaches and an atmosphere of unbelievable peace and tranquility.

The charming town of Pangai, the group's capital on Lifuka, was once the seat of the Royal Family. Captain James Cook anchored off the coast near the town in 1777 on his third visit to Tonga. Today, Pangai is the headquarters of the kingdom's fishing industry. The island group's airport is located at the north end of Lifuka, a short distance from Pangai.

Know Before You Go

The following practical information will help you plan your trip.

Entry/exit procedures. Visitors to Tonga staying 30 days or less need only a valid passport, a confirmed onward ticket, and adequate funds for their stay.

Visitors need a smallpox vaccination and inoculation against yellow fever only if they have been in an infected area prior to their arrival in Tonga. (Note: Since health requirements change from time to time, check with your local public health department before leaving on your trip.)

Departing international air passengers pay an airport departure tax of T$2.50, payable only in local currency.

Currency. The Tongan currency is the Tongan dollar or *pa'anga*.

The exchange rate is approximately T$1 = U.S. $1.15, Australia $1.00, and New Zealand $1.06.

Tipping. Tipping is neither customary nor encouraged.

Time. Tonga is 13 hours ahead of Greenwich mean time. When it is noon Saturday in Nuku'alofa, it is 11 A.M. Saturday in Auckland, 9 A.M. Saturday in Sydney, and 3 P.M. Friday in Los Angeles.

Weather and what to wear. The climate on Tonga is surprisingly cool for the tropics. Temperatures range from lows just over 21°C/70°F between May and October to highs around 32°C/90°F in December and January. The humid, rainy season (summer) runs from December to April.

You'll be most comfortable in casual, lightweight attire. Short shorts and bathing suits are fine for the beach but are frowned upon in villages. Tongan law prohibits any person appearing in a public place without a shirt.

Articles you'll want to pack include a sweater or stole for evenings during the cooler months, a lightweight raincoat and umbrella for the rainy season, sunglasses, suntan lotion, and beach shoes for reef walking.

For more information. You can get additional information on Tonga by writing the Tonga Visitors Bureau, Box 37, Nuku'alofa. In North America write Transportation Consultants International, 700 South Flower St., Suite 1704, Los Angeles, CA 90017. In Australia write Hugh Birch, 61 Cross Street, Double Bay, Sydney.

COOK ISLANDS

For years isolated from major tourist routes, the Cook Islands offer the visitor untouched beauty and a peaceful way of life. Here you'll stroll along beaches edged with swaying palms and swim in warm lagoons protected by coral reefs. But most of all, you'll enjoy the warm and hospitable people of the Cook Islands.

Fifteen Scattered Islands

Located near the center of the Polynesian triangle, the Cook Islands include 15 specks of land scattered across 2,202,073 square km/850,000 square miles of the South Pacific. Their closest neighbor, French Polynesia—lies over 1,126 km/700 miles to the east. New Zealand is some 3,059 km/1,900 miles southwest and Fiji is about 2,414 km/1,500 miles west.

Totaling a mere 241 square km/93 square miles in area, the islands divide naturally into two groups. The eight islands of the southern Cooks include the tourist destinations of Rarotonga and Aitutaki. All of the southern Cooks are volcanic islands, except for Manuae and Tukutea, which are coral atolls. The seven islands of the northern group are all low lying, remote atolls.

Named after Captain Cook

Spaniard Alvaro de Mendaña was the first European explorer to venture into Cook Island waters. In 1595 he sighted Pukapuka in the northern Cooks. His countryman Pedro Quiros discovered Rakahanga 10 years later.

During the 1770s Captain James Cook charted five more islands, and eventually the island group was named after him. In 1789, Fletcher Christian and fellow mutineers of the *Bounty* wandered into the southern Cooks, anchoring off Rarotonga to barter for food.

Missionaries soon followed. Arriving in 1823, John Williams and other members of the London Missionary Society soon converted most of the islanders.

The Cook Islands became a British Protectorate in 1888, and in 1901 they were annexed by New Zealand. Political changes began in 1947 that finally led to the country's internal independence in 1965.

The Cook Islanders

Over 96 percent of the 18,130 Cook Island residents are Maori (Polynesian); most of the remaining 4 percent are European.

Many of the Cook Island Maoris trace their ancestry to the country's early settlers, who arrived by canoe from the Society Islands between A.D. 600 and 800. According to Cook Island legend, the Maoris sailed from Rarotonga to colonize New Zealand. Strong similarities in language, traditions, and customs exist between the two Maori groups.

A simple life

Many Cook Islanders enjoy a gentle, quiet pace of life. They live in houses built of coral lime and concrete block, clustered in villages along coastal areas. They respect the traditions of their ancestors, believe in the extended family, and owe allegiance to their tribal chief.

Religion. The church plays an important role in the lives of Cook Islanders. There are Sunday services and several religious holidays. Visitors are welcome to attend services and enjoy hymn singing.

Economy. Agriculture is the mainstay of the Cook Island economy. People grow fruits and vegetables not only for their own consumption but also for export.

Island festivities

A love of sports and music is reflected in the Cook Islanders' special events and festivals. Many include sports activities and dancing and singing contests.

Bareback horse races are held about every 6 weeks on Muri Beach. However, there's no guarantee that the ponies will finish the race. Some stop running at the halfway point and others detour into the ocean for a swim.

The Cook Islanders also enjoy lawn bowling, tennis, sailing, rugby, netball, and cricket.

Planning Your Trip

Few travelers visited the Cook Islands until 1973, when the international airport capable of handling big jets was completed. Before that time, international transportation relied on passenger ships and flying boats.

Now travelers fly to the Cook Islands from New Zealand, Tahiti, Fiji, the United States, and Western Samoa.

(Continued on page 52)

Pineapple *and citrus fruits thrive in rich volcanic soil of southern Cooks. Avarua factory processes juice for export.*

Children *dressed in bright costumes gather to perform religious plays outdoors on Gospel Day, October 26.*

You'll arrive on Rarotonga, the country's main island. The airport is just a 5-km/3-mile drive west of Avarua, the capital. Most hotels provide airport shuttle service and a few taxis are available.

Both cruise and passenger/cargo ships stop in the Cook Islands on South Pacific voyages. Since the Avarua harbor can't accommodate large ships, passengers can be ferried by launch to the downtown wharf.

Traveling around the Cooks

The islands of Rarotonga and Aitutaki are the two main tourist destinations in the Cook Islands. Regular scheduled air service by Cook Island Airways links the two islands.

Small interisland cargo vessels provide service when needed to outer islands in the northern and southern Cooks. Used mainly by the local people, these vessels have limited passenger accommodations.

Sightseeing on your own. Public transportation is limited on Rarotonga and Aitutaki. If you want to tour the islands independently, rent a bicycle, car, or motorscooter—the Cook Islanders' favorite form of transportation. Traffic moves on the left in the Cook Islands.

Tours. On Rarotonga, you can take a variety of interesting tours. Aitutaki also has tours.

Where to stay in the Cooks

Tourist accommodations in the Cook Islands are just beginning to expand. With 150 rooms, the Rarotongan—8 km/5 miles south of the international airport—is the country's only large international class resort hotel.

Rarotonga's other hotels and motels are small (3 to 40 rooms) but comfortable. Most are located near Avarua, and many of the rooms have kitchen facilities. These accommodations include the Trailways Hotel, Arorangi Beach Motel, Motel Marie, Little Polynesian Motel, Puaikura Reef Lodges, and KiiKii Motel.

On Aitutaki you'll find just one small comfortable motel—the Rapae.

Since accommodations are limited in the Cooks, visitors must have confirmed reservations prior to arrival. Camping is prohibited in the Cook Islands.

Dining and entertainment

One of the best ways to see Cook Islands entertainment and sample local foods is to attend a special island night. These are held regularly at the Rarotongan, Trailways Hotel, and Arorangi Beach Motel

In addition to the above-mentioned restaurants, you may want to try the Vai Ma in Titikaveka, the Kumete in Avarua, and the Outrigger in Arorangi.

Shop for handicrafts

You'll find examples of Cook Island crafts for sale at the Women's Federation Handcraft Shop at Constitution Park in Avarua. You can select from carved wooden bowls; shell jewelry; woven straw baskets, hats, and mats; and ukuleles made from coconut shells. The intricate, brightly colored designs of the *Tivaevae* (bedspreads) will catch your eye. These are painstakingly hand sewn, then appliquéd.

Most stores are open from 7:30 A.M. to 3:30 P.M. Monday to Friday and from 7:30 to 11:30 A.M. Saturday. Some village stores near entertainment centers stay open in the evenings. Bargaining is not customary.

Recreational activities

You can enjoy both water sports and land sports in the Cook Islands. Reef walking is popular on the reef surrounding Rarotonga. If you're interested, join a guided tour to learn about the reef marine life.

For a closer look at aquatic creatures, go skin diving, scuba diving, or snorkeling in the lagoons of Rarotonga and Aitutaki. Snorkeling equipment and some diving equipment are available for rent. Inquire at your hotel.

Fishermen can contact the Cook Island Tourist Authority in central Avarua for information on deep-sea fishing. Catches include tuna and marlin.

Land sports include golf and tennis. You can golf at the Rarotonga Golf Club at Nikao and at a course near the airport on Aitutaki. The Rarotongan has tennis courts.

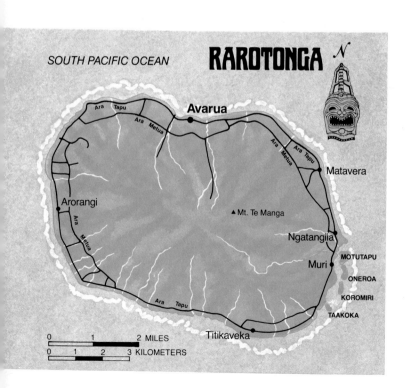

Seeing the Cook Islands

During your visit, you will spend most of your time on Rarotonga Island. Many travelers consider this mountainous island one of the most spectacular in the South

Pacific. A tiny piece of land—only 67 square km/26 square miles—it has 12 peaks over 305 meters/1,000 feet.

The smaller island of Aitutaki is a less mountainous island. Only an hour's flight from Rarotonga, it has a beautiful 10-km/6-mile-wide lagoon dotted with islets.

Touring Rarotonga

The country's capital of Avarua—located on Rarotonga's north shore—is the place to begin your exploration. Over a third of Rarotonga's population of 9,800 lives in the Avarua area.

Avarua sights. The Avarua area offers several historic sights to explore. The old Mission House—built in 1847 to house the headquarters of the London Missionary Society in the Cooks—is being restored and serves as a Church Museum. Many of the first missionaries are buried in the churchyard of the nearby Cook Islands Christian Church.

You'll also want to visit the busy wharf area. All fishing boats and interisland traders arrive and depart from here. Laden with flowers, whole families gather on the dock to greet or bid farewell to friends and relatives traveling on the interisland boats.

Circling Rarotonga. Venturing beyond Avarua, you can take the 32-km/20-mile road (Ara Tapu) skirting the perimeter of Rarotonga. On this road travelers see beaches, lagoons, villages nearly hidden among coconut palms, flowering trees and bushes, and towering mountain peaks covered in vegetation. You'll see fishermen out on the reef, children riding ponies along the beach, and men working in taro patches. Be sure to stop at Ngatangiia Harbor. From here, legend states, one of the last great Polynesian migrations sailed for New Zealand.

Historical road. Inland from the main road, you can still travel on sections of Ara Metua, a road built over 1,000 years ago. Cook Island legend says that this coral block road—now potholed and overgrown by vegetation in places—was engineered by a powerful warrior king named Toi about A.D. 900.

Trip to Aitutaki

The island of Aitutaki is located 224 km/139 miles north of Rarotonga. With a population of 2,500, Aitutaki is even more tranquil than its sister island.

Aitutaki achieved recognition in the 1950s when Tasman Empire Airway's (now Air New Zealand) Coral Route flying boat service used the island of Akaiami in Aitutaki's large lagoon as a refueling base. This was the first time that an uninhabited island had been visited by an international airline.

Know Before You Go

The information below will help you plan your trip to the Cooks.

Entry/exit procedures. If you are staying in the Cook Islands 31 days or less, you won't need a visa, just a valid passport and onward ticket.

Baggage of arriving passengers from Fiji, Western Samoa, and Hawaii will be fumigated. Since this process can take up to 3 hours, it's advisable to pack items needed on arrival in your hand luggage. Fumigation is necessary to prevent agricultural pests from entering the islands.

Smallpox vaccinations are required if you're arriving from an infected area. (Note: Since health requirements can change, it's advisable to check with your public health department before your trip.)

There is no airport departure tax.

Customs. Visitors may bring in duty-free personal effects plus 200 cigarettes, 50 cigars, or a half pound of tobacco; 1 quart of wine and 1 quart of spirits; and 2 still cameras or 1 still and 1 movie camera.

Currency. New Zealand dollars and Cook Islands coins (up to NZ $1). The recent exchange rate is NZ $1 = U.S. $1.09, and Australian $.95.

Tipping. There is no tipping.

Time. The Cooks are 10½ hours behind Greenwich mean time. When it is noon Saturday in Avarua, it is 2:30 P. M. Saturday in Los Angeles; 8:30 A. M. Sunday in Sydney; and 10:30 A. M. Sunday in Auckland.

Weather and what to wear. The Cook Islands have a warm tropical climate tempered by the trade winds. The cool season runs from May to October with temperatures averaging 25 °C/77 °F. During the warmer, wetter months (December to March), temperatures average 28 °C/82 °F.

Visitors dress in casual resort wear all year. If you plan to attend a church service, remember that Cook Islanders dress up for church. Women visitors should plan to wear a dress and men long trousers and a dress shirt. You'll need beach shoes for reef walking.

For more information. Your best source of information is the Cook Islands Tourist Authority, P.O. Box 14, Rarotonga, Cook Islands. You can also get information from your local Air New Zealand office.

In the United States, contact the Pacific Islands Tourism Development Council, represented in North America by Transportation Consultants International in Los Angeles, San Francisco, and Seattle.

MELANESIA

Fiji, New Caledonia, New Hebrides, Papua New Guinea, Solomons

Situated between the equator and the Tropic of Capricorn, the Melanesian islands include the countries of Fiji, New Caledonia, New Hebrides, Papua New Guinea, and the Solomon Islands.

The word Melanesia is derived from a Greek word meaning "black islands." Seafaring explorers may have given this name because of the dark-skinned inhabitants. Or they may have chosen the word to describe the jungle covered mountainous islands that appeared dark and forbidding from a distance.

The islands of Melanesia offer far more than dark vine-entangled jungles. Visitors can walk through rain forests rich in exotic tropical flowers and birds, ride across grassy plateaus dotted with grazing cattle, travel to primitive river villages by comfortable riverboat, swim in turquoise lagoons, or hike to mountaintops to enjoy wide-ranging views.

The Melanesian People

The people of these fascinating islands are as diverse as their landscape. Physically, they range from small and stocky types to medium or tall. Skin tones vary from deep brown to blue black. Most have wiry, curly hair. You'll see some traces of Polynesian and Micronesian ancestry; both of these groups stopped briefly on some Melanesian islands during their Pacific explorations.

The Melanesian migration

Scientists believe that the Melanesian islands were inhabited long before the first Polynesians explored the Pacific Ocean. They believe that at the end of the last glacial period, nomadic tribes migrated from the freezing forests of Asia south through the warm Malay peninsula, finally settling in New Guinea. Carbon dating of artifacts indicates that New Guinea was inhabited as early as 8000 B.C. Unlike the Polynesians, the Melanesians have no legends telling of migration from a homeland.

Over the years, additional tribes migrated into the area. These latecomers were physically larger than their predecessors, causing the first nomadic clans to retreat into the remote interior mountain regions.

Creation of separate cultures

The ruggedness of the land isolated many individual tribes and clans, who developed their own languages, traditions, and cultures that still exist today. Each clan or tribe held itself apart from the others. All strangers were suspect and automatically considered enemies.

These feelings made war between the clans and tribes inevitable. Elaborate preparations for war and fighting were part of normal village life. When a person from one tribe was killed by a member of another, a "payback" war or killing was customary. Some rituals demanded human sacrifice, and cannibalism was common in some areas.

Arrival of White Men

The first white men to land on Melanesian islands—mainly explorers—quickly discovered that the people of

Hideaway retreats *such as Fiji's Mana Island offer carefree relaxation on palm-fringed beaches. Overnight guests stay in thatched cottages.*

Melanesia were less friendly than their Polynesian neighbors.

The Melanesians were highly suspicious of these light-skinned people who had oddly shaped heads (hats) and removable skin (clothing). Many tribesmen feared that these white men could only be the evil spirits of their ancestors. They felt these evil spirits must be driven away with bows and arrows and spears. When the white men responded to the attacks not with spears but with magic sticks that smoked and killed (guns), the natives knew for certain that these evil spirits had supernatural powers.

The explorers who survived fled back to their home-lands, spreading tales of the hostility and cannibalism existing in the dark islands. This news kept many travelers from visiting Melanesia.

The lure of money

Some adventurers ignored the stories of bloodthirsty savages because of the lure of money. Sandalwood traders had learned that the Melanesian islands were rich in sandalwood, so they talked the natives into helping them cut down the trees. Later, some traders destroyed entire villages, killing all the people before sailing away. Others exchanged firearms for sandalwood. The natives learned to use these "magic sticks" on each other, and massive warfare ensued, resulting inevitably in the deaths of many islanders.

Another money-hungry group of white men arrived in the Melanesian islands during this period. Not interested in the riches of the land, these "blackbirders" wanted the people for use as slave labor on South Pacific sugar cane plantations. Thousands of young Melanesian men were sold by their chiefs in exchange for guns—or simply shanghaied away from their villages and shipped off to a strange land. Many of them never saw their island homes again.

Christianity arrives

Inspired by success in the Polynesian islands, mission-aries ventured into Melanesia to spread the Christian word, but they didn't always receive a cordial welcome. After continued hardship and many deaths, they finally began to make inroads, converting many Melanesians to Christianity.

However, in some remote areas today, there are tribes that still cling to traditional practices and ancestor worship.

Foreign rule

As more missionaries and other foreign settlers began to arrive in the Melanesian islands, they began to demand protection from their own governments.

One by one, the Melanesian islands came under for-eign rule. Great Britain claimed the Solomons and Fiji. France began to govern New Caledonia. The Dutch and the British divided Papua New Guinea (later Australia took over), and Britain and France shared the responsi-bility of ruling the New Hebrides with a condominium form of government.

Today, the Melanesian countries are again gaining their independence from outside control. Fiji, Papua New Guinea, and the Solomons are all independent nations, and recently the New Hebrides received the right to internal self government.

World War II influences

In the early 1940s, war came to many Melanesian islands. Natives who had known little about the world outside their primitive villages were suddenly exposed to modern technology. People from across the sea brought in a bewildering array of military equipment—airplanes, tanks, bombs, battleships, kerosene lamps, tents, and radios.

Many of the Melanesians, so recently removed from the Stone Age, fought bravely beside the Allied soldiers to drive the Japanese invaders from their land during World War II.

Melanesia Today

Today the Melanesian countries are struggling to enter the modern technological world while maintaining the customs, crafts, and culture of their ancestors. Visitors traveling to these countries see a sharp contrast in life styles between modern concrete towns congested with motor vehicles and the peaceful, thatch hut villages in the countryside where the only traffic moves by foot or horse.

In your travels, you'll experience the influences of foreign rule on the architecture in the towns, the res-taurant food, and the language. You'll also learn of the Melanesian people's cultural heritage reflected in their crafts, their dances, their music, their architecture, and their dress.

One important element has changed since early ex-plorers set foot on Melanesian soil. Unlike the reception accorded some of these first visitors, you will be welcomed as a friend, not an evil spirit or enemy. Everywhere you travel, Melanesian smiles will greet you.

Today Melanesia is a place where traces of the Stone Age and modern society live side by side.

Fiji, a friendly country

You can't help liking Fiji. From the moment you arrive by plane or ship, the friendliness of its people warms you like the waters of the South Seas. Dignified Fijians smile and greet you with "Bula" (hello)—not just once but repeatedly. Travelers enjoy a standing invitation to play or relax in modern towns, thatch hut villages, or on sandy beaches.

Towns and villages. In Suva, Fiji's capital, you stroll streets lined with aging, colonial-style wood buildings and modern concrete high rises. In the public market, you'll mingle with sari-clad Indians and sulu-wrapped Fijians. Visitors find a fascinating combination of ethnic groups in Fiji.

Outside the relative sophistication of Suva, you discover traditional villages of thatch-roofed *bures* (huts) where the people cling to the ways of their ancestors. Villagers don't need clocks or watches—they live a sun-and-tides existence geared to their fishing and agricultural economy.

Beach resorts. After you've explored Fiji's towns and villages, you can relax on its beaches. Scattered along the southern shore of Viti Levu, you'll find numerous Coral Coast resorts where visitors enjoy a variety of recreational activities ranging from water sports to golf and tennis.

If you yearn for a brief Robinson Crusoe existence, take a short boat trip to any of several offshore hideaway islands. Here you can stay in a thatch bure with the beach and clear blue lagoon just a few steps from your door.

Fijian culture. The Fijian people retain many traditions of their ancestors. You'll discover some of them as you view the ritualistic preparation of *yaqona* (a ceremonial drink made from a pepper plant root) and enjoy dances and songs at a *meke* (Fijian celebration). At a firewalking ceremony, visitors watch in amazement as barefooted Fijian men walk across white-hot rocks without getting burned.

New Caledonia, a touch of France

New Caledonia has been a possession of France since 1853. For more than a century, French influences have created a touch of France in the South Pacific.

Nouméa. These French influences are most prevalent in the country's capital, Nouméa, sometimes affectionately called the Paris of the Pacific. Here you'll find French boutiques, old houses with "gingerbread" iron grillwork, sidewalk cafes offering French dishes and wines, and bakeries selling long, crusty loaves of French bread.

Beyond Nouméa. Outside the capital, you can explore the other attractions of Grande Terre (the main island) plus some of New Caledonia's offshore islands. You'll see villages of thatch huts and smiling Melanesian women bedecked in colorful Mother Hubbards (loose fitting dresses). A trip to the Isle of Pines offers vistas of haunting beauty—short-branched pine trees; incredibly white, velvet-soft beaches; and shimmering lagoons of brilliant turquoise.

The French call New Caledonia "L'Île de Lumière," the Island of Light. After you have strolled its beautiful beaches, explored its lush mountain valleys, and swum in its sparkling sea, you'll agree.

New Hebrides, land of primitive rituals

In some ways, the New Hebrides islands seem more distant and foreign than any of the other island groups in the South Pacific. The visitor finds offbeat travel experiences in these islands where volcanoes smoke and erupt and the New Hebrideans still perform primitive rituals.

Men on Pentecost Island still dive headfirst from high platforms—restrained only by vines around their ankles—in a century-old ritual. Other New Hebrideans cling to the belief that "John Frum" will eventually send them cargos of riches from across the sea; their red, wooden crosses dot the countryside and villages of Tanna Island.

World War II touched these islands, and the rusting scrap of military debris remains. Luganville on Espirito Santo was one of the key staging areas for U.S. troops advancing on the Solomon Islands.

Papua New Guinea, a multicultured country

More than 700 languages and 700 different cultures exist in Papua New Guinea—a place where primitive traditions retain a strong appeal. Many tribes have emerged only recently from a dominant Stone Age culture. Hidden among Papua New Guinea's isolated plateaus and secluded valleys are areas where tribespeople remain untouched by the 20th century, living just as their ancestors did.

Meeting the people. Touring, especially in the Highlands, is a fascinating experience. On ceremonial occasions, tribesmen adorn themselves in unusual costumes; each tribe has a distinctive personality. Here you'll find wig men, top-heavy with huge elaborate bull-horn hats of woven human hair; mud men, grotesque in baked earthen masks, their bodies caked with mud; and basket men, encased from head to foot in cones of wicker. Other tribal men and women paint their faces and bodies in brilliant reds, blues, and yellows and adorn their heads with large headdresses made of colorful bird of paradise feathers.

In contrast to the Highlands, you can cruise along the Sepik River, meeting people who live in stilt houses and fear the crocodiles lurking nearby. The primitive art of these people is renowned as some of the best in the South Pacific.

Seeing the land. Papua New Guinea offers a varied landscape ranging from soaring mountain peaks—sometimes topped with snow—to mist-shrouded, alpine meadows; white, sandy beaches; vine-entangled jungles; and mangrove swamps.

You can visit Port Moresby, the country's capital, or travel out to Rabaul on New Britain. Rabaul, the Japanese center of operations in the southwest Pacific in World War II, has been completely rebuilt since it was destroyed during the war.

The Solomons, World War II battleground

Many World War II veterans who fought in the South Pacific will never forget the Solomon Islands. Places like Guadalcanal, Bloody Ridge, Iron Bottom Sound, and the "Slot" all recall memories of the fierce battles that were fought here.

Guadalcanal marked the point where U.S. Marines succeeded in stalling the formidable Japanese military offense, changing the course of the war in the Pacific. On the tiny island of Olasana (now known as Plum Pudding Island), John F. Kennedy and 10 other survivors of PT-109 were marooned.

As you tour the Solomons today, you travel past rusting war remains and military battlegrounds. You can meet Solomon Islanders who live in stilt house villages and barter with money made from shells.

FIJI

"Bula!" You'll hear this friendly Fijian hello often as you explore these tropical islands. Smiling strangers greet you warmly on city streets and wave on rural roads. Little wonder visitors from all parts of the world consider Fiji one of the South Pacific's most hospitable countries.

In Fiji (locally pronounced "Fe-*gee*"), visitors discover a fascinating population representing many ethnic groups—in addition to Fijians, you'll see Indians, Chinese, and Europeans as well as other South Pacific islanders. Strolling the streets of Suva, Fiji's capital, you pass turbaned Sikhs, sari-clad Indian women, and Fijians wrapped in skirtlike *sulus*.

Beyond the bustle of Suva's urban communities, villagers live much as their ancestors did generations ago—a sun-and-tides existence geared to their agricultural and fishing economy. They dwell in thatch-roofed houses and cling to the old communal life style.

Beyond the villages and urban centers, Fiji offers golden sandy beaches and beautiful blue lagoons.

A Tropical Archipelago

Situated just west of the 180th meridian south of the equator, the Fiji Islands are approximately 2,736 km/1,700 miles northeast of Sydney, 1,770 km/1,100 miles north of Auckland, and 9,012 km/5,600 miles southwest of Los Angeles.

How many islands comprise the Fiji archipelago? Estimates range from 300 to 500, depending on whether you count every little coral atoll (many of them underwater at high tide) or only the large atolls and islands. Of these, only about 100 are inhabited.

Viti Levu, the largest island, covers about 10,363 square km/4,000 square miles—over half of Fiji's land area. Fiji's main towns dot the Viti Levu coast at Suva, Lautoka, and Nadi.

A short distance northeast of Viti Levu is its smaller sister island, Vanua Levu. Other lesser islands and island groups include Taveuni, Ovalau, Vatulele, Beqa, the Laus, the Mamanucas, and the Yasawas.

Volcanic mountains, navigable rivers

Volcanic mountain ranges span Fiji's larger islands in a northeast-southwest line. Heavy rains—up to 3,048 mm/120 inches per year—fall on the eastern, windward side of these mountains, producing dense, dark green, tropical forests. Yellow green, rolling grasslands and sugar cane fields border the islands' western, leeward side where rainfall is only half as much.

Many navigable rivers and small streams drain the mountain ranges. Local people ply these waterways in punts and motorized launches, visiting nearby villages and going to market. One of the largest navigable rivers is the Rewa, located on Viti Levu east of Suva.

Countless palm-lined beaches border turquoise lagoons. Offshore, coral lies in broken patches and fringing reefs. Largest of Fiji's coral reefs is the 193 km/120 mile Great Sea Reef north of Viti Levu. Colorful coral and marine life inhabit the lagoon and reef areas.

Exotic flowers—among them poinciana, bougainvillea, hibiscus, frangipani, and orchids—bloom profusely in the warm, tropical sun. Abundant fruits such as breadfruits, mangoes, and bananas provide an important part of the Fijian diet.

Wildlife includes flying foxes (a type of bat), lizards, and several types of snakes—all nonpoisonous. One of the islands' more prevalent mammals is the mongoose, introduced in the 19th century to eliminate the burgeoning mice and rat population. Instead, the ferretlike animal developed a fondness for villagers' poultry and has become a pest.

A Pacific crossroads

Fiji has long been a Pacific crossroads. Archeologists believe the Fiji Islands were inhabited as early as 1500 B.C. Migrating Polynesians presumably stopped here on early journeys to Tonga and Samoa.

The first recorded European discovery of the Fiji Islands was made by Abel Tasman in 1643. His stories of cannibalism and treacherous coral reefs kept explorers away from Fiji until 1774, when Captain James Cook briefly sailed through the southern islands. Fifteen years later, Captain William Bligh (of *Mutiny on the Bounty* fame) reported barely escaping pursuing cannibals when he ventured into the area.

But the profitable lure of sandalwood and *bêche-de-mere* (sea cucumber, a marine animal consumed mainly by the Chinese) finally drew traders and sailors to the Fiji Islands in the early 19th century. These adventurers introduced European firearms which the native tribes began to use against each other. Fierce intertribal warfare and increased cannibalism plagued the country for the next 40 years.

During this period the first missionaries came to these "cannibal isles." They helped to abolish the practice of cannibalism and transcribed the Fijian language into writing.

Fiji didn't become unified and relatively peaceful until the mid-19th century, when a tribal chief of Bau, Ratu Cakobau, assumed leadership. However, Cakobau found himself unable to resolve all of the country's secular and religious problems. In 1858 he offered the islands to Great Britain, but his offer was refused. He next offered the islands to the United States, but since

Tropical islands *off Viti Levu attract visitors for day excursions or longer stays. Resorts like Plantation Village feature white sand beaches, water sports, simple accommodations, buffet meals.*

Costumed Fijian entertainers, *their soot-painted faces grimacing in mock fierceness, brandish spears to accompaniment of loud, forceful chants. Tribal warriors formerly performed intimidating war dance preceding battle.*

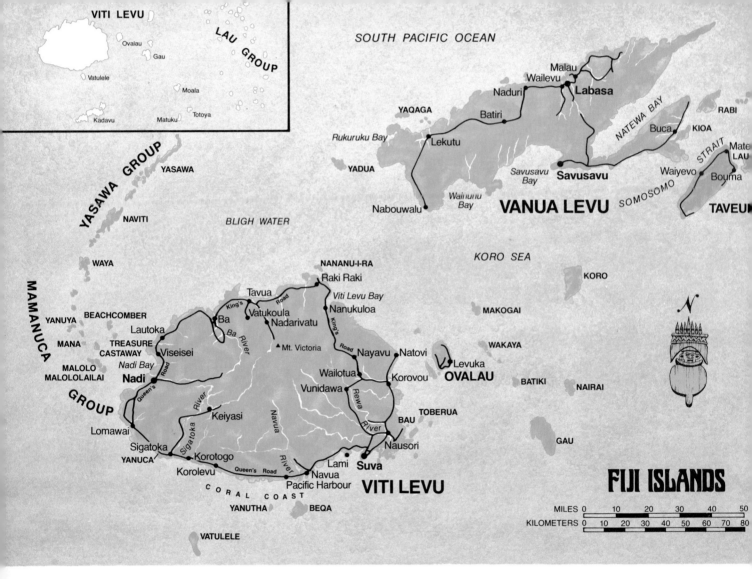

that country was engaged in its Civil War, this offer was ignored. Britain finally accepted a second offer, and, under a Deed of Cession, Fiji was annexed as a British Crown Colony on October 10, 1874.

Nearly a century later, Fiji achieved full independence. On October 10, 1970, the country became a member of the British Commonwealth with Dominion status.

Today Fiji has an elected House of Representatives, an appointed Senate, a Prime Minister, and a Governor-General representing the British Crown. King Cakobau's war club has now become the mace of the Fijian legislature.

Fiji's People

The people of Fiji provide an interesting contrast of cultures. Of the 586,000 people, nearly 259,000 are Fijian and 292,000 Indian. Most of the remaining 35,000 inhabitants are of Chinese or European ancestry or are from other South Pacific islands.

Village and rural life

The tall, handsome, easygoing Fijians are mainly Melanesian, with a trace of Polynesian ancestry. Most of them live in small, rural villages in thatch-roofed *bures*—small walled huts constructed from natural materials such as grass, dry leaves, bamboo, and reeds. They participate in a communal life style where rewards and obligations are shared equally, and all activity is governed by a chief. Even those who work in town feel a continuing obligation to their village and contribute financially when they can.

Fijian villagers grow yams, taros, *cassava* (tapioca), *kumalas* (sweet potatoes), and other vegetables and fruits in their gardens. Crops not consumed are sold or used for trade.

Missionaries—particularly Methodist—left a lasting mark on village life, and the church still plays an important role in community activities.

Many Fijian men and women wear the traditional *sulu,* a wrap-type skirt. Men's sulus are calf-length and worn with western-style shirts or flowered, loose-fitting tops called *bula* shirts. Women wear ankle-length sulus (they feel their legs should not be exposed —a vestige of missionary influence) with long tops.

The Indian influence

Indians originally were brought to Fiji from India as indentured servants in the early days of British colonial rule. European settlers imported them to work the sugar plantations—a job the Fijians didn't want.

Descendants of these indentured servants who remained in Fiji have prospered. They dominate Fiji's town life as merchants and professional people.

Some still work on or manage sugar cane plantations. However, over 85 percent of Fiji's land is community property, owned by the native Fijians and administered by the Native Lands Trust Board.

Many of these island-born Indians—some of them third generation—have never been to India, yet they observe traditional customs and religious beliefs. Hinduism is the predominant religion of the Indians; Moslems and Sikhs are also represented. Unlike India, Fiji has no caste system.

You can identify Indian settlements by their brightly painted, multicolored wooden houses. Many Indian women still wear flowing silk saris, but most Indian men choose western-style dress.

Sugar, copra, and a little gold

Sugar leads the list of Fiji's agricultural exports. Large processing plants are located in Lautoka and Ba (on Viti Levu) and Labasa (on Vanua Levu). Other exports include copra and a little gold.

In recent years tourism has become an increasingly important source of revenue.

Sporting enthusiasts

Fijians love athletic competition, either as spectators or participants. Rugby, soccer, hockey, cricket, boxing, and wrestling all arouse fervent enthusiasm. Various Fiji teams compete both locally and internationally. They have played in the United Kingdom, Canada, Australia, and New Zealand.

Competitions in skin diving, deep-sea and river fishing, swimming, lawn bowling, bicycling, yachting, and power boating are also popular.

Planning Your Trip

Since the days of canoe exploration, Fiji has been at the hub of South Pacific travel. Today, it lies on an important route between North America and Australia and New Zealand. Several international airlines and various cruise ships and cargo/passenger liners stop in Fiji.

When you arrive, you'll land on Fiji's main island

YAQONA
It's a Drink of Welcome

In Fiji as well as other South Pacific islands, the ceremonial drinking of *yaqona* serves as a symbol of welcome, an expression of hospitality and friendship. Outside Fiji, the drink might be called *kava,* or perhaps *ava* or *sakau.*

Although preparation may differ slightly from country to country, the drink is made primarily from powdered pepper plant roots blended with water. Many travelers who taste the liquid for the first time claim it tastes like what it looks like—muddy water. However, those who have acquired a taste for the cloudy mixture find it refreshing. After several bowls, the nonalcoholic drink can produce a slightly numb tongue and lips.

A solemn, stylized ritual—requiring total silence on the part of the honored guests—accompanies the ceremonial preparation and drinking of yaqona in Fiji. As a guest, you sit cross-legged in front of a large *tanoa* (wooden bowl with legs) to witness the preparation of the drink. Words are chanted and the *lali* (wooden drum) sounded. When the yaqona is the right consistency, your portion is served in a half coconut shell *bilo* (cup). You clap once, accept the bowl in both hands and down it in a single draught while your host claps three times. Both you and your host then clap three more times and your host shouts *"maca"* (meaning "it is drained").

At various hotels, the yaqona ceremony precedes an evening of native dancing and feasting. It is also held before a Fijian firewalking demonstration.

Venerable *Grand Pacific Hotel, built in 1914, adds colonial accent to Suva's Victoria Parade. Locally called the GPH, hotel exudes languid South Seas atmosphere. Lobby accents include ceiling fans and rattan chairs.*

Shaded *by parasols from tropical sun, Indian women draped in saris display vegetables for sale in Suva market near King's Wharf. Early morning is busiest time.*

FIJIAN PRONOUNCING PRIMER...

Mind Your Bs and Qs

In the Fijian language, there's more to the printed word than meets the eye. Take for instance, the town name—Nadi. It's pronounced "*Nan*-dee." Or the island of Beqa, home of the firewalkers. It's pronounced "M*beng*-ga." Sigatoka is pronounced "*Sing*-a-toka." Cakobau Road, "Tha-*komb*-au" Road.

Keeping track of these added consonants can boggle the mind of the visitor who'd like to pronounce his bs and qs and other consonants correctly while he's in Fiji. You even hesitate saying *bula* (hello), wondering whether it shouldn't come out sounding something like "mboula." (It should.)

Actually there are just five consonants in the Fijian language that take special treatment. Fix in your mind the pronunciations of b, c, d, g, and q and you'll have an easier time. If you memorize the following rules and words, they'll help you in your Fiji travels:

- B is pronounced "mb"; the "m" is almost a silent murmur. Try saying "M*ba*" (Ba) and "M*bau*" (Bau).
- C is pronounced "th." Try saying "Ma-ma-*nu*-thas" (Mamanucas) and "Ya-*nu*-tha" (Yanuca).
- D is pronounced "nd." Try saying "*Nan*-dee" (Nadi).
- G is pronounced "ng." Try saying "*Sing*-a-toka" (Sigatoka).
- Q is pronounced "ng-g." Try saying "M*beng*-ga" (Beqa).

Now that you've mastered a little of the Fijian language, remember that as you drink a cup of *yaqona* (Fiji's national drink) someday you'll be telling a friend about a drink called "yang-*gona*."

---

of Viti Levu—at Suva Harbour if you come by ship, Nadi International Airport if by plane. (Some flights from Tonga, New Zealand, and Western Samoa land at Nausori Airport near Suva.)

Getting around Fiji

Air Pacific and Fiji Air provide the fastest mode of travel within the Fiji Islands. Regularly scheduled flights link the main towns on Viti Levu and the other islands. Daily flights also depart for resort areas along Viti Levu's Coral Coast.

If you have the time to explore the countryside beyond Fiji's towns and resorts, you can take a coach or rent a car. Coaches allow passengers to enjoy the scenery without worrying about the curving road ahead. If you prefer to travel at a more relaxed pace and don't mind tackling dusty (sometimes muddy) roads, drive yourself.

Taxicabs are plentiful in Viti Levu's main towns. They also operate on Vanua Levu, Taveuni, and in Levuka on Ovalau. Drivers are well informed and rates are moderate. Taxis are metered in town. However, for trips of more than 16 km/10 miles, driver and passenger should mutually agree on the fare before departure.

In Suva, Lautoka, and Levuka on Ovalau you can take a local bus around town.

Traveling by bus. Island buses—without air conditioning—provide regular service between main towns on Viti Levu, Vanua Levu, and Taveuni. For a short trip, these commuter buses provide a colorful experience. Buses have no glass windows; instead, canvas blinds are raised during dry (dusty) weather and unfurled when it rains. Accompanying you and your fellow passengers may be live chickens and freshly caught fish.

On Viti Levu, an air-conditioned coach follows the Queen's Road between Suva and Nadi International Airport, stopping at all the major hotels.

Driving in Fiji. Fiji has 3,138 km/1,950 miles of public roads, yet outside the towns, very few of them are paved. The unpaved roads are narrow, winding, and bumpy. Dusty during the dry season, they become muddy and subject to flash floods during rainstorms.

Following British tradition, traffic moves on the left side of the road. Visitors who plan to drive will need a valid driver's license issued by their own country.

If you are renting a car to drive long distances over unpaved roads, check to see that the car's tires (including the spare) are in good condition. Repair shops are infrequent.

Rental car agencies are located in Nadi, Suva, Lautoka, Pacific Harbour, Sigatoka, and Labasa (on Vanua Levu). The traveler who enjoys the freedom of motoring —but who doesn't want to drive—can hire a chauffeur-driven car.

Cruising. If you have a leisurely itinerary, consider interisland cargo vessels as another way of seeing Fiji's islands. The boats make more-or-less regular stops at most of the inhabited islands, where they leave supplies, pick up copra, and take on an occasional passenger.

Don't expect luxurious accommodations, since these ships are designed for hauling cargo. Your schedule must be flexible, because weather, cargo loading, and related conditions affect departure times.

Posh resorts or simple bures

Fiji's accommodations suit a range of tastes and pocketbooks. You can stay in a convenient downtown hotel or try one of several elegant beach resorts complete with tennis and golf. If total escape is what you're looking for, you can settle into a simple but comfortable thatch or tile-roofed country *bure* (a small bungalow with steeply peaked roof and louvered windows). Additional choices include budget-priced, family-oriented housekeeping units; inexpensive guest houses with breakfast included in the price; and large luxurious condominiums, each with a private swimming pool.

Most accommodations include coffee and tea-making facilities in each room, so you can enjoy a "cuppa" any time. Some rooms contain small refrigerators.

Accommodations can be found on Viti Levu, Vanua Levu, Ovalau, the Mamanuca Group, and Taveuni. Information on the types of accommodations available in each area can be found under specific destinations.

Fiji's tourist season peaks in May, August, and from mid-December through mid-January. Reservations for this holiday period are sometimes made a year in advance.

Eating—Fiji-style

Fiji's wide range of ethnic cuisines offers some new experiences in dining. Stone-roasted suckling pig, spicy Indian curries, and Chinese noodles are just three of the items from which to choose. Hotel restaurants provide the best places to enjoy these dishes, though some local restaurants feature Chinese, Indian, British, and American foods.

Island fare. Local specialties include a variety of fish, fresh from the ocean and well prepared. A favorite Fijian first course is *kokoda*—chopped raw fish, onions, and coconut milk (*lolo*).

Lolo—milk obtained from grating and straining fresh coconut—is an ingredient in many Fijian dishes. It is used to flavor anything from a fish specialty like kokoda to the simple *dalo* (vegetablelike taro root).

In Fiji you'll find an abundance of tropical fruits such as mangoes, oranges, *paw paws* (papayas), bananas, pineapples, and coconuts. Other local desserts include tapioca, British-type puddings, and ice cream.

Many hotels hold buffet-style feasts and barbecues featuring Fijian-type foods at least once a week. Tasty specialties include crab, shrimp, oysters, fish, suckling pig, *kumalas* (sweet potatoes), several types of yams, baked bananas, and Indian curries. Some items may be cooked traditionally—wrapped in banana leaves and baked in a *lovo* (earth oven) for several hours.

Buffet-style meals are very popular in Fiji for both lunch and dinner—and sometimes even for breakfast.

The country's traditional drink is *yaqona,* made from pepper plant roots. A ritualistic ceremony accompanies the preparation and drinking of this liquid (see page 61). One of the most popular beverages is locally brewed Fiji beer. All wines and liquors are imported.

Flashing spears and joyful song. Feasts (also called *magitis*) held at the hotels often include a *meke*—a Fijian celebration in song and dance. To the beat of the *deruas* (thick bamboo lengths) and *lali* (hollow log drums), costumed Fijians perform generations-old dances and songs.

Tall, muscular, grass-skirted men—their faces painted with soot—leap toward you, brandishing spears or clubs.

Their flashing eyes and loud, forceful chants remind you that this was once a war dance performed before battle.

On a gentler note, the women—attired in floor-length *masi* (Fijian tapa cloth) garments—sing of domestic village life and the planting of crops. Much of their dance movements are performed seated, their hands moving gracefully to tell the story. When they stand, they sway in a kind of slow hula, their hands still the prominent feature of their dance.

During a *meke*, you might be invited to join the Fijians in the *taralala*. In this popular dance, partners move side by side, their arms about one another. They take several quick steps forward and several back in time to the music.

A shopper's paradise

Shops in Fiji offer everything from modern Japanese stereo equipment to traditional Fijian woodcarvings—sometimes sold side by side in the same store.

Before buying, try to do some comparison pricing. Some storekeepers have fixed prices; others like to bargain. Bargaining is common in the public markets. The prices are in Fijian dollars (see page 73).

Most shops are open weekdays from 8 A.M. to 4:30 P.M. (until 5 on Fridays) and from 8 to 12:30 on Saturdays. When cruise ships stop at Lautoka or Suva on Saturday afternoons and Sundays, duty-free shops in the area will open 1 hour after docking and remain open for 4 hours.

Duty-free shopping. Fiji is noted for good shopping values. Items you can buy include radios, cameras, projectors, stereo equipment, watches, French perfume, tape recorders, and diamonds.

Suva is the most popular duty-free shopping area because of its large number of stores. However, you can also shop in Nadi, Lautoka, and Sigatoka.

Fijian and Indian products. Locally made crafts and Indian products vie for your attention in many stores. Handwoven mats and baskets, shell jewelry, colorful sulus and flowered bula shirts, woodcarvings, *masi* (Fijian tapa cloth), and pottery head the list of Fijian craft items. Indian imports include bright silk saris and shiny brassware.

Public markets. Don't miss browsing through at least one public market. Tables laden with fresh fruits and vegetables are intermingled with bins of exotic Indian spices. The marketplace buzzes with excitement—conversation, punctuated with laughter, is carried on in Indian, Fijian, and English.

Though other towns have public markets, the best known is in Suva near King's Wharf. The most colorful time at any public market is early morning on Friday or Saturday when the place abounds with activity.

A South Pacific playground

Visitors to Fiji can choose from a multitude of recreational activities.

Fiji's many calm lagoons are a perfect playground for sailing, canoeing, coral viewing, snorkeling, skin diving, and fishing. You can collect shells on miles of deserted beaches or set off on a trek across a coral reef at low tide.

At the resort hotels, you can participate in archery, horseback riding, tennis, volleyball, ping pong, badminton, golf, or lawn bowling.

Skin and scuba diving. Divers won't be disappointed in Fiji. Major reefs provide a wide range of waters—shallow areas inside the lagoons for snorkelers and spear fishermen, deep waters outside the reefs for skin and scuba divers.

Around the larger islands, waters are the clearest during the cool, dry months from June through October. Scuba diving and snorkeling are possible the year around, but during the rainy season, rivers discharge muddy water into the surrounding sea.

You can find good diving spots at Astrolabe Lagoon (a 6-hour boat trip south of Suva); Argo Reef in the Lau Islands; Beqa Island waters (a 1-hour boat trip from Suva); Taveuni's Rainbow Reef; Mamanuca Group waters, especially around Mana Island (near Lautoka); and the Queen's Road coast between Suva and Nadi.

You can charter diving boats with scuba tanks at Mana Island, Suva, and Taveuni. Masks, snorkels, and flippers can be rented at most beach hotels.

Scubahire, with facilities at the Tradewinds Hotel marina in Suva, offers a complete selection of diving equipment for rent or sale. They also give diving instruction.

It is illegal to use spear guns fired with cartridges in Fiji waters unless you are a member of a spear fishing group and have received special permission from the Fiji police. (Police will only exempt equipment brought in for temporary use.) In an effort to protect marine life, diving organizations in Fiji actively discourage the use of spear guns.

Fishing. Fishermen will revel in Fiji's year-round fishing season. Most black marlin and sailfish strike between October and April; peak season occurs in January and February. Yellow-fin tuna are plentiful from December to June. Billfish, dolphin, barracuda, bonito, walu, and wahoo are caught throughout the year.

You can hire deep-sea fishing boats in Nadi (at the Regent of Fiji); at offshore island resorts near Lautoka (Castaway, Dick's Place, Plantation Village, Mana Island); along Viti Levu's Coral Coast (The Fijian, Naviti Resort, Korolevu Beach, Paradise Point, Pacific Harbour); in Suva (Tradewinds); and in Taveuni (Taveuni TraveLodge). Charter rates run $F100 to $F250 per day.

At some hotels you can rent smaller boats by the hour for lagoon fishing. If you stay on shore, you can

FESTIVAL TIME

Fiji's varied cultural background and the people's lively interest in sports provide Fiji with an active calendar. Below are a few events that will add to your Fiji visit.

January—April

New Year's Day. Fireworks, floral decorations, and festivities herald "Vakatawase" (the welcoming of the new year) on the first Monday in January.

Easter. Good Friday to Easter Monday activities include the Annual Easter Cricket Tournament in Suva and the Annual Easter Sports Meeting (track events) in Levuka.

Rugby. Early April marks the beginning of rugby season in Suva, where matches are held every Saturday through October at Albert and Buckhurst parks.

May—August

Queen Elizabeth's birthday. The queen's official birthday is celebrated on the Monday closest to June 14.

South Pacific Bowling Carnival. In June, lawn bowlers from Fiji, Australia, and New Zealand compete in this 10-day event in Suva.

Bula Festival. In mid-July, Nadi hosts this weeklong event, including floats, processions, and the crowning of a Bula Queen.

Hibiscus Festival. Late August marks one of Suva's most lively events. The week of activities features Fijian, Chinese, Indian, and Polynesian entertainment, as well as sports events, youth rallies, a fashion show, baby shows, and a parade.

Indian firewalking. People of the East Indian community hold this solemn religious ritual once a year between June and August at various locations in Fiji. The biggest firewalking event takes place in August on Howell Road in Suva.

September—December

Suva Orchid and Horticultural Show. Tropical plants and flowers are displayed at this September event in Suva.

Cricket. Early October marks the opening of the cricket season throughout Fiji. The season ends in March.

Fiji Day. On the Monday closest to October 10, Fiji's independence from Great Britain is heralded.

Diwali Festival. In late October or early November, Fiji's Indian population celebrates the Hindu New Year. Houses, porches, and paths come alive with twinkling lanterns and candles.

Prince Charles's birthday. The prince's birthday is celebrated on the Monday closest to November 14.

Christmas Day. Fijians honor this day with feasts, special church services, and Christmas programs.

enjoy fishing along the shallow flats, estuaries, and mangrove streams for salmon, cod, and mangrove snapper. Freshwater streams and rivers yield *ika droka* (jungle perch), trout, and bass.

No fishing licenses are required.

Yachting. Yachtsmen who are accredited members of overseas yacht and power boat clubs are welcome at the Royal Suva Yacht Club. Yachts and cruisers are available for charter by the day or for longer periods in both Suva and Lautoka.

Shell collecting. Several easily accessible areas just off Viti Levu offer a great variety of specimens for avid shell collectors. The Coral Coast is noted for gold cowries, while the area off Queen's Road between Navua and Suva is known for cowries and mitres. Be wary of cone shells in these areas—some are poisonous. The area around Suva is also a shell collector's paradise. Natewa Bay, off the east coast of Vanua Levu, is another area worth exploring.

Governmental restrictions prohibit taking triton shells out of the country.

Golf. If you plan to golf, you'll be pleased to find a dozen courses —11 on Viti Levu and 1 on Vanua Levu. You can play on 18-hole courses in Suva at the Fiji Golf Club or at Pacific Harbour Resort's championship course on Viti Levu's Coral Coast.

On Viti Levu, 9-hole courses are located at Nadi, Lautoka, Nausori, Ba, Vatukoula, and Penang (near Raki Raki), as well as at the Fijian, Naviti, and Korolevu Beach hotels on the Coral Coast. Vanua Levu's one course is at Labasa.

The Dominion International, Sunlover, Nadi Hotel, and Hotel Tanoa (all near Nadi), plus the Sandy Point Cottages (Sigatoka) have putting greens.

Tennis. Visitors who enjoy a game of tennis will find courts at the Suva Lawn Tennis Club in Albert Park, just across from the Grand Pacific Hotel. Fiji has 12 lawn tennis clubs whose seasons run from May to late November (before the rains start). Check with your hotel to arrange an introduction with a club official. Players are required to wear white attire. Albert Park also has Municipal Courts (hard court).

You'll find tennis courts (either lawn or hard court) at some of Fiji's hotels, including the Fiji Mocambo, Sunlover, Hotel Tanoa, Nadi Hotel, Regent of Fiji, Nadi Airport TraveLodge (all in the Nadi area); Pacific Harbour Resort, The Fijian, and Reef Hotel (all on Viti Levu's Coral Coast); Plantation Village (Malololailai Island); and Namale Plantation (Savusavu).

Exploring Viti Levu

Viti Levu, Fiji's main island, occupies more than half the land mass of the Fiji Islands. Volcanic in origin, the oval island possesses several navigable rivers. Many of its mountains rise above 914 meters/3,000 feet.

On the western side of the island, broad plains of sugar cane and grasslands stretch upward from the coast toward the densely wooded peaks. Junglelike tropical forests replace the grasslands on the island's wet east side.

Nearly 70 percent of Fiji's population live on Viti Levu. Main towns include Suva, the capital, on the island's southeast coast, and Nadi and Lautoka on the west coast.

Most visitors to Fiji spend most of their time on Viti Levu, where they enjoy duty-free shopping, miles of beaches and blue bays, and an array of recreational activities. Excursions depart from major towns to nearby offshore island retreats.

Nadi-Lautoka area

Situated on Viti Levu's west coast in the heart of lush sugar cane country, the Nadi-Lautoka area offers a composite of Fiji's scenic attractions. For many visitors —en route to other South Pacific destinations—it is their only glimpse of Fiji.

Miles of cane fields surround peaceful villages of thatch-roofed huts and Indian settlements of brightly painted, wooden houses. In Nadi and Lautoka you'll find opportunities to shop, or you can relax at nearby resorts.

A definite plus for this area is its climate. Because it's located on the leeward, "dry" side of the island, the average annual rainfall is only about 1524 mm/60 inches. (The Suva area gets nearly twice this much.)

Nadi. Fiji's main airline gateway, Nadi is a town of 23,000 located 6 km/4 miles southwest of Nadi International Airport.

Strolling down the one main street of Nadi Town (as it is affectionately known), you'll mingle with shoppers from nearby sugar plantations. Duty-free shops flank the thoroughfare, their bold signs luring prospective buyers. Along the side streets you'll discover thatch-roofed huts and wooden houses topped by rusting tin roofs. Cows and horses quietly graze in adjoining fields.

Lautoka. Fiji's second largest town, Lautoka is 32 km/20 miles north of Nadi. Primarily a port and sugar mill community, Lautoka has a population of 22,000. A number of ships—many of them passenger liners—dock here annually.

If you have only a short time in Lautoka, explore one of its tree-lined streets. On Vitogo Parade, the main street, you'll find both department stores and duty-free shops.

Another stop might be the local market, on Naviti and Vakabale streets, where you'll see an enticing variety of tropical fruits and vegetables. At Churchill Park on Verona Street, sports fans can watch local groups lawn bowl or play cricket, rugby, or soccer in season.

Discovering sugar cane country. During crushing season—May to December—you can see how sugar cane is processed at the South Pacific Sugar Mill near the outskirts of Lautoka. Phone ahead for reservations for the guided tours, which depart daily except Tuesday and Sunday. The mill tour leads you through each step of the processing—from cane crushing and the forcing out of juice to the purifying and refining of sugar.

Sugar cane fields abound near both Nadi and Lautoka. On a short drive, you're apt to see patches of sugar cane in varying shades of green. The darker cane is new growth; as it matures it grows lighter.

The harvested cane is loaded on small railroad cars and hauled to nearby sugar mills. You'll see tracks of the narrow-gauge sugar train weaving in and out of the plantations.

Nearby excursions. The village of Viseisei, located midway between Nadi and Lautoka, is the site where ancient Fijians supposedly first landed. The chief and leader of the migration is considered the legendary ancestor of the tribes of northwest Viti Levu.

Offshore island cruises. Both Nadi and Lautoka are embarkation points for cruises to Fiji's outer islands (see page 72).

Where to stay. More than a dozen hotels in the Nadi-Lautoka area offer visitors comfortable accommodations with restaurants, swimming pools, and a variety of recreational activities.

You can stay right next to the Nadi International Airport at the Gateway Hotel; or 5 to 10 minutes away at the Dominion International, Fiji Mocambo, Westgate Hotel, Nadi Airport TraveLodge, Sunlover, or Hotel Tanoa. Fifteen minutes from the airport is the Regent of Fiji beach resort, a large complex where you can enjoy a variety of water sports, tennis, and cruise excursions.

In Lautoka, travelers can stay at the Cathay Hotel.

After the sun goes down. Many hotels have special island nights with buffet dinners and Fijian song and dance. The Fiji Mocambo and the Regent of Fiji have weekly Fijian firewalking demonstrations.

Suva, Fiji's capital

Fiji's major city is Suva, located on Viti Levu's southeast coast 209 km/130 miles east of Nadi. The town's peninsula site facing a natural harbor made it an excellent choice for Fiji's capital, which was moved here from Levuka in 1882. Today, Suva is the country's main port, accommodating ships of all sizes from throughout the world.

Backed by lush, dark green hills of the Suva-Rewa Range, much of the town's waterfront is built on land

Indian woman *greets acquaintance outside Chinese general store at Savusavu, where merchandise ranges from hardware and dishes to groceries and soccer balls. Village residents meet here to exchange island news and gossip.*

reclaimed from tangled mangrove swamps. This waterfront district and intersecting streets provide the hub for much of Suva's activity.

The town's center is a conglomeration of British colonial-style and modern architecture. Wooden, two-story, arcaded buildings—their upper levels decorated with sagging verandas—intermingle with more recently built utilitarian concrete structures. Spreading up the hills from the waterfront, the residential area features gracious, colonial-style homes set in gardens rich with tropical flowers and spreading shade trees.

A multiracial settlement of 64,000, Suva is populated by Fijians, Indians, Europeans, Chinese, and other South Pacific islanders. You'll notice the contrast of cultures as you stroll the busy town streets—passing sulu-clad Fijians, Indian women in beautifully elaborate saris, and Tongans in *lava-lavas* (wrapped skirts similar to Fijian sulus) with plaited straw sashes.

Many people carry umbrellas, since Suva is located on the "wet" side of Viti Levu. Brief thundering downpours, South Seas style, are not unusual.

Getting there and getting around. The fastest way to travel to Suva from Nadi is by air, landing at Nausori Airport 23 km/14 miles north of town. International flights from other South Pacific islands also land at Nausori.

For a more scenic trip, you can follow the coast road from Nadi to Suva. The bus trip takes at least 6 hours. If you drive, you'll want to make a slower journey—2 days perhaps.

Some passenger liners cruising the South Pacific make brief stops at Suva.

In addition to taxis, you may want to ride one of Suva's commuter buses—a great way to see the town on a limited budget. The circular route through the city takes only 45 minutes. Buses depart from the bus station, located next to the public market near King's Wharf.

Strolling Victoria Parade. Despite the possibility of showers, Suva is an excellent town to explore on foot. Many of the main points of interest are located on Victoria Parade and its extension, Queen Elizabeth Drive.

Beginning your stroll south of Cakobau Road on tree-shaded Queen Elizabeth Drive, you glimpse Government House—home of the Governor-General—on a hillside surrounded by landscaped grounds. A stern military sentry—clad in a red jacket and white sulu—stands guard in front of the pillared gate. The Changing of the Guard that occurs here once a month is reminiscent of the parade and pomp at Buckingham Palace.

North of Government House is Thurston Gardens, Suva's botanical park lush with flowering plants, shade trees, and green lawns. Objects reflecting 3,000 years of Fijian history are exhibited at the Fiji Museum in the middle of this garden. The museum has fine displays of Melanesian artifacts, objects from Fiji's maritime era, and reminders of cannibal days. The museum is open daily except Saturdays.

Albert Park, across Cakobau Road from Thurston Gardens, became the "First Pacific International Airport" in 1928 when Sir Charles Kingsford-Smith landed his *Southern Cross* here on the first transpacific flight from California to Australia. Today, sports-loving Fijians use the park for rugby, soccer, hockey, and cricket.

The venerable Grand Pacific Hotel, built in 1914, faces Albert Park on the seaward side of Victoria Parade. As you enter the lobby with its stately columns, giant ceiling fans, and high-backed rattan chairs, you will be reminded of Fiji's colonial past when the hotel was the fashionable place to stay.

Immediately behind the hotel, you'll often see Fijians standing waist deep in the harbor netting fish.

Suva's wharves. One other stop on your walk might be the Prince's Landing-King's Wharf area just north of Suva's shopping district bordering Usher Street. Tying up here are international passenger liners and cargo ships; work-worn, interisland copra boats; local Fijian commuter vessels; and glass-bottomed tourist boats. Many a cruise ship passenger vividly remembers the colorful greeting and marching serenade of the Royal Fiji Police Band or Royal Military Forces Band. In their navy blue shirts or red jackets and white sulus, the bandsmen briskly perform on the dock.

Shopping around. You'll find good browsing in the heart of Suva's business district at the northern end of Victoria Parade and on nearby side streets bordering Nubukalou Creek.

Lining the streets are boutiques selling locally manufactured resort wear; tour and airline offices; shops featuring Mikimoto pearls and French perfume; department stores; and camera, radio, and stereo dealers. Everywhere sign-burdened shops proclaim they have "duty-free" goods. Between Thomson Street and Renwick Road is Cumming Street—a narrow, block-long lane lined with these shops.

Another Suva shopping adventure is the City Market on Usher Street. Located near the heart of wharf and port activity, the market dazzles the senses with its array of fruits, vegetables, fish, and flowers.

Handicrafts such as masi cloth, woven mats, baskets, shells, jewelry, and woodcarvings can be purchased nearby at the handicraft center on Stinson Parade. Other shops featuring handicrafts include Fiji Museum's gift shop in Thurston Gardens, The Cottage on Ellery Street, and the Fijian Women's Society Handicraft Center, about 5 km/3 miles from town in Mabua.

Other Suva sights. Suva Aquarium, on Matua Street in the suburb of Walu Bay, contains artistically landscaped tanks with colorful displays of tropical fish; a turtle pool; and an exhibit of "beautiful but dangerous" reef species. Open daily, the aquarium may be reached by taxi or cruise boat (from Stinson Parade).

The hills above Suva's waterfront are resplendent with tropical flowers and shrubbery in a residential setting. Explore the streets on your own or take a tour of several private gardens.

The Bay of Islands, a short distance north of town, provides a peaceful contrast from Suva's busy harbor. Pleasure craft lie quietly moored in a blue bay dotted with tiny green isles.

Cruising Suva's harbor. Glass-bottomed boats ply the coral-ringed harbor, then cruise to an outer island for a day of swimming and sunning. Evening island cruises include a dinner and Fijian entertainment. Most cruises depart from Stinson Parade jetty.

Orchid Island-Fiji on Display. Fijian life, both past and present, is represented at this exhibit. Located 11 km/7 miles west of Suva on Queen's Road, it features

FIREWALKING

A Mystifying Ceremony

The hushed audience stares in wonder as the Beqa Islanders use long poles to casually toss aside the burning logs. Chanting "O-vulo-vulo" as they work, they reveal a circular firewalking pit of white-hot rocks that have been heating beneath the pile of burning timbers for 6 hours.

With the pit finally readied, the *Bete* (leader) shouts "Vuto-O" and the barefoot firewalkers enter the arena.

Dressed in colorful skirts of dyed pandanus leaves and frangipani leis, they calmly step single file into the pit. Standing momentarily on the glowing rocks, they smile, wave at the audience, and shout "Bula." Their faces show no pain as they walk around the pit.

Following the ceremony, the firewalkers proudly display their feet to the audience. There are no signs of burns.

Firewalking, or *Vilavilairevo* as the Fijians call it (literally meaning "jumping into the oven"), has been practiced by the Sawau tribe of Beqa Island for generations. According to legend, firewalking began when a Sawau warrior, Tui-na-iviqa-lita, promised a famous storyteller that he would give him whatever he caught while fishing. He caught an eel which transformed itself into a spirit god. Pleading to be set free, the spirit god offered in exchange the gift of immunity to fire. To prove the validity of his gift, the spirit god built a fire pit, leaped onto the white-hot stones, and commanded Tui to follow. Tui did so and was unharmed.

Today the islanders believe the Bete is a direct descendant of Tui-na-iviqa-lita. He and his tribesmen have inherited Tui's ability to walk on fire. For 2 weeks before a ceremony, all firewalkers must adhere to two rules—separation from their wives, and no eating of coconut.

Firewalking ceremonies are held several times a month on Viti Levu at hotels in Suva, Nadi, and along the Coral Coast. Check locally for dates.

The East Indians who have settled on Fiji also have a firewalking custom. Traditionally an annual ritual during a religious festival, it is based on different concepts and is conspicuously different from that of the Beqa Islanders.

---

a model Fijian village and pagan temple *(bure-kalou)*. Orchid Island, connected to the village by a bridge, includes displays of native flora and fauna.

You'll see museum bures, including one containing a detailed portrayal of Fiji's history; a handicraft center; and Fijian entertainment.

The exhibit is open daily except Sunday.

Visiting other villages. You can journey to several other Fijian villages in the Suva area.

Marau Model Village, located 10 minutes from Suva in Tamavua, is an authentic replica of an early Fijian native village showing its way of life and handicrafts. It is open daily except Sunday.

Local operators offer tours to nearby villages by both bus and boat. Adventurous travelers can take 6 and 8-day trips into the interior by foot, horse, and boat.

Royal home. Bau, former island fortress home of King Cakobau and his royal tribesmen, lies just off Viti Levu's east coast northeast of Suva. Visitors travel to Bau by launch. Permission for visiting Bau must be obtained from the Fijian Affairs Board on Victoria Parade in Suva.

(Continued on page 71)

Rowboat transports villagers *from interisland ferry to Taveuni shore. Sailing daily from Buca Bay on Vanua Levu, ferry carries passengers, produce, copra, and domestic animals. International Date Line once split island into two time zones.*

When cannibalism was practiced, the tiny island—connected to Viti Levu at low tide by a narrow, coral causeway—harbored over 3,000 people armed with 100 war canoes. Although the island's population has diminished to about 400 and war canoes are a thing of the past, Bau is still home of Fiji's highest chiefs.

Bau's major sights are the Cakobau Memorial Church, a council house, and an ancient tree peppered with notches—each notch said to be the record of a villager who met his fate in the oven of an old-time cannibal chief.

Where to stay. Downtown Suva offers a wide range of modern hotels for travelers, including the Suva TraveLodge, Hillcrest, Suva Courtesy Inn, and Southern Cross. Several apartment hotels are also available. The venerable Grand Pacific Hotel appeals to nostalgia buffs seeking South Seas colonial atmosphere.

A short distance from town are the Hotel Isa Lei at Lami overlooking Suva Harbor and the Tradewinds Hotel on the Bay of Islands.

After the sun goes down. Many local hotels feature a special weekly buffet dinner or barbecue. The Tradewinds Hotel has a Fijian firewalking show on the second and last Friday of each month.

Levuka, Fiji's original capital

To glimpse a bit of Fiji's frontier past, take the day excursion from Suva to Levuka on Ovalau.

Raucous sailors, traders, whalers, plantation owners, and beachcombers once reeled through the streets of Levuka in pursuit of adventure at any of a multitude of wine and grog shops. Today Levuka is a sleepy fishing village—its brawling port days just a memory.

Until 1882 Levuka was Fiji's capital and main port, harboring many wooden sailing ships. After the capital was moved to Suva, its harbor soon became the country's major port.

Levuka today. The town drowses on a narrow shelf of land with little room to expand—even if it wanted to. The steep crags and mountain mass of volcanic Ovalau rise abruptly just behind the town. Part of the residential area struggles up the mountainside, its streets no more than flights of stairs. For a rewarding view, climb the 199 steps to Mission Hill, site of an 1837 Methodist mission.

Relics of the past survive in this quaint coastal town. A sprinkling of old, iron-roofed, wooden buildings line the crescent-shaped, main street fronting the harbor. Traces of missionary influence are still apparent in the town's aging churches, convent, and mission house. Visit the town hall to see photographs of early Levuka.

Just outside of town, a monument marks the spot where King Cakobau signed the Deed of Cession with the British. A stone marker commemorates Fiji's independence from Britain. Nearby is a large native bure, still used for Fijian chief tribal meetings.

The town's main industry is the Pacific Fishing Company—a tuna canning operation. Call if you'd like to tour the premises.

Getting there. You can reach tiny Ovalau (the island is only 13 km/8 miles by 11 km/7 miles) daily on Fiji Air flights from Suva's Nausori Airport. The 20-minute scenic trip passes over several smaller islands on the way. From the Ovalau airport it's a 21 km/13 mile trip to Levuka. Besides scheduled service, a special day tour departs from Suva for Ovalau on Fiji Air.

You can also reach Ovalau by launch from Natovi, a 2-hour bus trip north of Suva. The daily boat trip takes another 2½ hours.

Where to stay. Reminiscent of yesteryear, Levuka's homey accommodations feature ceiling fans, beaded curtains, wicker furniture, and an unpretentious atmosphere. Visitors can stay at the Royal Hotel, Ovalau Guest House, Mavida House, Old Capital Inn, and Rukuruku Resort (located 19 km/12 miles from town on the northern end of Ovalau).

Circling Viti Levu

A 531 km/330 mile road—longest in Fiji—circles the island of Viti Levu. One portion of it—Queen's Road—skirts the western and southern coast between Lautoka and Suva. King's Road continues inland from Suva up the eastern part of the island and along the northern coast to Lautoka.

Nearly two-thirds of Queen's Road is now paved, but all of King's Road remains unpaved though graded. Unpaved roads can be bumpy and muddy when it rains. A more leisurely trip on either road will include an overnight stop along the way.

If you don't wish to drive, you can hire a car and driver or take a bus. Air-conditioned buses operate daily between Nadi and Suva on Queen's Road, stopping at several resorts along the way. Non-air-conditioned buses travel King's Road daily. A local tour operator offers a 5-day, circle-island tour, departing Nadi on Monday and returning on Friday.

No matter what transportation you choose, the resorts and scenery you'll see on the journey make the trip worthwhile.

Queen's Road. Winding along the palm-fringed coastline on Queen's Road, you'll pass deserted beaches and blue lagoons. Villages of thatch-roofed huts stand in forest clearings. As you pass, villagers will stop their activities to smile, wave, and shout "Bula." If you stop, don't be surprised if you're invited to visit the village.

One of the most popular sections of Queen's Road is the 97 km/60 mile Coral Coast stretching from Yanuca Island to Pacific Harbour. Sprinkled along this section of road are numerous resorts, both large and small, offering accommodations ranging from luxurious villas —each with individual swimming pools—to modest bure-style bungalows.

Major hotels along the Coral Coast—The Fijian, Reef, Ramada Naviti, Korolevu Beach, Paradise Point, and Man Friday—operate as resorts with pools, boats, tennis courts, stables, and water sports. Some have golf courses. One resort, the multimillion dollar Pacific Harbour development, not only offers accommodations (Beachcomber Hotel and Villas) and sports facilities but also has a Fijian cultural center featuring craft demonstrations and colonial-style marketplace.

Many of the hotels are departure points for day tours to local villages, cruises to nearby islands, or a Navua River trip.

Firewalking (see page 69) is the greatest nighttime

attraction at Coral Coast resorts. Hotels featuring this entertainment include the Beachcomber (Pacific Harbour Resort), The Fijian, Ramada Naviti, and Korolevu Beach. All the major hotels in this area have a buffet dinner or barbecue and *meke* (Fijian entertainment) at least once a week.

King's Road. To discover a more primitive part of Viti Levu, take the drive between Suva and Nadi by way of King's Road. Traversing the eastern interior and northern coast, this route is for the more adventurous traveler. None of the narrow, winding road is paved.

Again you will experience the beauty of the Fijian countryside. The eastern "wet" side of the island is thick with bamboo, banana trees, ropelike vines, and hibiscus. As you travel westward along the northern coast, waving sugar cane fields replace the jungle vegetation. As on Queen's Road, fishermen and farmers will stop working to greet you.

For an interesting side trip, leave King's Road at Tavua on the north coast and head 11 km/7 miles inland to Vatukoula, site of a working gold mine. Guided tours of the Emperor Gold Mine can be arranged by contacting the supervisor at the mining company office 24 hours in advance.

Small hotels, located in villages along King's Road, include the Tailevu Hotel, Raki Raki Hotel, Tavua Hotel, and the New Ba Hotel.

Romantic getaways

Island hideaways and long leisurely cruises through quiet tropical waters characterize the Fiji experience.

Island retreats. No journey to Fiji is complete without a day trip to an island hideaway off Viti Levu. Several tiny island resorts—renowned for their palm-lined beaches and coral-rimmed lagoons—can be reached by a short cruise or flight. You'll have most of the day free to relax and enjoy the beach and water.

If you want more time, stay several days. Accommodations range from bures (cottages), many of them family-size, to bunk-bedded dormitories. In addition to lavish buffet-style meals, several resorts present Fijian entertainment.

Island hideaways off Viti Levu's west coast possess such intriguing names as Castaway, Beachcomber, Treasure, Plantation Village, Dick's Place, and Mana. Several tour operators sail to one or more of these islands daily, either from Lautoka or the Regent of Fiji Hotel. Connecting boat service links some of the island resorts. Fiji Air flies from Nadi to Malololailai Island (Plantation Village, Dick's Place) several times daily. Turtle Island Airways has charter seaplane service to these Nadi Bay island resorts.

Visitors to the Suva area can relax at Toberua Island Resort. Launches sail daily from Nakelo Landing, 29 km/18 miles east of Suva. The 1-hour cruise takes you 8 km/5 miles down the Rewa River past villages before entering the ocean.

One added attraction at Toberua—besides its tropical setting and numerous water sports—is a monthly fish drive. Villagers from neighboring islands gather to demonstrate this ancient art of catching fish. Guests take a launch to a nearby reef to watch the villagers, and perhaps join in, as the scare line is spread in a circle; the water pounded amidst excited yells; and the frightened fish caught. Some of the day's catch become a part of a *lovo* feast (food baked in the ground).

Cruising. Another kind of Fiji-type escapism can be enjoyed on a 3-day Blue Lagoon Cruise through the Yasawa Group northwest of Viti Levu. Motorized boats, complete with comfortable accommodations and conveniences, depart daily except Thursday from Lautoka. They ply 241 km/150 miles of ocean, docking nightly at different island lagoons.

Days are filled with visits to villages, a shell market, underwater caves, and deserted beaches. As the sun sets, feasting begins followed by Fijian entertainment.

If you are seeking the passenger/cargo boat experience (with comfortable accommodations), try Blue Lagoon Cruises' 6-day round trip aboard the *Salamanda*. Departing Lautoka on Saturdays, the boat heads for Labasa on Vanua Levu for cargo delivery. Frequent stops along the way offer opportunities for swimming and village visits.

Because of the popularity of Blue Lagoon Cruises, reservations should be made well in advance. Write to Blue Lagoon Cruises, P.O. Box 54, Lautoka.

Fiji's Other Islands

Many visitors miss relatively undeveloped Vanua Levu and Taveuni—two of Fiji's other islands. The charm of these islands lies in their unspoiled beauty, friendly people, and gentle pace of life.

Vanua Levu, second largest island

Located northeast of Viti Levu is Fiji's second largest island, Vanua Levu. About half the size of the main island, Vanua Levu covers an area of about 5,544 square km/2,140 square miles. Volcanic mountains, thermal hot springs, waterfalls, sugar cane fields, and copra plantations landscape this island. Savusavu and Labasa are Vanua Levu's two main centers.

Most visitors arrive by air. Regularly scheduled flights serve the towns of Labasa and Savusavu and the nearby island of Taveuni from both Nadi Airport and Suva's Nausori Airport. The three centers are also connected by regular air service.

Blue Lagoon Cruises' *Salamanda* sails weekly from Lautoka to Labasa. Even though it serves primarily as a round-trip passenger cruise with cargo deliveries and tourist visits to remote villages, one-way passage can be arranged. Regular interisland cargo vessels also stop at Vanua Levu.

Taxi service is available on the island and fares are reasonable. If arrangements are made ahead, a tour can be included in the taxi ride. Rental cars are available only in Labasa, but Vanua Levu has very few roads, and most of them (except in town) are unpaved.

Savusavu. Surrounded by copra plantations, the small harbor town of Savusavu sits on Vanua Levu's southern coast. Peaceful tropical beauty is its main attraction.

From Savusavu you can enjoy long scenic drives through the countryside, visit local villages, and cruise to a nearby, uninhabited island.

Visitors can stay at the Savusavu TraveLodge overlooking an island-studded bay, hilly peninsula, and downtown Savusavu.

Namale Plantation combines a working copra plantation and hideaway tropical paradise located on a bay headland only 10 km/6 miles from Savusavu. Surrounded by the plantation, bures nestle in a garden setting of brilliant, tropical flowers. Beautiful beaches and lagoons can be found nearby.

Labasa. Situated on a river on Vanua Levu's north coast and surrounded by sugar cane fields, Labasa is a bustling, sun-baked town. Its predominantly Indian population works as cane farmers, shopkeepers, lawyers, and accountants.

Things to explore in and around Labasa include the colorful public market, sugar mill, hot spring, floating island, waterfalls, and nearby villages.

While in Labasa, you can stay at the Hotel Takia.

Taveuni, the garden isle

Renowned for its lush vegetation, many streams, and a plummeting waterfall, Taveuni is known as the "Garden of Fiji." Just 42 km/26 miles long and 11 km/7 miles wide, it ranks third in size in the Fiji island group.

Copra is the mainstay of the Taveuni economy, although cotton, coffee, sugar, arrowroot, and cinchona have all been grown in the past. Tropical trees, flowering shrubs, fruits, and vegetable gardens all compete for space on this verdant isle.

From Buca Bay on Vanua Levu, you can board the ferry to Taveuni daily—sharing your ride with local villagers, produce, copra, and perhaps a few roosters. Or you can fly from Labasa, Savusavu, or Suva to Taveuni's Matei Airstrip. Taxis provide island transportation.

One gravel road extends the length of the island along the northwest coast's beaches. Along this route you might see women, waist deep in ponds, fishing with nets for their evening meals.

Midway down the island road, a sign reads "180th Meridian, International Date Line, Where One Can Stand With One Foot In Yesterday and One Foot In Today." The 180th meridian normally marks adjustment of time from one day to the next. Once, Taveuni was split into two time zones—the eastern half of the island was one full day (23 hours) behind the western half. To resolve the obvious problem, the Date Line was adjusted so all of Fiji falls on the west side of it. Although the Date Line has been relocated, the sign still remains.

Taveuni TraveLodge, located on a beach midway down the island (near the Date Line sign), provides a good center for island excursions.

Know Before You Go

The following are some practical details to help you in planning your trip to Fiji.

Entry/exit procedures. You will need a valid passport and an onward travel ticket. Nationals of most countries don't need a visa. Upon your arrival, you will receive a 30-day visitor's permit, which may be extended for up to 6 months.

If you are arriving from an infected area, you need cholera, yellow fever, and smallpox shots. Arrivals from India must have smallpox certificates.

When you leave Fiji by air, you will pay a F$2.50 airport departure tax.

Customs. Visitors are allowed to bring in duty-free personal effects, including 200 cigarettes, 25 cigars, or a half pound of tobacco; one

quart of liquor; and F$20 worth of new merchandise.

Currency. The Fijian dollar. The recent exchange rate is F$1 = U.S. $1.25, Australian $1.09, and New Zealand $1.25.

Tipping. Heavy tipping is not expected in Fiji. Visitors are requested to tip only when they wish to reward particularly good service.

Time. Fiji is GMT (Greenwich mean time) +12. For example, when it is noon Sunday in Suva, it is 4 P.M. Saturday in San Francisco, noon Sunday in Auckland, and 10 A.M. Sunday in Sydney.

Weather and what to wear. Fiji's "cool" season extends from May to November with temperatures rarely below 16°C/60°F. The hot rainy months include December through April when temperatures

can reach nearly 32°C/90°F.

You can dress in casual resort wear the year around in Fiji, though it is not considered appropriate for women to wear shorts in town. Useful items for you to pack include an umbrella, a lightweight sweater, and sunglasses. Bring tennis or beach shoes to wear when swimming in coral-infested areas.

For more information. Your best source of travel information is the Fiji Visitors Bureau. You can contact the bureau in Fiji at P.O. Box 92, Suva. In North America write to Holmes Associates, P.O. Box 126, Ross, CA 94957. In Australia, F.V.B. offices are located at 38–40 Martin Place, Sydney, N.S.W.; 343 Collins St., Suite 311, Melbourne, Victoria; or Russ Gribble & Assoc., P.O. Box 761, Southport, Queensland 4215. The New Zealand address is P.O. Box 1179, Auckland.

NEW CALEDONIA

New Caledonia lingers in the memory long after you have taken a last look at Grande Terre and its small offshore islands.

You remember the haunting beauty of the Isle of Pines, renowned for its short-branched pine trees, white, velvet-soft beaches, and abundant wild orchids; Amédée Island, a mere sand spit in the sea topped by a lighthouse built in the time of Napoleon III; Nouméa, noted for its atmosphere of *la vie française,* its excellent restaurants and stylish boutiques; and the remote reaches making up the rest of New Caledonia, where neat, well-tended Melanesian villages peek out from forest clearings.

More than the sights, you remember the people—smiling Melanesian women bedecked in colorful Mother Hubbards, children on the roadside waving hello, and hospitable French innkeepers offering home cooking.

Grande Terre and Other Islands

The cigar-shaped island of New Caledonia—402 km/250 miles long and 48 km/30 miles wide—lies halfway between Fiji and Australia. Scientists believe it was once part of an ancient land mass linked to Australia.

Scattered around the main island are New Caledonia's small island dependencies. They include Ouvéa, Lifou, and Maré (the Loyalty group) situated off the east coast; the Isle of Pines and Ouen Island to the south; and the Belep group to the north.

Called "Grande Terre" by the locals, the main island of New Caledonia is rich in minerals, tropical plants, and white sand beaches. The island (also known as the "mainland") is divided geographically by the Chaîne Centrale. This mountain range—scarred by nickel mining—runs the length of Grande Terre, creating two distinct climatic and geographic regions. Blessed by heavy rains, the east coast boasts rich plant life and large rivers that plummet through mountainous countryside to the ocean. In contrast, the "dry" west coast appears savannalike with broad, grassy plains ideal for cattle ranching. Two major peaks of the Chaîne Centrale are Mount Panié and Mount Humboldt.

Unique plants and wildlife

Nearly 2,000 species of plant life have been found in New Caledonia, many of them unique to these islands. Of particular note are the *niaouli* (native gum trees), plentiful along Grande Terre's west coast; and the *Araucaria cookii,* an unusual looking species of pine on the Isle of Pines.

The call of the country's rare *cagou* bird might fool you—it sounds like a young dog barking. The gray-plumed cagou is a flightless running bird similar to New Zealand's kiwi. Unfortunately, the cagou faces extinction because it can't run as fast as its predators which, ironically, include the canine population.

A Captain Cook discovery

New Caledonia remained virtually undiscovered until 1768, when French navigator Louis de Bougainville noted the island in his ship's log as he sailed south from the New Hebrides. However, it wasn't until 1774 that Captain James Cook actually discovered and landed on the island on his way to New Zealand. Because its pine-clad ridges reminded Cook of Scotland (called Caledonia in ancient times), he named his discovery New Caledonia.

During the late 18th and early 19th centuries, various navigators, explorers, missionaries, traders, and runaway seamen sailed to New Caledonia's shores. Although it seemed likely that Great Britain would annex the island, France did it first in 1853, when soldiers were sent in to protect French missionaries who had occasionally been attacked by cannibalistic tribes.

From 1864 to 1897 New Caledonia served as a French penal colony noted for brutal treatment of felons. Long-term political prisoners and convicts were deported from France to the colony.

During World War II, New Caledonia served as an important Allied military base. It became a French Overseas Territory in 1946. A Governor, appointed in Paris, administers governmental policy.

The people of New Caledonia participate in government through a 35-member Territorial Assembly elected locally. They also send locally elected representatives to the French Parliament in Paris.

The New Caledonians

Of the 135,000 people that inhabit New Caledonia, only 55,000 are Melanesians. The country has a sizable European population—about 52,500—many of them descendants of 19th century settlers. Other residents have immigrated here from Wallis, Tahiti, Indonesia, Vietnam, and other areas.

Melanesian with a French influence

When the first explorers journeyed through these islands, the indigenous Melanesian population numbered 50,000 to 70,000. Living in small tribal groups,

Shady pedestrians' haven *in bustling Nouméa, Place de Cocotiers contains bright yellow benches where townspeople pause to converse and watch passersby. Greenery and flowering plants brighten city streets.*

French influence *permeates all phases of New Caledonian life. Officers in tropical white uniforms participate in awards ceremony.*

the dark-skinned, curly-haired natives existed on subsistence agriculture and fishing.

Village life today. Most of the Melanesian people today dwell in small villages scattered through the islands. Existence is still eked from the land and the sea.

In the villages, thatch-roofed dwellings cluster around a large square carpeted with well-kept lawn. Many of the rounded, beehive-shaped, windowless abodes have been replaced by rectangular windowed structures.

City life. In Nouméa, the country's major city, the population of 60,000 is predominantly French. Smaller numbers of Tahitians, Indonesians, Vietnamese, New Hebrideans, Martiniquais, and New Caledonian Melanesians are also represented. Old French colonial cottages and modern, government-built housing projects provide living accommodations.

The reigning economic force in Nouméa is not agriculture, it's nickel. Société le Nickel, the French nickel mining company, employs many Nouméans.

Dress. New Caledonian dress reflects both native and French influences. On the streets of Nouméa you'll see barefoot native women chatting in missionary-inspired

Mother Hubbards—loose fitting, lace trimmed, floral print or solid color dresses. Other women pass them adorned in the latest Parisian fashions purchased from local boutiques.

Countryside attire leans to traditional Mother Hubbards. Men wear *sulus,* wrap-type skirts.

Language and religion. French, New Caledonia's official language, is spoken everywhere. Though a knowledge of the language is helpful, visitors get along quite easily with English in Nouméa and the resort areas. Few people in the countryside understand or speak English. They mainly speak Melanesian or French. Most islanders are Catholics or Protestants.

Cricket and other diversions

New Caledonians have enthusiastically adopted many games and sports introduced by the 19th century European settlers.

One such sport, English cricket, takes on a different look when played in New Caledonia. (See the special feature on page 77.)

The French game of *pétanque* has also become a part of New Caledonian life. Similar to English bowls, it is played with baseball-size metal balls which players toss across a dirt game area. On weekends and public holidays Nouméan men play pétanque in the Place de Cocotiers or near the waterfront.

Other popular sports include horse racing (early August to the end of September), soccer and rugby (October to April), judo, and track and field events.

Mineral exports dominate the economy

Minerals—primarily nickel—dominate New Caledonia's export trade. The country contains one of the world's largest reserves of nickel oxide ore.

The two main agricultural exports are coffee and copra. Crops grown for local use include yams, taros, mangoes, maize, sweet potatoes, rice, and bananas. Other New Caledonian products such as meat and salt-water fish are also consumed locally. Food production in New Caledonia has not matched the country's demands, so much of the country's food must be imported, contributing to the high cost of living.

Planning Your Trip

New Caledonia is located midway between Fiji and Australia in the southwest Pacific Ocean. Its closest neighbor is the New Hebrides, 536 km/333 miles northeast of Nouméa.

Several international air carriers and passenger ship lines stop in the country. Visitors arrive on Grande Terre, the main island of New Caledonia. Air passengers land at Tontouta International Airport about 51 km/ 32 miles northwest of Nouméa, the country's capital and largest city. At the airport you'll find bus, taxi, and airport limousine service into town. Ship passengers dock at the wharf in Nouméa.

Getting around New Caledonia

Visitor transportation runs the gamut from "baby cars" —Nouméa's local bus service—to regularly scheduled air service to main island towns and island dependencies.

Driving in New Caledonia. Rental cars are available in Nouméa. You'll need a valid driver's license and passport to obtain a temporary driving permit. Minimum age for rental is 25.

Traffic moves on the right side of the road. Refrain from honking your horn in Nouméa; this privilege is reserved for wedding parties.

Traveling by bus. An inexpensive way to explore Nouméa and its nearby suburbs is to hop on a Transport en Commun "baby car." You can board one of these colorful, small buses at Place de Cocotiers, the main square.

Taking a taxi. Traveling by taxi in New Caledonia is relatively expensive. Expect to pay an extra charge for

LADIES' CRICKET
In Mother Hubbards

"That's cricket?" might be the question raised by Englishmen upon viewing New Caledonia's version for the first time. Although it differs from the more sedate game played back home, the shouting, riotous matches are ladies' cricket, New Caledonian-style. The game has been played here since it was introduced by the missionaries.

Watching a match, you'll see that the ladies take this competitive sport seriously. It also provides an entertaining show.

The bat, for instance, is as big as an oversize loaf of French bread. Each team sports its own "uniform": loose Mother Hubbard dresses made from the same color material. Usually each player wears a twisted ribbon or scarf headdress in the same color as the uniform.

Bare feet are *de rigueur*, and they pound up and down the field to the noise of flat-sounding whistles, blown by both the referee and lady spectators. From the sidelines come shouts of advice or encouragement—from husbands, boyfriends, offspring, relatives, and friends.

Action takes place on school grounds, at local cricket fields, or in vacant lots, usually on Saturday mornings during the winter months, July to April.

Gleaming *white sands and clear waters lure visitors to Isle of Pines. One-time prison home to 19th century French exiles, island is now quiet retreat.*

service after 7 P.M. on weekdays and on Saturday afternoons, Sundays, and public holidays.

Flying. Air Calédonie provides frequent domestic air service from Nouméa to outlying towns on Grande Terre and to the Isle of Pines, Ouen Island, Belep Islands, and the Loyalty group. All local flights leave from Magenta Airport, located within the Nouméa city limits.

Cruising. If you're traveling on a leisurely schedule, you can journey to the outer islands on a small trading vessel—the local villagers' mode of interisland transportation. Schedules are often irregular. Check with the Harbor Authority office in Nouméa for current information.

Resort hotels, wayside bungalows

Most of New Caledonia's accommodations are located in the Nouméa area. Resort beach hotels (Chateau Royal, Isle de France, Hotel Le Lagon, Mocambo, Nouméa, Le Nouvata) lure visitors to the Anse Vata/Baie des Citrons areas (15 minutes south of downtown).

In downtown Nouméa, you'll discover several modest hotels offering comfortable accommodations, including La Perouse Hotel and Hotel Sebastopol. The downtown hotels might not front the ocean, but their rates are lower than the beachfront resorts.

At towns and villages on the east and west coasts of Grande Terre (and on several outer islands, as well), small casual hotels and an occasional *relais* (country inn) provide comfortable overnight stopping points.

Make reservations for accommodations well in advance of your visit. The peak tourist season comes in January; August is the least crowded month to visit.

Mini-meals to native feasts

Dining in New Caledonia is a gastronomic adventure. New Caledonians love to eat—and so will you upon discovering the variety of tempting offerings available.

In Nouméa you can sample French, Cantonese, Mandarin, Vietnamese, Indian, Tahitian, Indonesian, and Spanish cuisine. If you prefer a mini-meal, stop at one of numerous snack bars and fancy pâtisseries. Better yet, tote a *casse-croûte* (lunch of crusty French bread, fresh fruit, and French wine) to the beach for a picnic. For breakfast, treat yourself to fresh-baked croissants and café au lait.

Outside of Nouméa, most relais and local restaurants offer simple French provincial cooking featuring fresh seafood and locally grown vegetables and fruit.

Native feasting and dancing. To sample Melanesian specialties, attend a *bougna*. Usually held on a beach, this native feast features fruits, vegetables, pig, fish, and chicken that have been wrapped in banana leaves and baked for several hours on hot stones covered with sand.

Following the feast, visitors are entertained by grass-skirted Melanesian dancers.

After the sun goes down. Much of Nouméa's night life centers around the hotels and their discos. You might also enjoy seeing a European or Polynesian floor show; the latter includes the Tahitian *tamure* and Wallisian saber dances. At Chateau Royal's casino you can try your hand at baccarat, roulette, or blackjack.

FESTIVAL TIME

Join New Caledonians as they revel on their special holidays. Two of the most colorful to enjoy are Bastille Day and Anniversary Day. Important occasions include the following:

January—April

Mardi Gras. In February or early March, costumed children parade through Nouméa's streets to the Place des Cocotiers, where prizes are given for the most original costumes.

Easter. This day marks the beginning of the winter sports season. Events are usually held weekly.

May—August

Arts Season. During the first week in May, works of artists from all over the South Pacific are displayed at the Museum of Nouméa. In addition, Theatre de l'Île (10 minutes from Nouméa) presents independent stage productions.

Bastille Day. New Caledonians herald France's July 14th independence day with a torchlight parade and fireworks in Nouméa on the night of July 13. Celebrating continues the following day with special sports events and local festivities.

September—December

Anniversary Day. On September 24, a military parade at Anse Vata Beach and sports events commemorate the 1853 raising of the French flag in New Caledonia. Week-long activities include a cycling race around Grande Terre.

All Saints Day ("Fête des Morts"). On November 1 families journey to cemeteries to leave armloads of flowers at graves.

Pére Noël Day. Pére Noël arrives in Nouméa on December 24 by an unusual means of transportation—the conveyance is always a surprise.

Shop for French perfume, tapa cloth

Strolling the streets of Nouméa, you'll discover a multitude of boutiques. Each store prides itself in having the latest in fashions.

Imports from France include women's lingerie, shoes, clothing, men's ties and shirts, and perfume. You'll also want to look at Italian sandals and London sportswear. Chinese and Tahitian dressmakers can whip up beachwear from locally made "pareo" cloth in 1 or 2 days.

Don't miss the local handicrafts such as woodcarvings, woven place mats and other articles made from pandanus bark, shell and mother-of-pearl necklaces, tapa cloth, and handpainted fabrics.

Shops open early in New Caledonia and close for a lengthy lunch hour. Shop hours are 7:45 to 11 A.M. and 2 to 6 P.M. Monday through Friday. Most stores are closed Saturday afternoons and Sundays.

Fun in the sun

New Caledonia has one of the world's largest barrier reefs, Grand Récif, offering an ideal playground for water sport enthusiasts. Snorkeling and scuba diving are excellent in the warm, clear, reef-protected lagoons. Both snorkeling and diving equipment are available for rent locally; check with your hotel.

Many resort hotels and relais have small boats available for visitors' use. Larger boats can be chartered in Nouméa for diving, cruising, or fishing. Best fishing months are November through February for marlin, sailfish, tuna, bonito, and mahi mahi.

If you want to play tennis, you'll find courts in Nouméa at the Château Royal and at the Mont Coffyn Tennis Club. There are also courts at some relais on Grande Terre and Isle of Pines.

Nouméa, the Capital

Often labeled "the Paris of the Pacific," Nouméa as a city blends a light-hearted zestful quality with a bit of French sophistication. *La vie française* permeates almost every facet of Nouméa: the good French restaurants, the Paris-style boutiques, streets named for Republic heroes, Frenchmen playing *pétanque* (see page 77), the predominance of the French language.

Attractively situated on a hilly peninsula on Grande Terre's southwest tip, Nouméa overlooks a succession of lovely, curving bays and a magnificent, almost landlocked harbor. The site was chosen as the country's capital and main port in 1854 by Commandant Tardy de Montravel, a French naval officer.

As you explore the city, stop in the Tourist Information Bureau on the Place de Cocotiers at the corner of Rue Jean Jaurès and Rue d'Austerlitz.

Exploring the city center

Downtown Nouméa offers many walking and browsing possibilities. Stroll the shady, narrow streets lined with French colonial-style, wooden buildings fitted with shuttered windows and rusting metal roofs. Interspersed with this early architecture, you'll find white, concrete modern structures.

Place de Cocotiers. Start your city explorations at Place de Cocotiers ("Coconut Palm Tree Place") or Central Square. Bordered by palms and flamboyant trees (laden with red flowers in November and December), this pedestrians' oasis extends 4 blocks through the center of the city.

It is actually two adjoining squares, one marked by a turn-of-the-century bandstand, the other by a fountain. Between the two stands the Fontaine Monumentale, focal point of Place de Cocotiers.

The Market Place. Nouméa comes to life early (5 A.M.) at the local market. Housewives and chefs haggle with food vendors over the best buys in everything from breadfruit and coconuts to squawking poultry and live fish. Fishermen wheel their catch in tanks to the market, where the fish are lifted out alive for customers. (Local law forbids the sale of dead fish unless cooked.) The market is located near the Place de Cocotiers, at the corner of Rue Anatole France and Rue Georges Clemenceau.

The Museum of Nouméa. This modern building covers an entire city block bordering Baie de la Moselle on Avenue du Maréchal Foch between Rue August Brun and Rue Tourville. You can visit the museum Tuesday to Saturday from 9 to 11 A.M. and 2:30 to 5:30 P.M.

The main exhibit hall contains artifacts from New Caledonia and many other South Pacific islands. Another part of the museum houses an art gallery.

Along the waterfront

You'll leave the city center behind when you take the relaxing drive south along the Rue Jules Garnier, skirting boat-filled bays, to the beach resort area. The best beaches are Anse Vata and nearby Baie des Citrons, both a short 15-minute ride from Place de Cocotiers.

On the peninsula separating the Baie des Citrons and Anse Vata, you'll find the famed Aquarium de Nouméa. The aquarium offers insight into a tropical marine world —observe dangerous creatures that haunt reef waters as well as some beautiful fish. In the Hall of Fluorescent Corals you'll see these marine deposits glowing eerily under ultraviolet light.

Aquarium de Nouméa is open daily except Mondays and Fridays from 1:30 to 5 P.M. The Hall of Fluorescent Corals opens its doors from 3:30 to 4:30 P.M.

Nearby excursions

Having explored Nouméa, you will discover more of New Caledonia's charm by taking brief trips through the countryside and to outlying islands.

Villages and vistas. Near Mount Dore, 26 km/16 miles northeast of Nouméa, visitors often stop at the Mission of St. Louis to see its large church and Melanesian village of thatch-roofed bungalows.

Amédée Lighthouse. At night Amédée Lighthouse's intense beacon guides ships through the narrow coral passage into the calm lagoon near Nouméa. Built in France, the metallic lighthouse was shipped to Nouméa in sections, reassembled, and put to work in 1865.

Tour companies operate day cruises (lunch included) to tiny Amédée Island, 18 km/11 miles south of Nouméa.

Ouen Island. This get-away-from-it-all island is just a 15-minute flight or a 2½-hour cruise southeast from Nouméa.

Stay overnight at the Turtle Club, the island's one small resort, or just spend the day enjoying the beach before you return to the mainland.

Touring Grande Terre

The hinterlands of the island of New Caledonia provide an unexpectedly peaceful world of gentle, sometimes spectacular, beauty.

If you don't wish to explore on your own, you can take a guided tour from Nouméa. Air Calédonie schedules regular flights to several villages on the east and west coasts.

Along the west coast

From Nouméa, the road rambles nearly 483 km/300 miles along the Coral Sea coast to Poum, its northernmost point. On this route you enter the world of the "stockman," New Caledonia's counterpart to the gaucho or cowboy. Herds of cattle and horses graze on broad savannas punctuated with stands of white-barked niaouli trees.

For a shorter trip, take an overnight trip to Bourail (171 km/106 miles northwest of Nouméa). You'll see some of New Caledonia's small towns, Melanesian villages, cattle ranches, and mining districts along the way.

East coast destinations

The jungle vegetation and Melanesian thatched villages of New Caledonia's east coast contrast with Nouméa's urban activities and Rivieralike climate. You have three alternatives for east coast exploration—the Yaté area, the Thio area, and the coast road north from Houaïlou.

Yaté area. Yaté, known as the Paradis Botanic, lies about 64 km/40 miles east of Nouméa in the Plaine des Lacs region. More than 2,000 different kinds of plants— many found nowhere else in the world—thrive here.

Thio area. From Nouméa it's a 2-hour drive (140 km/ 87 miles) to New Caledonia's major mining center. Head northwest along the coast and turn east at Boulouparis to climb through the mountainous Chaîne Centrale. The descent to the east coast brings you to Thio. Sheared mountain tops and deeply scarred slopes reveal the town's major industry.

In the Canala area north of Thio, deep green coffee trees heavy with bright red berries and mandarin orange trees line the road. Many Melanesian tribes live in thatch-roofed villages in this area.

Complete your loop trip by traversing the mountain range once more, returning to the west coast just north of La Foa.

To the north. If you have time for a longer journey along the east coast, you can strike inland just north of Bourail, following a winding mountain road across the Chaîne Centrale to the east coast town of Houaïlou, then turn northward.

As you pass through rich, verdant fields and vine-entwined forests, you'll see little villages tucked into clearings. The well-preserved, beehive-shaped communal hut at Baye was built over a century ago.

Outer Islands

Several of New Caledonia's satellite islands can be easily reached by plane or boat. On these islands, visitors relax on quiet beaches and meet friendly villagers.

Excursion to Isle of Pines

Called Kounié Island by its inhabitants, the Isle of Pines is probably the best known of the outer islands. Located 126 km/78 miles southeast of Nouméa, the Isle of Pines has a dry climate with temperatures consistently lower than on Grande Terre. By air, it's a 35-minute flight from Nouméa.

The island's coast is one of those places you dream about—quiet and serene. Powdery white sand rims transparent, turquoise lagoons. Standing along the shores are majestic *Araucaria cookii,* a species of pine that inspired Captain Cook to name the island for them. Silhouetted against the sky, these trees become 61-meter/200-foot columns trimmed with short 2-meter/6-foot-long bristling branches.

In the late 1800s French prisoners were exiled to this island. You can still see the prison ruins.

Relais de Kanuméra, the island's only hotel, sits on a narrow isthmus flanked by beaches at Kuto Bay.

The seldom-visited Loyalty Islands

Not many tourists visit the main Loyalty Islands of Maré, Lifou, and Ouvéa that lie off New Caledonia's east coast. They are about an hour's flight from Nouméa's Magenta Airport.

The people of these islands maintain many traditional customs and follow deep-rooted folklore. Only local people may acquire land on these Melanesian reserve islands.

Ouvéa, smallest of the islands, has the only tourist accommodations in the group—a 16-bungalow hotel.

Know Before You Go

The following practical information will help you plan your trip to New Caledonia.

Entry/exit procedures. You will need a valid passport and a confirmed onward travel ticket for a stay no longer than 30 days. A tourist visa may be obtained at nominal cost from a French consulate or embassy for stays up to 90 days.

Travelers arriving from an infected area will need smallpox, yellow fever, and cholera vaccinations. Vaccinations are also recommended against typhoid and paratyphoid fevers. (Since health requirements change from time to time, check with your local public health department before going.)

New Caledonia has no airport departure tax.

Customs. Travelers may bring into New Caledonia duty free 400 cigarettes, 50 cigars, or 8 ounces of tobacco; one bottle of liquor; and personal effects.

Currency. The French Pacific Franc (CFP or FR). The recent exchange rate is approximately CFP 83.33 = US $1; CFP 72.46 = Australian $1; and CFP 76.45 = New Zealand $1.

Tipping. Tourists should not tip. Tipping is against tradition.

Time. New Caledonia is GMT (Greenwich mean time) +11. For example, when it is noon Sunday in Nouméa, it is 5 P.M. Saturday in San Francisco, 1 P.M. Sunday in Auckland, and 11 A.M. Sunday in Sydney

Weather and what to wear. Nicknamed the "Island of Eternal Spring," New Caledonia enjoys a balmy, semitropical environment tempered by the trade winds. However, definite seasonal variations do exist. Summer extends from January through March with temperatures averaging 27°C/81°F. During these humid months, an occasional hurricane or thunderstorm pummels the area. The winter months from April through December are drier and cooler—a better time to visit. Temperatures average 21°C/70°F during these months, though they can drop as low as 14°C/57°F.

You can wear informal, lightweight attire the year around. Bring a light raincoat and sweater for cooler weather. You'll need beach shoes for reef exploring.

For more information. To obtain more information on New Caledonia, write to the Office du Tourisme, Box 688, Nouméa. In Australia, write to the New Caledonia Tourist Office, 12 Castlereagh Street, Sydney, 2000.

NEW HEBRIDES

The New Hebrides provide the visitor an off-the-beaten-path experience. In this land of smoking volcanoes, New Hebrideans still perform primitive rituals, and the Melanesian culture remains alive. Dotting the countryside are aging colonial-style plantation houses and the rusting scrap of World War II military operations.

A Land in Constant Motion

The New Hebrides archipelago forms an elongated, y-shaped chain of islands stretching north-south for 724 km/450 miles through the southwest Pacific Ocean. Nearest neighbors include New Caledonia to the southwest; the Fiji Islands to the east; and the Solomons to the northwest.

With a total land mass of 14,767 square km/5,701 square miles, the New Hebrides consist of 13 large islands and 60 smaller islands and islets. Principal urban centers are Vila (the administrative capital) on the island of Efate and Luganville on Espiritu Santo.

Volcanic in origin, the islands in the New Hebrides chain are geologically young and still growing. There are five active volcanoes: two on Ambrym and one each on Tanna, Lopevi, and the ocean floor near Tongoa.

Frequent earth tremors are common in the New Hebrides, and seismograph records indicate that the archipelago is in nearly constant movement. Most of the tremors—except for a few major ones each month—are not even felt by the people, and damage is rare.

Jungles, orchids, and native birds

Edged by a narrow coastal plain, most New Hebrides islands are mountainous with slopes rising steeply from the sea. The highest mountain is Mount Tabwemasana (1,879 meters/6,165 feet) on Espiritu Santo.

Dense black-green jungles resembling those of the Solomons and Papua New Guinea cover the mountain sides. Along the coast you'll see patches of cultivated land and narrow, winding beaches edged with palms.

Brightening the islands are vividly colored flowers —bougainvillea, hibiscus, orchids, and plumeria—and birds such as bright green pigeons and multihued parrots. Fifty-four types of native birds include warblers, fantails, robins, mynas, peregrine falcons, Australian goshawks, island thrushes, and trillers.

Charted by Captain Cook

Pedro de Quiros, a Portuguese navigator sponsored by the King of Spain, discovered the New Hebrides in April 1606. Thinking he had found the sought-after "Southern Continent," he anchored off an island which he named "Terra Australis del Espiritu Santo." Though he attempted to establish a permanent settlement on the island, his efforts failed as a result of illness and disagreements with native villagers.

Some 160 years later, the French navigator Louis de Bougainville sailed through the islands, landing at Aoba. He determined that Quiros's discovery was not the "Southern Continent."

Captain Cook charted the islands in 1774, naming them after the Hebrides located west of his Scottish homeland. Following Cook came another navigator, Captain William Bligh, who sighted several previously undiscovered islands in 1789.

After sandalwood forests were discovered in the early 1800s, greedy traders destroyed both property and lives. "Blackbirders" also visited the New Hebrides, kidnapping islanders for use as laborers on sugar plantations in Australia. The missionaries arriving in the wake of these wrongdoings felt the wrath of native hostility, but they remained to build churches, schools, and settlements.

Foreign settlers, predominantly English and French, purchased land in the New Hebrides and established coconut plantations in the late 19th century. In 1887, a Joint Naval Commission was formed to protect British and French subjects. So began the British-French connection that led to the creation of the Condominium (joint administration) of the New Hebrides in 1906.

During World War II, Luganville on Espiritu Santo served as a key staging area for U.S. troops advancing on the Solomons.

A new government takes shape

In January 1978, the New Hebrides Government was established. The new government's Representative Assembly elected a Chief Minister who appointed a Council of Ministers. The power to govern most internal affairs has been given to the new ministries.

Before 1978 the New Hebrides was ruled jointly by French and British Resident Commissioners in a Condominium form of government. Duality applied in matters large and small—there were two separate school systems, two separate medical services, and two flags—the British Union Jack and French Tricolor. In judicial matters, four separate courts of law functioned: British; French; a court of New Hebridean native affairs; and the Joint Court, for settling matters of internal concern such as land claims.

Today the country's external affairs still are managed jointly by the French and British. However, much of the internal duality is disappearing. The country hopes to gain its independence in 1980.

Children play *beneath upright slit log drum topped by carved, painted mask. Primitive New Hebrides art and carvings depict island legends and indicate social ranking.*

Anchored boats *dot Vila's harbor. From waterfront business area, narrow streets climb steep slopes to hillside viewpoints.*

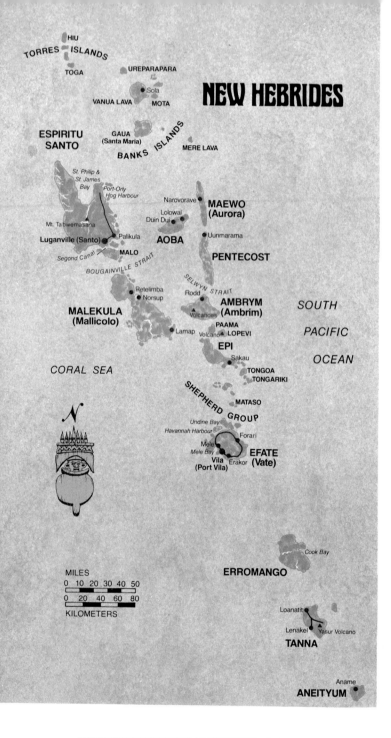

A rural society

Nearly 80 percent of the New Hebrideans reside in rural communities; the rest live in either Vila or Luganville. The customs, traditions, and language of the rural villagers vary from island to island—and even from village to village on the same island.

Most rural inhabitants live in round or rectangular huts known as "leaf houses" constructed of bamboo walls topped by steeply pitched roofs covered with leaves. Often these leaf roofs almost touch the ground.

One of the chief occupations is the raising of pigs. Not valued as food, these animals are prized for their fine circle of tusks. Possessing pigs gives a person capital and power within the tribal system. The pigs are used in trade and even as a bride-price.

Some rural villagers still dress in the attire of their ancestors—grass skirts for the women and penis sheaths called "nambas" for the men. Other villagers and city dwellers have adopted western-style clothing. The women wear loose fitting, floral print Mother Hubbard dresses and the men don shirts and shorts or slacks. Some townspeople retain the dress of their homeland; you may see Indian women draped in saris or Vietnamese wearing oriental-style pajamas and conical hats.

Language. French and English are the official languages of the New Hebrides. However, Pidgin English (Bichelamar in French) is the *lingua franca,* the common language allowing people of different tribes to communicate even though their native dialects might differ. (Several hundred different dialects are spoken in the New Hebrides.) Pidgin English is even used in the Representative Assembly.

New Hebrides' Pidgin English is a mixture of basic English plus French words and local expressions.

Religion. Missions have been established by many religious groups—including Presbyterian, Anglican (Melanesian Mission), Roman Catholic, Seventh-day Adventist, Church of Christ, and Apostolic Church—all working to convert native New Hebrideans to Christianity. However, tribespeople living inland on the islands of Malekula, Espiritu Santo, Pentecost, and Tanna still follow indigenous ancestral customs.

Sports. In New Hebridean towns, you see people enjoying golf, cricket, and *pétanque* (see page 77). Other popular sports include basketball and horseback riding. Soccer is played throughout the country wherever a flat piece of ground can be found.

The New Hebrideans

Native New Hebrideans account for more than 90 percent of the country's population of 97,000. Most are Melanesian, but a few Polynesian clans—descendants of early Pacific migrations—live on several of the islands.

Nonindigenous New Hebrideans include Europeans, Wallis and Gilbert islanders, Tahitians, Fijians, Australians, New Zealanders, Chinese, and some Vietnamese agricultural workers.

Wealth of the land

Chief New Hebrides' export is copra, followed by manganese, fish, and timber. The manganese is mined at Forari on Efate.

Other exports include small amounts of cocoa, coffee, and beef. Cattle were first introduced to the islands to control weeds and grass on the coconut plantations.

The growing tourist industry also contributes additional income to the New Hebrides economy.

An impressive number of overseas companies have established their headquarters in the New Hebrides since the country has no direct income or capital gains tax.

Planning Your Trip

The New Hebrides' first visitors arrived by canoe after an arduous journey across the Pacific Ocean. Today, you can arrive by international air carrier or ship.

By air, the country is a 50-minute flight from either Nouméa, New Caledonia, or Nadi, Fiji; and a 2-hour trip from Honiara in the Solomons. Many cruise ships and passenger/cargo liners stop in the New Hebrides on South Pacific voyages.

Arriving by plane, travelers land at Bauerfield Airport, 6 km/4 miles from Vila on Efate. You can take a taxi or bus into town. Ships dock at Vila or at Luganville on Espiritu Santo.

Getting around the New Hebrides

Beyond the towns of Vila or Luganville, the best way to explore the New Hebrides is by tours originating in Vila. Air tours feature volcano viewing, flights over the smaller islands near Vila, and an aerial view of Efate. You can also take land trips around Espiritu Santo and Efate, and fly to Tanna on a tour.

No public bus service is available in the New Hebrides. Travelers can obtain rental cars in Vila and Luganville. Except for short stretches of paved road on Efate and Espiritu Santo, all the roads are crushed coral. Traffic moves on the right side of the road.

Vila and Luganville have the only taxi service.

When studying maps of the New Hebrides, you'll see that some islands and towns have two names—one English, one French. We use the English names in this

LAND DIVING
Pentecost Island-style

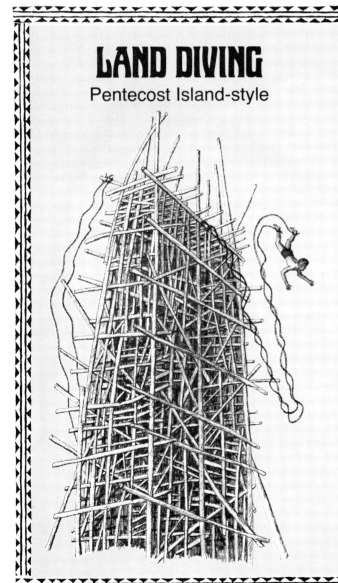

Each year during the harvest period (generally May), the men and boys of Pentecost Island gather to perform the land-diving ceremony. After climbing to various levels of a 21-meter/70-foot tower, they then dive headfirst from it. Liana vines tied around their ankles stop the fall just short of the ground.

Certain procedures are followed in building the tower. It is constructed on a hillside around a large tree. All brush is cleared in front of the tower, and the ground is dug up to soften it. (Throughout the jumping ceremony, villagers rake the ground.)

Each diver builds his own diving platform at the desired height and location. He carefully selects the vines for his legs, calculating the length so his head just brushes the ground at the end of his jump.

After the vines are secured around his ankles, the diver climbs the tower. With the vines fastened to his platform, he falls. The vines extend fully just before he reaches the ground. The platform he has constructed breaks with the pull of the vines tied to it, minimizing the vines' recoil on his legs.

According to legend, land diving originated when a woman trying to escape her husband climbed a banyan tree. He followed her, and when he had nearly caught up with her, she jumped from the tree. He followed, not realizing that she had tied lianas from the tree around her ankles before jumping. She survived her fall, but he perished. Today, only the men have the right to land dive.

If the weather permits and the Pentecost Islanders agree to have visitors, tour operators will take groups on 1-day outings to the island to witness this ceremony. During the last several jumps, no photography has been allowed.

book; the map on page 84 also shows the French version in parentheses.

Flying. Air Melanesiae, the local airline, flies from Bauerfield Airport in Vila to Aneityum, Erromango, Malekula, Aoba, Pentecost, Espiritu Santo, Sola in the Banks Islands, Tanna, and Tongoa.

Cruising. Tour operators offer short boat excursions from Vila. Local people ride interisland copra boats between islands in the New Hebrides chain; the boats sail "almost weekly" from Vila.

Where to stay

You'll find most of New Hebrides' accommodations in the Vila area on Efate. Travelers who prefer large, resort-type accommodations will enjoy the Hotel Le Lagon or Port Vila Inter-Continental Island Inn. Both are located on the shores of beautiful, sheltered Erakor Lagoon less than 3 km/2 miles from town.

If you want to stay in downtown Vila, you can choose from several small hotels including the Hotel Rossi, Hotel Vate, or Vate Marina Motel.

Ten km/6 miles west of town on Mele Island, you will discover Hide Away Island Resort's island-style bungalows. Other small, bungalow-style hotels on Efate include Takara Beach on the island's north coast and Manuro Beach Resort on the east coast.

On Espiritu Santo, Luganville has several small hotels including Hotel Santo, Les Castors Hotel, and Bokissa Island Resort. A few self-contained bungalows accommodate visitors on Sola in the Banks Islands, on Erromango, and on Tanna.

International cuisine

New Hebrides' restaurants feature an international array of offerings. French cuisine predominates, but you also can sample Chinese, Vietnamese, or Italian dishes. Among local island favorites are marinated fish, coconut crab, prawns, lobster, and flying fox (a bat).

In Vila popular restaurants include Le Pandanus,

Tanna Island children *herd goats on Mount Yasur lava flow. Island's active volcano attracts visitors, who journey to rim by jeep and foot. Painted red crosses, symbols of John Frum cargo cult, dot Tanna's countryside.*

FESTIVAL TIME

New Hebrides holidays reflect French, British, and Melanesian traditions. Important occasions you can witness include these:

January–April

John Frum Day. On February 14 members of the John Frum cargo cult hold dances and feasts on Tanna. (See page 89.)

May–August

Pentecost Island land diving. Men and boys of Pentecost Island gather, generally in May, to perform the land-diving ceremony (see page 85).

Queen Elizabeth II Birthday. In early June, the British militia parade at Vila, Luganville, Tanna, and Malekula. Sports events and a Grand Ball are also held.

Bastille Day. On July 13–14 this French holiday is celebrated in the larger town centers with torchlight processions, fireworks, and sports events.

Toka. Featuring dancing and a pig kill, this native feast is usually held at the end of August on Tanna.

September–December

Agricultural Show. Artifacts, local produce, pets, flowers, plants, and cattle are on display in September during a 2-day show in Vila, Luganville, and on Tanna. Rodeos and dances are also held.

Christmas holidays. Special church services, choir singing, and holiday balls take place December 23 to 25.

Rossi, L'Houstalet, La Mer, Kwang Tong, and those at the Hotel Vate and Hotel Le Lagon. The Hide Away Island Resort has buffets featuring South Pacific delicacies. In Luganville, try the Hotel Santo's restaurant.

Duty-free treasures...

The New Hebrides is a duty-free port with prices on imports that compare favorably with those in other free-port areas in the Pacific. (No sales tax nibbles away at your wallet here.)

Stores in Vila and Luganville sell cassette recorders, stereo equipment, transistor radios, cameras, watches, French perfume and clothing, and Chinese curios.

You can purchase colorful and varied New Hebrides handicrafts in both Vila and Luganville. Articles made in outlying Melanesian villages include carved, brightly painted, tree fern masks from Ambrym; grass skirts from Tanna; and baskets and mats from Pentecost. Also available are carved wooden objects from Tongoa and Espiritu Santo.

Most prices in stores are fixed.

Shop in Vila and Santo stores between 7:30 and 11:30 A.M. and 2 and 5 P.M. Monday through Friday, or on Saturday between 7:30 and 11:30 A.M. Larger stores close on Saturday afternoons and Sundays.

...Outdoor pleasures

Warm waters, calm lagoons, and miles of beaches provide the New Hebrides with a perfect setting for varied recreational activities. You can swim, water-ski, snorkel, ride horseback on the beach, hunt for shells, or rent a small boat.

Skin and scuba diving. Beautiful reefs and marine life lure divers into New Hebrides waters. An added diving bonus is the opportunity to explore shipwrecks in Vila Harbour as well as the World War II ship relics— *President Coolidge* and *U.S.S. Tucker*—that lie at the bottom of the Segond Canal off Espiritu Santo.

Compressors are available in both Vila and Luganville. Check locally for information on diving guides and diving tours.

Golf. In Vila golfers can play at 9-hole courses at the Hotel Le Lagon and Port Vila Inter-Continental Island Inn. Luganville also has a golf course.

Tennis. Tennis buffs will find courts in Vila at the Hotel Le Lagon, Port Vila Inter-Continental Island Inn, and Vila Tennis Club (small fee). Luganville also has courts available.

Exploring Efate

The small, oval island of Efate (Vate in French), lies near the center of the New Hebrides chain. On the southwest coast is Vila (Port Vila in French), the nation's capital and largest urban center (17,000 residents).

Vila, the capital

Vila's main business district clings to a narrow stretch of land bordering a harbor punctuated by two islets. Inland from the waterfront, narrow streets climb steep slopes graced with flowering bougainvillea. On the hillsides you'll see a few wooden, colonial mansions with wide verandas, relics of another era. Alongside Vila's old colonial-style buildings have sprouted new concrete structures. As the town grows, the new buildings are fast replacing the old.

Cultural Centre. Located on the waterfront next door to the Hotel Rossi, Vila's Cultural Centre houses fascinating displays of primitive art, island crafts, plants, and other wildlife.

Public market. Activity starts early at Vila's public market, located on Rue Higginson along the shady waterfront opposite the government buildings. Market days are Wednesdays, Fridays, and Saturdays from 6 A.M. to noon.

Smiling village women dressed in colorful Mother Hubbards will try to sell you giant coconut crabs, fish, and home-grown fruits and vegetables. Prices in the market are now fixed, and there is no bargaining.

Art gallery. Another good browsing spot is the studio and art gallery of Nicolai Michoutouchkine and Aloi Pilioko at the edge of the Erakor Lagoon just a short distance from the Hotel Le Lagon. The wood and thatch building houses more than 800 pieces of Oceanic art.

Other town sights. For a good view of Vila, climb the hill from the waterfront to the French government offices. Since many French people live in this area it has become known as the "Quartier Français."

South of the French government offices, you find the British government offices housed in a large, rambling wooden building bordering a well-tended lawn called the "British paddock." On weekends avid cricket fans gather here to see their favorite sport played. Many of the town's British residents make their homes nearby.

Boat cruises. Several tour operators offer short cruises from Vila. Enjoy a trip aboard a glass-bottomed boat to the harbor's outer reef or sail to Mele Bay.

Touring the island

Efate has about 145 km/90 miles of all-weather roads encircling the island. By metropolitan standards, these roads range from fair to poor condition.

From Vila you can take short trips or longer full-day excursions. Local operators offer organized tours of the island and a flightseeing trip.

Traveling around the island, you'll see rugged terrain, dense vine-tangled jungles, coco palm-bordered lagoons, native villages, coconut plantations, and white and black sand beaches.

Lama Mountain. Just 10 km/6 miles north of Vila on Efate's west coast, you can explore the natural forests and jungle scenery of Lama Mountain. Visitors are welcome daily between 8:30 A.M. and 5 P.M. Here you'll find an aquarium, aviary, and waterwheel.

Havannah Harbour. Near the north end of Efate this quiet expanse of water sheltered U.S. Navy ships during World War II.

East coast. You'll pass some of Efate's most beautiful beaches on your drive along the east coast. A short distance south of Forari, visitors can enjoy the hospitality of the Manuro Club. You can participate in water activities, have a quiet lunch or dinner, or just relax on the beach. The club is located only 55 km/34 miles from Vila on the southeastern coast.

Visiting Other Islands

For different glimpses of the country, travel to some other New Hebrides islands.

Espiritu Santo's urban center of Luganville offers a small town where touches of World War II are still visible. You can take a tour from Vila to Espiritu Santo or fly there on your own.

Another island to explore is Tanna, where you can climb an active volcano and peer into its fiery depths. On Pentecost Island you might be fortunate enough to witness a land-diving ceremony (usually held in May). Both of these trips are best taken on a tour.

A trip to Espiritu Santo

Until World War II, the quiet island of Espiritu Santo —located in the northern part of the New Hebrides chain—remained little changed from the sight that greeted Pedro de Quiros in 1606.

During the war, Allied military forces used southern Espiritu Santo as a staging area—hospitals, barracks, roads, and airfields were built. Jungles were cleared and market gardens planted to feed the American and New Zealand troops based here. At one time nearly 200,000 men were stationed on Espiritu Santo.

The military personnel have since departed, but war reminders are still evident in the crushed coral roads, houses built of abandoned war materials, and vine-covered quonset huts. Jungle has claimed the market gardens and hidden most of the rusting military scrap.

Espiritu Santo (also called Santo by the locals) is a heavily wooded island 113 km/70 miles long and 72 km/45 miles wide. Largest island in the New Hebrides, it's just an hour's flight from Vila.

Luganville. The New Hebrides' second largest town (population 5,000) grew from the former U.S. military base on southern Espiritu Santo. Like the island, Luganville is sometimes called Santo, which creates some confusion. Planes land near Luganville at Pekoa Airport, an ex-bomber base.

Luganville stretches 10 km/6 miles along the shore fronting the Segond Canal. Chinese trading stores line the town's main street, and numerous cargo ships tie up at the wharf. Luganville is one of the New Hebrides' main copra exporting ports. Cattle raising also has become an important industry.

A day's tour from Vila includes a flight to the island; a visit to Palikula, port for a sizable Japanese fishing fleet; and a stop at the Santo Golf Club. It also includes a visit to a coconut experimental station, the old American military hospital, and the site of the Rene River bridge which was destroyed by an earthquake in 1971.

The town has several small hotels, and rental cars are available.

Beyond Luganville. You will find beautiful beaches 50 km/31 miles north of Luganville at Hog Harbour. Here translucent blue waters roll onto sugar white sand bordered by coconut palms.

If you wish to venture into Espiritu Santo's jungle interior, a local guide is necessary. Bush tribes still live here in tiny villages clinging to mist-enshrouded mountain sides.

Tanna's volcano

Near the southern end of the New Hebrides archipelago, the island of Tanna is one of the most fertile islands in the chain. Here you'll find an active volcano, a "cargo cult," and a large herd of wild horses.

From Vila, a 75-minute flight brings visitors to Tanna. You can take a round-trip day excursion or stay overnight on Tanna in a self-contained, thatch-roofed bungalow. The island has no restaurants, but food supplies can be obtained at a nearby general store.

Volcano trek. Airplanes land at the airstrip near Lenakel village on the island's west coast. A waiting jeep transports visitors the 29 km/18 miles to the active volcano of Yasur. On your journey you'll pass coconut and coffee plantations, rain forests, and villages.

Surrounded by a moonscapelike plain of black ash, quiet Lake Siwi shimmers near the base of Yasur. Occasionally, ground orchids break the monotony of the desolate landscape; these flowers apparently thrive in the sulfur fumes pervading the region.

A guide from a nearby village accompanies the group on the 45-minute trek to the rim of the volcano. Your reward: a close-up glimpse of bubbling, red-hot lava.

Occasionally you'll hear an awesome rumbling as it spews from the volcano's depths.

Visitors are asked not to remove any stones from the mountain. It is considered taboo because of the stones' importance to the spiritual beliefs of the people.

John Frum movement. Sulphur Bay, the nearby village that owns Yasur, is the home of the John Frum cargo cult. Painted red crosses—symbols of the movement—dot the village and the countryside. (You can photograph these crosses, but don't touch them.)

These villagers, and others on Tanna, believe that someday "John Frum" will send them cargos of refrigerators, jeeps, and other riches. The movement began when the islanders became disillusioned with the missionaries and white people who seemed to possess all the material wealth in the area. The islanders believed the material possessions were brought "free" by cargo ship. Military cargo shipped to the New Hebrides during World War II further prompted these islanders to believe that they, too, would soon receive riches from the flying bird in the sky or the ship much larger than their canoes. No one really knows who John Frum was—he may have been an American G.I.

Wild horses. A jeep tour takes visitors to White Grass, a plateau on northern Tanna where more than 500 wild horses run and graze. The stallions and mares are descendants of stock introduced by missionaries.

Know Before You Go

The following practical information will help you plan your trip to the New Hebrides.

Entry/exit requirements. All visitors need a valid passport. If you are not a British or French subject, you will need a visa, which must be procured in advance at any French or British consulate. Travelers will also need an onward ticket.

Travelers arriving from an infected area will need smallpox and yellow fever vaccinations. Since a malaria risk does exist outside of Vila, check with your doctor before your trip for anti-malarial treatment. (Note: Since health requirements change from time to time, check with your local public health department before leaving on your trip.)

Departing air passengers pay an airport departure tax of A $2.

Customs. You are allowed to bring in duty free 400 cigarettes or 1 pound of tobacco or cigars, plus 2 bottles of liquor.

Currency. The Australian dollar. The exchange rate is Australian $1 = U.S. $1.15, and New Zealand $1.06.

Tipping. Tipping is not customary in the New Hebrides; it offends the New Hebridean sense of hospitality.

Time. New Hebrides is GMT (Greenwich mean time) +11. For example, when it is noon Sunday in Vila, it is 5 P.M. Saturday in San Francisco, 1 P.M. Sunday in Auckland, and 11 A.M. Sunday in Sydney.

Weather and what to wear. Located 14 to 20° south of the equator, the New Hebrides islands enjoy a semitropical climate marked by two seasons. The

cool, dry winter runs from May through October with temperatures averaging 27°C/81°F. During the warm rainy, humid summer (November through April), temperatures rise to around 29°C/84°F. Yearly rainfall totals about 3048 mm/120 inches, and humidity averages 83 percent. The southern islands in the chain enjoy cooler weather and less rain than their northern neighbors.

Casual, lightweight attire is perfect for the New Hebrides' tropical climate. Bring along a sweater if you journey there during the cool season. You'll want sunglasses and sturdy walking shoes if you plan to hike up Tanna's volcano.

For more information. Write to Tourist Information Bureau, P.O. Box 209, Vila, New Hebrides for further information on the New Hebrides.

PAPUA NEW GUINEA

In Papua New Guinea visitors see startling contrasts between developing modern society and relatively unchanged primitive cultures.

Only in recent years has this country emerged from a dominant Stone Age culture to become an independent nation. Even today, primitive tribal traditions persist in secluded valleys and on isolated plateaus.

The rugged topography of Papua New Guinea—sometimes shortened to PNG—has not only insulated most of its people from the outside world, but it has also isolated them from each other. More than 700 different languages are spoken in the country, and some 700 different cultures have developed during centuries of isolation.

As a visitor, you'll want to discover some of these cultures. From Port Moresby, the capital, or one of the country's other major urban centers, you can take a tour back in time when you explore Papua New Guinea.

Within the Tropics

Papua New Guinea lies wholly in the tropics just a few degrees south of the equator, only 161 km/100 miles north of Australia's Cape York Peninsula.

Most of the country is located on the eastern half of New Guinea, the world's second largest noncontinental island. (Irian Jaya, a province of Indonesia, shares the island.) Large and small islands scattered off the mainland's east coast include the Admiralty Islands, New Britain, New Ireland, the Trobriands, Louisiade Archipelago, and—in the North Solomons—Bougainville and Buka. Papua New Guinea's land area totals 462,840 square km/178,703 square miles.

Highlands and lowlands

Soaring, jagged mountains with deep ravines and valleys characterize the country's topography. Extending across the central part of the mainland (called the Highlands), a massive mountain spine forms a complex chain of knife-edged ranges, high plateaus and valleys, and steep ravines.

Numerous great rivers drain the rugged pinnacles.

Two of the largest are the Sepik River, flowing north into the Bismarck Sea, and the Fly River, emptying into the Gulf of Papua on the southern coast. Where silt-laden rivers reach the flat coastal plains, large mangrove and sago swamps have been created.

Wildlife abounds in Papua New Guinea. Perhaps most famous are the birds of paradise.

Discovered en route to the "Spice Islands"

In the 16th century, Spanish and Portuguese sailors first spotted the island of New Guinea while en route to the Moluccas—the rich "Spice Islands." The first European to land was Jorge de Meneses, Portuguese governor of the Moluccas, who arrived in 1526. He called the island "Ilhas dos Papuas," meaning Island of the Fuzzy-Haired Men. Twenty years later Spanish navigator Inigo de Retes sailed along the north coast and named the island "Nueva Guinea" because of its resemblance to the Guinea coast of Africa.

Spanish, English, and Dutch explorers all visited New Guinea during the 16th and 17th centuries, but few people settled here until the 18th century.

In 1828, the Dutch annexed the western half of New Guinea (now Indonesia's Irian Jaya). Germany annexed the northeast part of the island in 1884, naming it German New Guinea. One week later, the British claimed the southeastern portion of the island plus the smaller islands to the east; they called their protectorate British New Guinea. In 1906, Australia assumed responsibility for this protectorate, changing its name to the Territory of Papua. After World War I, Australia also became the administrator of (German) New Guinea.

In 1942, during World War II, Japanese troops invaded the territories of Papua and New Guinea, but they were soon halted by the Australian and American Forces under the command of General Douglas MacArthur.

Today, the former territories of Papua and New Guinea are one nation administered by a freely elected government. Papua New Guinea achieved independence from Australia on September 16, 1975, and is now a sovereign state within the British Commonwealth of Nations.

Papua New Guinea's People

Nearly 3 million people inhabit Papua New Guinea; most are Melanesians. About 30,000 residents are of Australian, European, or Chinese ancestry.

Lifestyles—primitive and modern

Each of Papua New Guinea's 700 cultural groups has its own customs, culture, and language. Some of these people have felt the influences of modern civilization for a number of years; others scarcely knew a world outside their village existed until a short time ago.

Housing for Papua New Guinea's rural people ranges from A-framed, thatch-roofed stilt houses to round houses with dome-shaped thatch roofs. The land and

98
100
102
103
104
105

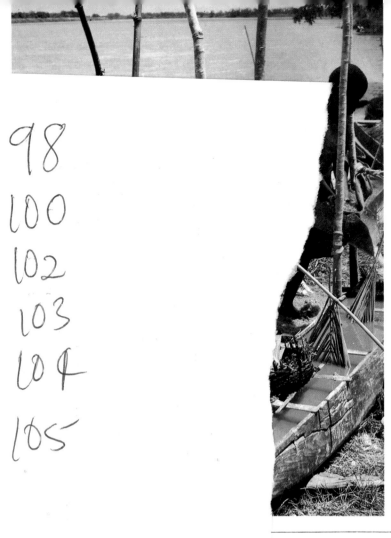

Sepik youths *process sago, a starchy food derived from sago palm. Travelers take cruises up Sepik River to view tropical wildlife, visit stilt villages, and shop for primitive art.*

Highlands tribesman *costumed for a sing sing paints face, wears feathered headdress, nose and neck ornaments. Villagers in native dress congregate for market days and Highland tribal celebrations.*

rivers provide such dietary staples as sago palm, taro, yams, and fish. More westernized city dwellers live in western-style houses and shop at the local supermarket.

Dress. Clothing in Papua New Guinea reflects both traditional and modern customs. Some Papua New Guineans wear western-style dress—loose fitting shirts and shorts or *lap-laps* (wraparound skirts) for men, "meri" blouses (long tops) and skirts for women.

Still others (living in the Highlands or Trobriands) retain their traditional tribal dress of grass skirts or apronlike string skirts. Many women wear *bilums* on their heads; in these multipurpose woven bags, they carry everything including produce and children.

Language. Because of the many different languages in Papua New Guinea, it is difficult for people to communicate with others outside their own tribe. For this reason Pidgin has flourished, particularly in the Highlands and northern part of the mainland.

English is being taught increasingly in the schools.

Religion. Even though Papua New Guineans are now Christianized, superstition and magic still play an integral role in their daily lives. Their beliefs—based largely on ancestor and spirit worship *(puri-puri)*—are reflected in much of their art and customs.

Sports. Papua New Guineans touched by western civilization have become sports minded. Major activities include football, cricket, softball, and golf. Around Port Moresby you'll find teams competing in canoe races.

Mining and forestry exports

Since 1972, when Bougainville Copper Ltd. began production, copper has become an important export for the country. An enormous open-cut copper mine is located at Panguna on Bougainville. Other mining exports include small amounts of gold and silver.

Forestry products are also a leading export item, along with copra, palm oil, and tea.

Planning Your Trip

Papua New Guinea, a newly developing South Pacific destination, can be reached by both air and sea.

Several major airlines—including the country's air carrier, Air Niugini—serve Jacksons Airport at Port

Moresby. (It's an 11 km/7 mile bus or taxi trip into town from the airport.) Connecting flights serve Papua New Guinea from Australia, the Philippines, the Solomons, Hong Kong, Indonesia, Japan, and Hawaii.

A few passenger and cargo/passenger liners make at least one PNG town a port of call. Seaport towns include Port Moresby, Rabaul, Lae, Madang, and Wewak.

Getting around the country

Because of the rugged and mountainous terrain, few roads have been developed. Many existing roads are narrow and extremely difficult to maintain because heavy rains frequently cause problems.

The easiest way to travel within Papua New Guinea is by air. Several local airlines offer scheduled and charter service to a number of airports and landing strips.

Taxi service is available in towns. However, cabs are in short supply so be prepared for a wait.

Renting a car. If you wish to explore the towns and their neighboring environs on your own, rent a car (or hire a car and driver) in Port Moresby, Lae, Rabaul, Mt. Hagen, Goroka, Madang, Wewak, Kieta, and Popondetta. Traffic moves on the left side of the road. It's advisable to reserve your car ahead of time.

Bus travel. Regular bus service links Goroka (Highlands) and Lae (coast), and Goroka and Mt. Hagen

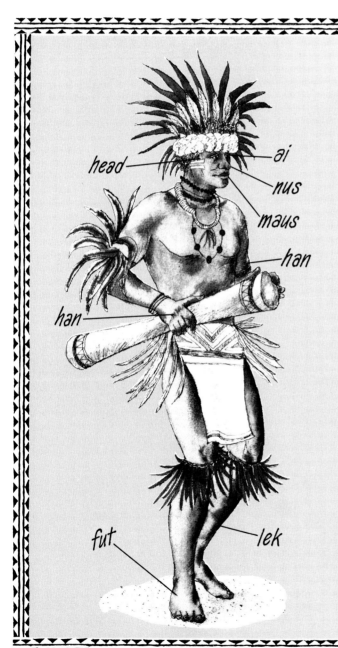

TOK PISIN
Talk Pidgin

"Yu save (savvy) tok pisin?" Do you speak Pidgin? About 1,000,000 Papua New Guineans do. With over 700 different languages in the country, Pidgin allows people from various tribes to communicate with each other, unifying the nation. Melanesian Pidgin is used extensively in the national parliament and in local government council meetings.

Pidgin originally developed more than a century ago in the sugar cane fields of Australia's Queensland. Workers from different tribes in Papua New Guinea couldn't communicate with each other or with their overseers. The overseers spoke English, and the workers arranged the English words according to their Melanesian grammar pattern. Thus, a language was born.

For a few kina, you can buy a simple Pidgin phrasebook. Below are a few phrases you might want to try. First read them aloud to yourself. You will probably understand the meaning of the words after you have heard them.

Don't be shy. Smile and try a phrase or two.

Good morning/good day—"Mornin"
Good afternoon—"Apinun"
Good evening—"Gud nait"
How are you?—"Yu stap gut (goot)?" or
    "Yu orait?"
What's your name?—"Wanem nem bilong you?"
Do you understand?—"You save (savvy)?"
How much does it cost?—"Em i kostim hamas?"
I want to buy it.—"Mi laik baim."
Please—"Plis"
Thank you—"Tenkyu"
Yes—"Ies"   No—"Nogat"
I'll be seeing you.—"Lukim yu."

Field workers pick tea *on Highlands plantation. Grown and harvested for export, tea contributes substantially to economy. Other main exports include lumber, minerals, copra, palm oil, rubber, spices, and pyrethrum (used in insecticides).*

(Highlands). Each trip takes about a day journeying mostly over unpaved roads.

Boating. Cargo/passenger service with limited accommodations is offered along the northeast coast between Madang and Lae. Contact Lutheran Shipping M.V. "Totol," Box 789, Madang.

Tours. Many visitors to Papua New Guinea see the country by arranged tour. Operators in both the United States and Australia offer packaged tours to and around Papua New Guinea. You also can arrange ahead (or on arrival) for a tour of the country originating in Port Moresby. Other major towns schedule short local tours of nearby points of interest. For further information on tour possibilities, check with your travel agent.

Hotels, lodges, and mountain huts

Papua New Guinea offers a wide selection of small to moderate-size accommodations. You will find comfortable hotels, motels, lodges, and guest houses scattered throughout the country. Travelers can stay in the major towns, in the jungle foothills, in the Highlands, near the Sepik River, or beside a beach. Architectural styles range from low-rise modern structures to individual thatch-roofed mountain huts.

Dining and entertainment

Hotel dining rooms offer a good menu selection as well as an occasional buffet. You also can sample Chinese, Australian, or Indonesian dishes at local restaurants.

Occasionally the Hotel Madang (in Madang) and Chimbu Lodge (in Kundiawa) present a small sing sing featuring costumed entertainers in traditional native singing and dancing. The native feast accompanying these sing sings might include roast pork, sweet potatoes, rice dishes, tropical fruits, and vegetables. Many feast items are cooked in a *mumu* (oven made of hot stones buried in the ground). Sometimes hotels hold these native feasts without sing sings.

Tourist officials caution visitors in outlying towns against wandering alone too far from the hotel after dark. Every country has its rascals.

A plethora of primitive art

Papua New Guinea craftspeople are noted for their excellent creations of primitive art. Regional arts and crafts include carvings, ceremonial masks and figures from the Sepik; crocodile carvings from the Trobriands; basketware from Buka; and arrows, bows, and decorated axes from the Highlands.

You can buy Papua New Guinea artifacts in the villages where they are made or at shops in the major towns. Shops are open from 8 A.M. to 4:30 P.M. Monday through Friday, and on Saturday mornings. In Port Moresby the government-run Village Arts Store, on Rigo Road about 2 km/1 mile from the airport, offers a representative selection of artifacts from all over the country. Store hours are 8 A.M. to 5 P.M. Monday to Saturday, 9 to 4 on Sunday.

The export of artifacts is government controlled, and no traditional village artwork over 20 years old may be

FESTIVAL TIME

One of the best ways to see some traditional aspects of Papua New Guinean life is to attend a local celebration or festival.

January–April

Chinese New Year. The Chinese communities celebrate this occasion near the end of January with traditional festivities.

May–August

Frangipani Festival. In early May, Rabaul celebrates the arrival of the first flowers after the 1937 volcanic eruption with an annual festival. Events include a sing sing and string band competitions.

Port Moresby Show. Held in June on the Queen's Birthday weekend, this event includes sing sings and agricultural displays.

Madang Music Festival. Musicians gather in Madang in August for a week-long schedule of performances.

September–December

Independence Day. Celebrations take place throughout Papua New Guinea on the weekend nearest September 16.

Hiri Moale. This September festival in Port Moresby marks the early voyages of the Motu people along the Papuan coast.

Annual Arts Festival. In September Port Moresby and Lae alternate in hosting this 2-week event featuring guest performers from other Third World countries.

Tolai Warwagira. During a fortnight of festivities in November, Rabaul schedules fireworks displays, sing sings, and choral group performances.

Morobe Show. An October weekend of festivities in Lae includes cultural and agricultural displays plus a major sing sing.

Pearl Festival. In November a weekend-long celebration in Samarai, Milne Bay Province, features beauty contests, art and crafts displays, and canoe races.

---

taken out of the country. Your port of debarkation might want a certificate of fumigation for artifacts purchased.

Outdoor pleasures

The warm, clear waters off Papua New Guinea provide a variety of excellent snorkeling and scuba diving opportunities. Many of the diving centers have diving clubs that hold weekly outings. In addition, specialized tour companies operating out of Madang and Port Moresby offer qualified instructors, scuba gear, and compressors.

Game fishermen catch small marlin, sailfish, mackerel, and tuna as close as 6 km/4 miles from Port Moresby. For further information, write Port Moresby Game Fishing Club, P.O. Box 5028, Boroko.

Golfers can try the 18-hole course at Port Moresby Golf Club. Other courses are located at Goroka, Lae, Madang, Minj, Wau, Rabaul, Kavieng, Popondetta, Mt. Hagen, Wewak, and Kieta.

You can also enjoy tennis, squash, boating, waterskiing, horseback riding, lawn bowling, and swimming.

Seeing the "Mainland"

Most visitors spend their time on the Papua New Guinea mainland, an extensive area covering the eastern part of the island of New Guinea. From Port Moresby, the country's main air and sea gateway, visitors can take 2 to 14-day tours of the country or travel independently to Lae, Goroka, and Mt. Hagen (to tour the Highlands) or Madang and Wewak (to cruise on the Sepik River).

Port Moresby, the capital

Most visitors stay only briefly in Port Moresby, the country's capital and government center, before continuing on to other Papua New Guinea destinations. Located on the mainland's southern coast, the city overlooks Fairfax Harbour. Many of its 117,000 residents live near the harbor or in suburbs spreading over low hills and valleys behind it. The new government buildings are in Waigani Valley, north of the old part of town.

Visitor accommodations include the Boroko Hotel, Davara Motel, Gateway Hotel, Islander Hotel, Outrigger Motel, Papua Hotel, and TraveLodge.

Touring Port Moresby. Within walking distance of most hotels is popular, palm-edged Ela Beach. On Sunday mornings, the local police band performs here.

Every day is market day at Koki Market, located near the water's edge east of Ela Beach on Healy Parade. Townspeople and villagers, including out-islanders who have arrived by canoe, gather to exchange gossip and sell and purchase supplies. Stall displays feature such items as parrot fish strung on racks, big green cassowary bird eggs, and mud crabs.

The National Museum and Art Gallery is located in Waigani Valley, a suburb 13 km/8 miles north of the town center. Open daily except Saturdays, it houses one of the largest displays of traditional Papua New Guinea pottery in the world.

Sogeri Plateau. The cool Sogeri Plateau, just an hour's drive northeast of Port Moresby, offers numerous places to explore. You can see teak and rubber plantations, waterfalls, and the Bomana War Cemetery.

Lae, a garden town

The garden town of Lae, on the Huon Gulf, is a 45-minute flight north of Port Moresby. The country's second largest city (75,000 people), Lae originally developed around an airfield that serviced the Morobe gold fields during the 1930s gold rush. Destroyed during World War II, the town has been completely rebuilt. Travelers can stay at the Huon Gulf Motel, Lae Lodge, and the Melanesian Hotel.

Touring Lae. Within walking distance of town center are Lae's lovely Botanical Gardens. Early morning is the best time to view the water lilies and glimpse some of Papua New Guinea's colorful tropical birds flitting through the jungle forest.

Other town sights include Lae War Memorial and several colorful markets.

Bulolo and Wau. You can drive or take a tour to Bulolo and Wau, located 122 km/76 miles southwest of Lae. These now-quiet towns bustled with activity during the 1930s gold rush. Some dredging equipment remains.

The fascinating Highlands

As you travel the Highlands Highway and side roads, you'll see tiny settlements of round houses near sweet potato fields fenced off by sharp stakes. You'll pass villagers—wearing brief apron skirts and carrying bows and arrows—walking their pigs alongside the road. Occasionally travelers come upon an impromptu sing sing—a colorfully costumed tribal celebration in song and dance.

You can get to the Highlands on a short flight from Lae, Port Moresby, or Madang; or by a long drive on the Highlands Highway out of Lae. Several Papua New Guinea tour operators offer special tours through the Highlands. If possible, schedule Highland tours at least 30 days in advance.

Goroka accommodations include the Bird of Paradise Hotel and Lantern Lodge; space is booked up to a year in advance for the annual Eastern Highlands Show (sing sing). In Mt. Hagen travelers stay at the Airport Hotel, Hagen Park Motel, The Highlander, and Kimininga.

Goroka. Largest town in the Highlands, Goroka is located at an elevation of 1,524 meters/5,000 feet in the Bismarck Range. Market gardens and coffee plantations surround this town of 30,000 people. If you journey to the Highlands from Lae, Goroka will probably be your first stop. It's a 40-minute flight or 8-hour bus trip from Lae to Goroka.

From Goroka, take a tour to Kominufa village to see the mud men of Asaro Valley. Covered in dried grey river mud and wearing ugly helmet masks made of mud, fiber, dog teeth, and pig tusks, these men perform their traditional chants and macabre dance for tour groups.

Kundiawa. In the heart of the Chimbu province 97 km/ 60 miles west of Goroka, you'll find Kundiawa. It's been less than 50 years since the first westerners explored this primitive and thickly populated region. The hard-working Chimbu people cultivate patchwork vegetable gardens on the steep mountain slopes.

On a tour of the area you might see Chimbu bush plays—spectacular performances of mime, dance, and song depicting scenes of everyday tribal life.

Mt. Hagen. Nestled in the Wahgi Valley amid coffee and tea plantations, Mt. Hagen is the provincial capital of the Western Highlands. A small town of 21,000, its population soars on the big market days (Wednesdays, Fridays, Saturdays) when the tribespeople converge from outlying districts.

The Highland Show. The big event of the year in the Highlands is the Eastern Highlands Show. Previously, this annual show has alternated between Goroka and Mt. Hagen, but it is now planned yearly in Goroka, probably in late September.

More than 60,000 tribespeople from all over Papua New Guinea gather to participate in and enjoy this 2-day event. Some come by foot, traveling for weeks to the show; others arrive by plane, bus, or truck.

Highlight of the show is the sing sing. Over 4,000 tribespeople dance and sing while swaying to ancient chants and the beat of drums. Costuming is spectacular. Many performers wear huge headdresses of brilliantly colored bird of paradise plumes, fur neck pieces, shell jewelry, and body paint in bright yellow, blue, and red.

Madang, a tropical Venice

Situated on a coral promontory 241 km/150 miles northwest of Lae, Madang has one of the country's most beautiful settings. A string of palm-covered tropical islands protects its fine deepwater harbor, and placid waterways meander through the town. Madang has been called the Venice of Papua New Guinea.

Originally settled by Germans, this sleepy tropical port was invaded by the Japanese during World War II. Today Madang is a starting point for some tours into the Sepik region and Highlands.

Accommodations include the Coastwatchers Motel, Hotel Madang Resort, and Smuggler's Inn Motel.

The wonderous Sepik

Navigable for about 1,127 km/700 miles, the Sepik River drains an immense northern region of grasslands, swamps, and jungle. Its expansive area is home for a remarkable collection of animals, reptiles, insects, birdlife, and flowering plants.

Cruising the Sepik. Travelers can take half-day, all-day, and several-day water tours on the Sepik and its tributaries traveling by canoe, small motorized boat, or houseboat. Tours, which include village stops for exploration and shopping, leave from Angoram, Amboin, Pagwi, and Ambunti. One popular 3 to 6-day cruise on the "Sepik Explorer" houseboat navigates the river between Angoram, Pagwi, and Ambunti.

Airstrips are located at Angoram, Amboin, Ambunti, Hayfield, Maprik, and Wewak. A road links Wewak with Pagwi and Angoram.

Wewak and Maprik. Wewak, on the coast northwest of Madang, is the East Sepik's administrative capital. It offers the principal road accesses to the Sepik River.

Lodging includes the Sepik Motel, Wewak Hotel, and the Windjammer Beach Motel.

From Wewak you can journey by air or road inland to the Maprik area, which is known as "*haus tambaran* (spirit house) country." You'll see full-scale models of these A-framed spirit houses with their murals and interesting carvings at the Maprik Cultural Center.

Primitive art. The Sepik people produce some of the finest examples of primitive art in the world including intricate carvings and decorated pottery.

Exploring Offshore Islands

In addition to Papua New Guinea's massive mainland area, the country includes numerous offshore islands. Those of interest to visitors include New Britain, Bougainville (in the North Solomons), and the Trobriands. All are easily accessible by air.

New Britain, the largest of these islands, lies due east of Madang. Rabaul, the island's main town, sits at the head of one of the Pacific's best natural harbors, surrounded by a backdrop of several volcanic cones—some of which are still active.

In 1942 the Japanese invaded Rabaul and made it their center of operations in the Southwest Pacific. A large number of interesting war relics remain.

Accommodations in Rabaul include the Hotel Ascot, Motel Kaivuna, Kulau Lodge, and Rabaul TraveLodge.

Bougainville, located northeast of the mainland at the northern end of the Solomon Islands chain, is famed for its enormous open-cut copper mine at Panguna. While visiting this island which also has World War II battlegrounds, you can stay at the Davara Motel or the Kieta Hotel.

The Trobriand archipelago, lying off the mainland's southeastern coast, contains 22 coral islands—some of them so flat they're at ocean level. These islands possess both natural beauty and a carefree population.

Know Before You Go

The following practical information will help you plan your trip to Papua New Guinea.

Entry/exit procedures. Visitors to Papua New Guinea need a valid passport, a confirmed onward ticket, and sufficient funds for their stay. Upon your arrival, you will be issued a 30-day visitor permit.

Visitors are required to have a smallpox vaccination; you'll also need inoculations against cholera and yellow fever if you come from an infected area. Since a malaria risk does exist, it is advisable to take antimalarial tablets. Check with your doctor a few weeks before departure for treatment. (Note: Since health requirements change from time to time, check with your local public health department before leaving on your trip.)

Departing international air passengers pay an airport departure tax of K2.

Customs. Travelers may bring in duty free 200 cigarettes or an equal amount of cigars or tobacco, 1 litre of liquor, perfume for personal use, and gifts totaling no more than K200 (U.S. $290, A $240, N.Z. $275).

Currency. The Papua New Guinea currency is the kina. The exchange rate is approximately K1 = U.S. $1.25, Australia $1.09, and New Zealand $1.15.

Tipping. Tipping is neither customary nor encouraged.

Time. Papua New Guinea is GMT (Greenwich mean time) +10. For example, when it is noon Sunday in Port Moresby, it is 6 P.M. Saturday in San Francisco, 2 P.M. Sunday in Auckland, and noon Sunday in Sydney.

Weather and what to wear. Because Papua New Guinea lies within the tropics, the climate is typically humid. There are two principal seasons: the season of the northwest monsoon (from December to April)—hot, with sudden squalls, heavy rains, high winds; and the season of the southeast trade winds (from May to November)—drier and cooler.

The rainfall varies. Lae averages about 457 cm/180 inches per year, whereas Port Moresby receives only about 102 cm/40 inches. Day coastal temperatures range from a minimum of 26°C/79°F to a maximum of 32°C/90°F. Night temperatures can drop to 19°C/67°F. The less humid Highlands have sunny warm days and cool nights.

As in much of the South Pacific, you'll be comfortable in lightweight summer clothes in most areas. In the Highlands you'll need warmer clothing for the evening. Bathing suits and shorts (except walking shorts and knee-high socks for men) should not be worn in towns or villages. Other articles to pack include walking shoes, an umbrella, sunglasses, suntan lotion, a rainhat, and beach shoes for reef walking.

For more information. Write to the Director, PNG Office of Tourism, P.O. Box 773, Port Moresby for further information on Papua New Guinea.

SOLOMON ISLANDS

Nowhere in the South Pacific are memories of 20th century wartime history more prevalent than in the Solomon Islands. Guadalcanal, Tulagi, the "Slot," and Iron Bottom Sound are all familiar names from the annals of World War II. The formidable Japanese offensive was stalled on Guadalcanal in 1943, changing the course of the war in the Pacific.

As you tour the Solomons, you'll still see vestiges of war—tanks overgrown with creeping vines, shell-torn landing craft ravaged by the seas, trenches gouging the land, and redoubts jutting from the hillsides. However, the islands' exotic flowers, towering palms, blue lagoons, and friendly people lessen the grimness of these war reminders.

Two Chains of Islands

The Solomon Islands cover an extensive area stretching for more than 1,448 km/900 miles across the Pacific in a northwest-southeast direction. The wide seaway of New Georgia Sound, called "The Slot," divides the island group into two chains.

The Solomons lie about 1,408 km/875 miles due east of Papua New Guinea, and 1,284 km/798 miles northwest of the New Hebrides.

Guadalcanal, with an area of 6,477 square km/2,500 square miles, is the largest island in the Solomon group. Other large main islands include Choiseul, Malaita, New Georgia, San Cristobal, and Santa Isabel.

Islands vary from large, mountainous, volcanic land masses to small atolls that are mere flat coral outcroppings. Steep mountains cut through the volcanic islands, sloping sharply to the sea on one side and descending more gradually in a series of foothills on the other. Swift-flowing rivers drain these peaks. Where limestone deposits exist, the rivers may disappear to surge through underground channels.

Some of the volcanoes remain active. In the Santa Cruz Islands southeast of San Cristobal, Tinakula Volcano briefly erupted in 1971. Although Savo Volcano last erupted in 1840, it still is considered potentially dangerous with numerous hot springs and thermal areas. A submarine volcano (Kavachi) near New Georgia occasionally erupts from the sea, then disappears once more underwater.

Mangrove swamps, rain forests

Extensive mangrove swamps rim the coastal areas of the islands and dense rain forests cover much of the interior. Ferns, mosses, orchids, climbing and creeping vines, and flowering shrubs such as hibiscus thrive in the rain forests.

Wild pigs, opossums, and bush rats forage through the forests, while crocodiles and lizards lurk in the coastal mangrove swamps. Though the Solomons have many snakes, few are venomous.

Over 140 species of birds—including king and pygmy parrots, sunbirds, kingfishers, cockatoos, and a variety of pigeons—dwell in the Solomons. In addition to an interesting bird population, you'll also see a colorful assortment of butterflies.

One bird of special note—the burrowing megapode—lives on Savo Island. Although this bird is smaller than a domestic fowl, it lays an egg twice the size of a normal chicken egg. The megapode then buries the egg in a burrow. The egg eventually hatches from the heat of the sun or the warmth of an adjacent thermal spring. You can see these birds on a 1-day boat tour from Honiara to Savo Island.

Numerous sharks prowl the open seas around the Solomon Islands.

Discovered by Mendaña

In 1567 the Spanish explorer Alvaro de Mendaña sailed from Peru in search of a southern continent. He reached the Solomons the following year, discovering Guadalcanal, Ysabel (Santa Isabel), and San Cristobal. In an effort to encourage Spanish migration, he hinted at the existence of gold in the area by naming the group the Solomon Islands. (Much speculation existed regarding the site of "King Solomon's lost mines.")

Mendaña returned to the Solomons in 1595 with a group of settlers to establish a colony at Graciosa Bay in the Santa Cruz Islands. Disputes and sickness plagued the group. After Mendaña fell ill and died, the colonists sailed for the Philippines.

In the following centuries, other explorers including Abel Tasman and Louis Antoine de Bougainville sighted or stopped at the islands.

During the 1800s whalers, traders, and missionaries all found their way to the Solomons. Their reception was not always cordial. Massacre and murder reigned here during this period. Some of the attacks on Europeans were in retaliation for "blackbirding"—the kidnapping of islanders for use as laborers on South Pacific plantations.

To provide protection for Europeans in the Solomons, Great Britain declared the South Solomons a Protectorate in 1893. The remainder of the Solomon Islands became part of the Protectorate between 1898 and 1900.

Early in the 20th century, private companies started a variety of plantations, but in later years—up until

Rusting debris *marks Guadalcanal landing beach where Allied troops stormed ashore in 1942. Abandoned relics litter countryside, providing vivid reminders of heavy fighting in Solomons during World War II.*

War memorial *near Rabaul honors Commonwealth military men who died in World War II battles in New Britain area. Center of Japanese operations in 1942, Rabaul was bombed by Allies, rebuilt after war.*

AD MAJOREM DEI GLORIAM

IN THIS PLACE ARE RECORDED
THE NAMES OF OFFICERS
AND MEN OF THE BRITISH
COMMONWEALTH OF NATIONS
WHO DIED DURING THE
1939-1945 WAR IN THE NEW
BRITAIN AREA, ON LAND, AT
SEA AND IN THE AIR, BUT TO
WHOM THE FORTUNES OF WAR
DENIED THE KNOWN AND
HONOURED BURIAL GIVEN TO
THEIR COMRADES IN DEATH

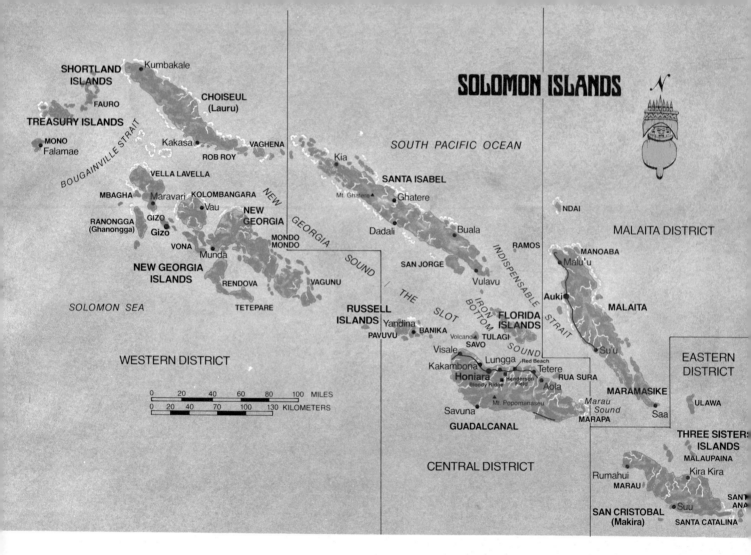

1940—the British Solomon Islands were largely neglected except for coconut plantings.

Then came World War II. In April 1942, the Japanese invaded the Solomons, and the islands became the focal point of fierce battles between Japanese troops and the Allies. These confrontations continued until the Japanese were driven out in early 1943. Many Solomon islanders, fiercely loyal to the Allied cause, distinguished themselves in battle.

One of the most important World War II naval battles—the Battle of the Coral Sea—took place near the Solomon Islands. The U.S. Marines captured a Japanese airstrip under construction on Guadalcanal. After its completion, Henderson Air Field played an important role in the Guadalcanal Campaign.

Until World War II, most Solomon islanders had little contact with the outside world. With the advent of war, however, they learned of aircraft (believed by some to be a huge kind of bird), and other marvels such as canned foods, bottled drinks, kerosene lamps, radios, and modern weapons.

On July 7, 1978, the Solomon Islands gained their independence after 85 years of British rule. The country is governed by an elected 38-member national parliament headed by a prime minister and by elected provincial assemblies in each of the Solomons' five provinces.

Solomon Islands People

Approximately 197,000 people reside in the Solomon Islands. Of that number about 184,000 are Melanesian and 8,000 Polynesian; Europeans, Micronesians (Gilbertese), and Chinese are also represented.

Most of the Melanesians live on the larger islands, while the Polynesians inhabit the smaller islands and atolls. The most heavily populated islands are Malaita and Guadalcanal.

Most live in villages

Except for a few urban centers—Honiara on Guadalcanal, Auki on Malaita, and Gizo in the New Georgia group—most Solomon islanders reside in small, thatched hut villages. Many of these villages lie near the coasts of the islands and their inhabitants are known as "saltwater" people. "Bush" people dwell inland on Guadalcanal and Malaita.

Villagers maintain a traditional way of life that has been in existence for hundreds of years. They grow their own fruits and vegetables, and hunt and fish for addi-

(Continued on page 102)

THE COCONUT PALM
A Tropical Supermarket

Symbol of the South Pacific, the coconut palm tree is more than a decorative addition to scenic views of the South Seas. It is a tropical supermarket of useful products that contribute substantially to island life. During your South Pacific travels, you'll discover its many uses. When you're standing in its shade, however, remember that a coconut can fall without warning.

The fruit of the tree—the coconut—is an important ingredient in many native recipes. For the local population, these nuts are no farther away than a quick climb up a tree. (Visitors usually find tree climbing a little more difficult than the local people do.)

Savor coconut in cakes, puddings, and fish cream sauces. For a refreshing cool drink, sip the slightly sweet liquid of the green immature coconut. Villagers living on arid islands and atolls without rivers or streams often drink this instead of water.

The tree itself offers another gourmet treat— heart of palm salad. But a tree must be sacrificed in the preparation of this dish, sometimes known as "millionaire's salad."

The coconut tree provides building materials for islanders. Hardwood tree trunks become the uprights and rafters of huts as well as the masts and spars of boats. Palm fronds are used to thatch the hut roofs.

From the coconut tree villagers create many useful household items. The coconut shell serves as a bowl, cup, or cooking vessel. Carved shells become buttons, bracelets, and other ornamental objects. Palm fronds are woven into handsome mats, hats, and baskets. Visitors purchase many of these locally made products to take home as useful souvenirs.

Copra—the South Pacific's economic mainstay —comes from the coconut palm. Islanders halve the nuts and dry them, either naturally in the sun or artificially in kilns. As you travel through the countryside, you'll see halved coconuts spread out to dry in the sun, and occasional small roadside kilns.

The islanders take the dried meat to the nearest port, where it is shipped to a crushing mill. Here the oil—about 70 percent of the meat —is extracted. The resulting high grade vegetable oil is used in the manufacture of soap, margarine, cosmetics, and other products.

The coconut palm's origin in the South Pacific is somewhat of a mystery. Not considered indigenous by botanists, the tree may have originated in the Indo-Oceanian area. Migrating tribes took these coconuts with them to plant upon arrival in their new homeland. Some coconuts may have been dispersed naturally by drifting ocean currents. Today the tree grows on large commercial plantations as well as in natural groves.

tional food items. Any needed cash can be obtained through the sale of copra or surplus produce. Transportation is by canoe or foot.

Solomon islanders need little clothing in their warm, tropical climate. Village men wear western-style shorts or a wrap-around skirt known as a *lap-lap*. Women prefer cotton dresses or just a skirt. Honiarians have adopted western-style casual dress.

Language. Although English is the official language taught in school, few people speak it. Since more than 80 different languages and dialects are spoken in the Solomons, most inhabitants communicate by Pidgin English, which combines an English derived vocabulary with Melanesian grammar.

Religion. Nearly 90 percent of the people follow a form of Christianity combined with traditional native customs. Most villages have a church, and services are conducted daily.

Sports. In Honiara (and main centers on other islands) you can join local residents as they cheer for their favorite team. Rugby and association football are both very popular spectator sports. Rugby season runs from November to April and association football is played between April and October. League games take place on Saturday afternoons.

Other island sports include cricket, volleyball, basketball, and amateur boxing.

An agricultural economy

The Solomon Islands depend primarily on agricultural products for income. Chief cash crops include copra, cocoa, timber, and spices. There is a limited amount of commercial fishing and a growing interest in cattle raising.

Planning Your Trip

Once relatively isolated from tourist routes, today the Solomon Islands can be reached easily by either air or sea.

Several international air carriers—flying from Papua New Guinea, Fiji, New Hebrides, Nauru, and Australia—make regularly scheduled stops at Honiara on Guadalcanal. From the airport (Henderson Field), travelers board a bus or taxi for the 11-km/7-mile trip into town.

Both South Seas cruise ships and passenger/cargo liners make occasional stops at Point Cruz in Honiara, the Solomons' major port of call.

Pilot supervises *baggage loading on small plane at Munda airport in New Georgia Islands. Quonset hut serves as ticket office and waiting room. Small planes provide vital link in interisland transportation.*

Getting around the Solomons

Visitors to the Solomons spend most of their time in and around Honiara, the country's capital located on the island of Guadalcanal. Here you'll find several comfortable hotels, good shopping for native crafts, and many wartime historical sights.

For your town and island exploration, you can rent a car or hire a taxi. Since cabs are not metered, negotiate the fare in advance. Other transportation options include scheduled buses, serving Honiara and its nearby suburbs, and chauffeur-driven cars available through the rental car agencies.

Local tour operators offer trips around Honiara and Guadalcanal and excursions to the western Solomons,

Savo Island, Tulagi, and Malaita. Since transportation facilities are limited on these outer islands (Malaita is the only other island with bus and taxi service), tours provide the best way to see them.

Air travel. Solomon Islands Airways Ltd. (Solair) schedules regular trips from Honiara to some 20 airstrips in the Solomons. From Honiara a flightseeing tour takes visitors over World War II battlegrounds on and near Guadalcanal.

Boat trips. Both private and government interisland cargo boats, carrying some passengers, travel to many of the islands. Schedules are subject to alteration or cancellation, and the boats can be crowded not only with people but also with their pigs, dogs, and chickens. There are limited cabin accommodations.

From Honiara you can board a boat for a scenic trip along the Guadalcanal coast, take a canoe up the Matanikau River at the edge of Honiara, or see marine life from a glass-bottomed boat. One tour operator offers an overnight boat trip to Gizo in the New Georgia group stopping at 10 ports en route.

Hotels and guest houses

In the Solomon Islands, visitor accommodations are limited, modest in size, and relatively simple. In all of these scattered islands, travelers find only nine hotels and guest houses.

In Honiara, you choose from medium-size Hotel Mendana or Honiara Hotel, each with swimming pool and restaurant, or the small Hibiscus Lodge where each room has its own cooking facilities and refrigerator.

If you're seeking a hotel away from the downtown area, try the Tambea Village Hotel Resort 48 km/30 miles west of Honiara on a quiet beach. Guests stay in Melanesian-style bungalows and enjoy water sports.

On the other islands, visitors stay in simple facilities ranging from two to six rooms. Tavanipupu Island Resort, 129 km/80 miles southeast of Guadalcanal on an island in Marau Sound, has several cottages with kitchens. Ngarando Resthouse, on Mohawk Bay in the Reef Islands 579 km/360 miles southeast of Honiara, also has several cottages equipped with kitchens.

Other accommodations include the Auki Lodge in the town of Auki on Malaita; and the Munda Rest House in Munda and the Kasolo Hotel in Gizo, both in the New Georgia Islands group.

Dining and entertainment

In addition to restaurants in Honiara hotels, try The Lantern (in Chinatown) and Pagoda Room (in Kukum, a short distance from town). Both feature western and Chinese dishes. The Tambea Village Hotel Resort features an occasional Melanesian feast or barbecue.

Enjoy an evening of Melanesian and Gilbertese songs and dances at the Honiara Hotel and Tambea Village Hotel. Some tours include visits to local villages where you'll sample native food and hear local music.

Shop for woodcarvings

Solomon Island craftsmen are noted for excellent woodcarvings enhanced by intricate patterns of pearl shell inlay. Traditional carvings still have an important ceremonial significance in parts of the country.

Carvings feature *nguzunguzus* (canoe prow heads symbolizing a protective spirit), model canoes, fish, turtles, birds, dance sticks (used in ritual dances), food bowls, and busts or full human figures. Woven fiber bags and traditional shell money are also of interest.

Several things should be noted before shopping for handicraft items. The asking price is considered reasonable for the workmanship involved; therefore, shoppers are requested not to bargain. Only replicas of Solomon Island artifacts can be freely exported; genuine artifacts may not be taken out of the country without special permission.

You'll find craft items for sale in Honiara shops and in some of the villages. The Women's Clubs of the Solomon Islands sell handicrafts at the Solomon Islands Museum on Mendana Avenue in Honiara.

A few duty-free shops in Honiara cater to visitors. Those who have sufficient time can have a reasonably priced suit made by one of Honiara's Chinese tailors.

You'll find most shops open from 8 A.M. to 12:30 P.M. and 2 to 5 P.M., Monday through Friday, and from 8 to 12:30 Saturday. Chinese shops stay open longer hours.

If you wish to avoid the risk of having woodcarvings or straw items confiscated by customs when you return home, the Customs Department office at Point Cruz in Honiara will fumigate articles for a small fee and issue a verifying certificate.

Recreational possibilities

In the Solomons most recreational activities center around the Honiara area. Private clubs offer opportunities for tennis, lawn bowling, snooker, darts, and golf; you also can go sailing and skin diving. Temporary club memberships are issued on request to visitors. Check locally with the Solomon Islands Tourist Authority.

If you enjoy water sports, arrange to go fishing, snorkeling, or boating at one of several resorts in the Solomon Islands including Tambea Village Hotel Resort, Munda Rest House, Ngarando Resthouse, and Tavanipupu Island Resort.

Skin diving. Numerous sunken World War II relics lie off the Solomon Islands. Iron Bottom Sound, located between Guadalcanal and the Florida Islands, is the world's largest graveyard of ships and planes.

The Skin Divers Association in Honiara sponsors diving trips on weekends. Information is available from the Solomon Islands Tourist Authority. Local tour operators also sponsor skin diving trips which include a professional diving guide and the use of scuba equipment. Tavanipupu Island Resort has scuba gear for hire.

Fishing. Fishermen catch sailfish, yellow-fin tuna, marlin, kingfish, bonito, and barracuda in the Solomons. Deep-sea fishing trips are arranged through the Point Cruz Yacht Club in Honiara. Tambea Village Hotel Resort also has facilities for fishing, and local tour operators have fishing boats available for charter.

Skin divers can enjoy spear fishing.

Golf. The Honiara Golf Club, located 6 km/4 miles from town, has a 9-hole golf course. Tambea Village Hotel Resort offers miniature golf.

Exploring the Solomons

Some of the fiercest battles of the World War II South Pacific campaign were fought in the Solomon Islands from mid-1942 through February 1943. Even today you'll still find numerous rusting battle relics on beaches, in jungles, and at the bottom of bays.

Besides touring the battlegrounds, visitors can enjoy the village life of Solomon islanders, a slow-paced existence that has remained relatively unchanged despite war and modern influences.

Honiara, the capital

The capital and main port of the Solomons—Honiara— was a wartime creation. Before World War II, its site on the north coast of Guadalcanal was merely a coconut plantation. The country's capital was Tulagi, on the island of the same name just north of Guadalcanal.

War destroyed the town of Tulagi. In 1945 Honiara— offspring of a collection of military quonset huts west of Henderson Air Field—became the new capital.

Today, little remains of the World War II quonsets. Instead, Honiara displays a modern look with air-conditioned, concrete and glass buildings. The business district extends along a narrow coastal plain on either side of Point Cruz, a peninsula containing the town's wharf area. It was named in 1568 by explorer Alvaro de Mendaña, who landed on Guadalcanal and erected a cross on the peninsula.

Before embarking on your town and island explorations, stop at the Solomon Islands Tourist Authority office in Coronation Gardens on Mendana Avenue. Here you can pick up maps and a booklet describing local walks and drives.

Solomon Islands Museum. As you stroll down tree-lined Mendana Avenue, Honiara's main thoroughfare, stop at this interesting museum in Coronation Gardens across the street from the Hotel Mendana.

Open daily, the museum offers an opportunity for learning about various facets of the Solomon Islands. It displays traditional artifacts including weapons, tools, and fishing gear; war relics from Guadalcanal and the surrounding area; geological exhibits; and collections of butterflies and shells.

Botanical gardens. Walk through these gardens in the coolness of early morning or late afternoon. You'll find them in a wooded valley at the west end of town off Mendana Avenue.

Paths wind through a rain forest and alongside a small meandering stream trickling through a series of pools. You'll see lily ponds and a herbarium.

Other sights. Another place to visit is the public market; its colorful array of fruits and vegetables is located on Mendana Avenue near the bay. A short distance east of the market, you'll cross a bridge and discover Chinatown sprawling along the Matanikau River.

Drive into the hilly residential area behind the town for a good view of Iron Bottom Sound, graveyard of countless sunken planes and ships.

Touring Guadalcanal

Guadalcanal's one main road follows the island's northern coast on either side of Honiara for a total length of about 97 km/60 miles. Winding through lush coconut and cocoa plantations, it passes peaceful villages, deserted beaches, and mission schools. Traveling this road, you'll see some of Guadalcanal's World War II battle-grounds—the scene of heavy fighting between Allied and Japanese forces during 1942 and 1943. Today, the rusting relics of battle still lie on beaches and in grass-lands near the road.

East of Honiara, you'll cross the Lungga River just before Henderson Field. Just across the bridge, a sign on your right indicates a foxhole where the airfield commandant took refuge during enemy attacks.

Allied forces had an underground field hospital near Lungga River. Some organized tours guide visitors through this facility.

Henderson Field. Located 11 km/7 miles east of Honiara, Henderson Field is the country's international airport. Begun by the Japanese in July 1942, the airfield was captured a month later by the U.S. Marines. After its completion, Henderson Field (named in memory of a Marine Corps hero of Midway) played an important role in the Allied campaign in the Solomons and other Pacific islands to the north.

Bloody Ridge. Looking south from Henderson Field, you'll see a low hill which became known as Bloody Ridge (or Edson's Ridge) during the Guadalcanal Campaign. Here one of the bloodiest battles between the U.S. Marines and Japanese forces occurred.

On September 12–14, 1942, the Japanese launched a counterattack in an effort to retake the airfield. The U.S. Marines, commanded by Colonel Merritt A. Edson, held their positions on Bloody Ridge and the Japanese were defeated.

Red Beach. Continuing east past Henderson Field, you'll come to the turnoff for Red Beach (Tenaru Beach). On August 7, 1942, the first U.S. Marines landed here on Guadalcanal—10,000 men and their equipment.

Rusting landing debris still litters the long, narrow strand of dark grey sand. A large landing barge juts into the waves and an antiaircraft gun points seaward.

West of Honiara. Traveling westward from Honiara, you pass through Kakambona village, the Japanese army command post during the Guadalcanal Campaign. The U.S. Marines attacked and captured it on January 23, 1943.

As you continue west, you'll see the rusted super-structure of a wrecked Japanese wartime supply ship lying close to the beach. Farther on you come to Cape Esperance with its steel tower and warning light.

Just before you reach Tambea Village Hotel Resort, you pass Kamimbo Bay. Many Japanese troops made their Guadalcanal escape from here at the end of the campaign in February 1943.

Malaita's manmade islands

For a different aspect of the Solomon Islands, take a trip to Malaita, 105 km/65 miles northeast of Honiara. Though most of the island's villages lie along the coastal plain or in the hills, a few are scattered off the coast on man-made islands situated in quiet lagoons.

Construction of these islands began more than 17 generations ago. They were built offshore as a retreat from warring hill tribes who knew nothing about using canoes or boats. These island settlements also provided easy access to fishing grounds and relief from mosquitoes.

Malaita islanders made the islands by stacking blocks of coral in the shallow waters of the lagoons. This coral area was then filled with rocks, sand, and soil, transported by canoe or log raft. As the villages grow, the islands' area also increases. Many of the homes are built on stilts over the water. Gardening takes place in nearby drained mangrove swamps.

A trip to Langa Langa Lagoon. From Honiara, you can take a tour to the Malaita manmade islands. You'll fly to Auki, Malaita's largest town, where a bus transports visitors south to Langa Langa Lagoon on Malaita's west coast. Here you'll board a boat to visit either Alite or Laulasi village.

Just before you reach your destination, a canoe bearing a custom priest will pass your boat. Waving his twig of leaves, he wants to ensure that no evil spirits accompany your group.

You leave your boat at the dock, then proceed onto the island where a threatening warrior party blocks your way. Appeased by a gift from the tour leader, your group will be allowed to pass.

On the tour, men will be allowed to see the men's custom houses and women will visit the women's custom houses. The structures are off limits to members of the opposite sex.

You'll also see shell money made. Village women gather in a special hut to make this money, still used on ceremonial occasions and as part of the "bride price."

Near the end of the tour you join in a native meal, served in a basket made of leaves. Sweet potatoes, cooked chicken, and fresh fruit are among the foods you'll sample. While you eat, villagers entertain with local songs and dances.

Visitors are expected to respect traditional beliefs and customs. Avoid wearing either black or red. Islanders believe these colors harm their fishing abilities and their skill in making shell money.

Other island explorations. If you stay on Malaita for several days, you might want to see other manmade islands. The Lau Lagoon, north of Malu'u near the northern end of Malaita has larger artificial islands then those of Langa Langa Lagoon. You reach this area by boat or canoe from the end of the road at Gwaunatolo.

Know Before You Go

The following practical information will help you plan your trip to the Solomon Islands.

Entry/exit procedures. You will need a valid passport. Citizens of the United States, British Commonwealth, and most west European countries don't need visas. Upon arrival you will be issued a 7-day transit visa after you show proof of onward transportation. For a longer stay, visitors' resident permits are available for periods of up to 4 months.

Visitors coming from an infected area are required to have vaccinations against smallpox, yellow fever, and cholera. Since a malaria risk does exist, it is advisable to take antimalarial tablets. Check with your doctor a few weeks before your departure for treatment. (Note: Since health requirements change from time to time, check with your local public health department before leaving on your trip.)

Departing air passengers pay an airport departure tax of Solomon Islands $2.

Customs. Visitors may bring in duty free personal effects such as clothing, jewelry, a camera, portable tape recorder, 200 cigarettes, two bottles of liquor or three bottles of wine, plus other dutiable goods not exceeding Solomon Islands $30 in value. If you bring in a portable radio, you must declare it specifically on arrival.

Currency. The Australian dollar: The exchange rate is Australian $1 = U.S. $1.15, and New Zealand $1.06. With its recent independence, the country will be getting its own form of currency.

Tipping. There is no tipping in the Solomons, and visitors are requested to honor this custom.

Time. The Solomon Islands are GMT (Greenwich mean time) +11. For example, when it is noon Sunday in Honiara, it is 5 P.M. Saturday in San Francisco, 1 P.M. Sunday in Auckland, and 11 A.M. Sunday in Sydney.

Weather and what to wear. The best time to visit the Solomons is between April and November when humidity is low and southeast trade winds cool the islands. Heavy rains and an occasional typhoon plague the area between November and April. Daytime temperatures seldom exceed 31°C/88°F, and evening temperatures rarely drop below 22°C/72°F.

You'll be comfortable in lightweight summer clothes the year around. Visitors should refrain from wearing bathing suits or skimpy resort attire in towns and villages. Don't forget to pack your umbrella, sunglasses, and beach shoes for reef walking.

For more information. Write the Solomon Islands Tourist Authority, P.O. Box 321, Honiara, for further information on the Solomons.

MICRONESIA

Guam, Northern Marianas, Caroline and Marshall Islands

The word Micronesia means "small islands." It's an apt description of the islet-studded northwest Pacific, where more than 2,000 small islands are sprinkled across about 8 million square km/3 million square miles of ocean.

The entire land area of the 2,141 islands in this vast region totals only 1,834 square km/708 square miles. The islands range from low-lying coral specks inhabited by few as 8 people to rugged volcanic masses where the population is more than 10,000. Less than 100 of the islands and atolls are inhabited. Total population exceeds 100,000.

These far-reaching islands are divided into three island groups—the Mariana Islands, the Marshall Islands, and the Caroline Islands. Each group is subdivided—Palau, Yap, Truk, Kosrae, and Ponape (Carolines); Marshall Islands (Marshalls); and the Northern Marianas and Guam (Marianas).

The First Inhabitants

How did Micronesia's first settlers discover these tiny specks of land in the vast Pacific? Why and when did they settle here? Where did they come from? Scientists still are seeking the answers to these questions.

Carbon dating of artifacts found in the Marianas indicates that people lived in this part of Micronesia as early as 1500 B.C. Many scientists believe that Micronesia's first inhabitants migrated from the Malay Peninsula. Competent seamen and navigators, they sailed north and east across the uncharted seas of Micronesia, discovering islands as they went.

Their reasons for migration were probably similar to those of other groups who arrived in various regions of the Pacific during the same period. Perhaps they left an overcrowded land at war, or they may have been lured by an urge for adventure.

The first Micronesians were of medium stature with brown skin and straight-to-wavy black hair. Their physical characteristics were Malaysian with Polynesian traces. Since the first settlers arrived, several foreign powers have ruled Micronesia. Intermarriage has resulted, and today's Micronesians show traces of Filipino, Mexican, Spanish, Japanese, German, and American ancestry.

Early Foreign Rule

Since Ferdinand Magellan discovered Guam in 1521, many Micronesian islands have been dominated by one foreign power or another. Spain was the first, taking possession of the Marianas in 1565. Spanish galleons stopped regularly at the islands on their trade routes between Mexico and the Philippines.

Missionaries bring Christianity

In 1668 Spanish missionaries and a garrison of Spanish soldiers settled on Guam. They faced many setbacks and much fighting before dominating the strong-willed Chamorros, local inhabitants of the Marianas. Most of the male Chamorro population was killed before the survivors finally agreed to embrace the Catholic religion. The widowed women and their daughters then married the Filipino, Mexican, and Spanish troops stationed in the islands by the Spanish Empire.

The art of canoe building and many of the ancient

Guiding canoe through shallow green waters of Truk lagoon, villagers travel by water between Micronesian coastal communities.

Chamorro ceremonies and traditions died with the men. Despite intermarriage with Spanish troops, the island women retained the Chamorro language, foods, and weaving skills.

Islands sold to Germany

Following their 1898 defeat in the Spanish-American War, Spain sold the Caroline and the Mariana islands (except Guam) to Germany, which had already established a protectorate over the Marshall Islands. After capturing Guam during the Spanish-American War, the United States was given the island during the peace settlement.

Seeking profits from the sale of Micronesian copra, the Germans set up copra production quotas for all the islanders. However, the German reign was short. Soon after the outbreak of World War I, Japanese troops captured the islands of Micronesia. In 1920 the League of Nations mandated the islands to Japan.

Development under Japanese rule

For the next quarter century, the Japanese worked hard to develop the Micronesian islands as an important part of the Japanese Empire. They cleared fields and planted sugar cane, rice, and pineapple. They built attractive towns with Japanese-style houses, temples, shrines, and geisha houses. They constructed many roads, railroads, docking facilities, water and electrical systems, and hospitals.

In 1935 Japan withdrew from the League of Nations and prohibited foreign travel through the islands of Micronesia. Under a cloak of secrecy, they erected a vast complex of naval and air bases and war fortifications. Ships of the Imperial Navy sailed from Kwajalein in the Marshall Islands to attack Pearl Harbor in 1941. The Americans later wrested Kwajalein from the Japanese in a bloody battle.

Little remains of the advanced culture which the Japanese brought to Micronesia. What bombs didn't destroy, the jungle has reclaimed.

World War II strikes Micronesia

World War II did not spare the Micronesian islands. Bombing and bloody fighting occurred on many of them, and even those not actually invaded were touched by the war. Ponape was bombed, but damage wasn't heavy. Yap also escaped extensive damage; however, you'll find wrecks of Japanese fighter planes near Yap's airport. Many pieces of ancient Yapese stone money were crushed to build roads, and others were used whole as anchors.

Before the war, Koror in the Palau district was a bustling community, the capital of Japanese Micronesia and a Japanese vacation spot. Bombs reduced this town to rubble, and only a few foundations remain. Much of the Japanese fleet lies at the bottom of Truk Lagoon—victim of a surprise, pre-dawn American air attack on Feb. 17, 1944.

Saipan was a bustling commercial food processing center before the war. During bitter and costly fighting, much of the island's vegetation was destroyed. Near the end of the war, Saipan was one of the final major Japanese strongholds taken by the Americans. During a month of desperate fighting, 3,144 Americans died. Many Japanese jumped to their deaths from cliffs at the northern end of the island rather than be captured.

Micronesia Today

In 1947 all the islands of Micronesia except Guam were included in the Trust Territory of the Pacific Islands—a United Nations trusteeship administered by the United States. Guam remained a U.S. territory.

The United States still maintains important military bases on Guam and Kwajalein. Both Bikini and Eniwetok in the Marshalls were used for post-World War II nuclear bomb testing. Radiation still is present on these islands, so the people of Bikini and Eniwetok cannot return to their home islands for some time to come.

Trusteeship to end soon

The U.N. Trusteeship Agreement over the islands of Micronesia is targeted to end in 1981, and political changes are now underway. The people of the Mariana Islands (except Guam) changed the islands' name to the Northern Marianas and voted to become a United States Commonwealth. Under this agreement, the Northern Marianas will be self-governing in all matters except defense and foreign affairs, which will be handled by the U.S. government. The autonomous new government has already been set up, although officially the Northern Marianas will remain part of the Trust Territory until it is dissolved.

The United States is negotiating with other Micronesian islands to establish some form of government allowing the islands to have control of internal affairs while the U.S. retains control of military operations and some foreign affairs.

Discovering today's Micronesia

Following the devastation of World War II, most Micronesians reverted to a simple village life where they farm their fields and fish the lagoons to satisfy their daily needs.

When you visit Micronesia, you'll meet these quiet, gentle, friendly people who have endured repeated invasions by foreign powers. You'll see remnants of occupation in the old Spanish fortresses on Guam, the remains of a Japanese hospital on Saipan, and the old American landing strips on Tinian. You'll also discover relics of ancient Micronesia: *latte* stones, believed to be supports for early Chamorro houses; Yapese stone money; and traditional Palau men's houses, virtually unchanged in architectural style over the centuries.

The past mingles with the changing present in Micronesia. Here you'll find motorboats and canoes; *carabao* (water buffalo) and motorbikes; lagoon-caught fish and canned food from the local grocery store; and disco as well as traditional dancing.

DIVING
A Fascinating Underwater World

Not all the delights of the tropical Pacific lie on the land. For the person who enjoys exploring the underwater world of the sea, the Pacific offers a fascinating and colorful variety of marine attractions.

You'll see an array of corals in varying shades of red, blue, purple, black, and white. There are staghorn coral growths, black coral trees, and clumps of brain coral. Exploring the watery depths you can see a variety of marine terrain—crevasses, caves, and overhangs. In some places vertical dropoffs plunge to depths of 305 meters/1,000 feet.

Darting among the colorful coral formations are brilliantly colored fish in all shapes and sizes—square, tubular, and flat. There are squirrel fish and groupers, parrot fish and butterfly wonders. Their colors—ranging from blue stripes on orange to black barred with silver—shimmer in clear water where visibility averages at least 30 meters/100 feet. In these waters, underwater photography is excellent.

For the shell collector, there are myriad choices. Families of shells represented in Pacific waters include augers, miters, helmets, olives, and cones.

Snorkelers also can enjoy the Pacific's fascinating underwater world, since colorful fish and coral are found just below the water's surface. Ideal water temperatures exist for both the snorkeler and diver. Year-round temperatures are a warm 27°C/80°F.

Besides interesting flora and fauna, the tropical Pacific waters are filled with sunken relics waiting to be discovered and explored. Over the centuries the reefs have claimed many sailing ships. World War II vessels and planes lie ghost-like at the bottom of the sea near the Solomons and other Pacific islands. More than 60 ships of the Japanese Imperial fleet rest at the bottom of Truk Lagoon. They were sunk during World War II in a surprise bombing attack. The lagoon has been declared a historical monument.

Other areas where divers find colorful marine life and an occasional sunken ship are the waters off Fiji's islands, Palau, French Polynesia, and New Caledonia. Most tropical Pacific islands have reef-protected lagoons ideal for exploring.

Be alert. When you venture into the tropical Pacific's underwater world, you should be wary of several things.

Coral cuts can be painful, and they become infected easily. Some divers and snorkelers wear long-sleeved shirts and long pants while exploring reef areas. Reef walkers should always wear protective footwear. If you do get a coral cut, clean it carefully.

A variety of stinging fish and shells inhabit tropical waters. Never grab a fish with your bare hands, no matter how harmless it may look. You should also be careful in picking up shells, for the occupants of some will fight back. The shells are equipped with small stingers which inject a paralyzing toxin into their prey—usually small fish. This toxin can be painful, even deadly.

Tours and lessons. Many operators offer organized package diving tours to tropical Pacific island destinations. These tours usually include hotels or other accommodations and daily excursions. In some cases, participants stay aboard a chartered dive boat for several days at a time so they can make more than one dive per day. The boats are equipped with air compressors, diving tanks, and hot showers. Most diving tours are designed for experienced divers.

Novices can obtain diving instructions and rent diving gear at many Pacific island resorts. Instruction ranges from simple snorkeling lessons without air tanks to 5-day basic certification courses in scuba-diving.

Guam boutique *displays locally made sportswear fashioned from bright, tropical print fabrics. Open 7 days a week, shops cluster along shore of Agana Bay.*

Scuba divers *glide through Palau's clear blue waters, viewing an incredible marine world. Vividly colored tropical fish dart among coral formations, past underwater cliffs and caverns. Visitors can rent snorkel and scuba equipment.*

MARIANA, CAROLINE, & MARSHALL ISLANDS

The islands of Micronesia stretch across the western Pacific like the beads of a far-flung coral necklace. Though bearing some of the deepest scars of World War II, they are among the most unspoiled and varied islands in the Pacific. Most are unknown to outsiders. However, a few—such as Saipan, Truk, Yap, Peleliu, Kwajalein, Ulithi, and Majuro—stir the memories of many Pacific war veterans.

How have these lesser-known islands maintained their solitude and lack of development? For many years they were off limits to the casual visitor. Once restrictions were eased, the prospective visitor faced problems of transportation and accommodations.

But times have changed. Now frequent flights transport travelers into the area. Modern accommodations range from small but comfortable hotels to large, luxury resorts. Local tour options offer varied sightseeing opportunities. Yet despite these new tourist developments, most of the islands remain unspoiled and uncrowded.

A Multitude of Islands

Micronesia's islands wind through vast reaches of ocean, extending about 2,200 km/1,367 miles from north to south and about 3,701 km/2,300 miles from east to west. More than 2,000 specks of land cluster into three island groups—the Marianas, the Carolines, and the Marshalls. Total land area covers only about 1,833 square km/708 square miles. Guam, the largest island in Micronesia, is the main center for exploring the other islands.

High islands and coral atolls

The many islands of Micronesia range from substantial high volcanic islands to tiny, low-lying coral islands and atolls. As island topography varies, so does the vegetation. On the high islands, mangrove swamps cluster at lower elevations and forests cover the uplands. Expanses of sand dotted with groups of coconut palms mark the atolls.

Island wildlife includes bats, large monitor lizards, deer, and coconut crabs. Crocodiles live in the Palau swamplands.

Micronesia's People

Micronesia is actually an umbrella term covering a collection of islands whose people have many similarities but also some striking differences. They all share the uncomplicated life patterns associated with tropical island villages and a deep love for the island on which they were born.

The indigenous population of the islands is Micronesian, descended from people who migrated from Southeast Asia as long ago as 1500 B.C. Islanders who live nearer the Philippines and the Asian mainland more closely resemble Filipinos and Asians. The people on the more easterly islands near Polynesia have Polynesian characteristics. Locally, the people of each island are known by the district in which they live— Yapese, Marshallese, Palauan. The native people from Guam and the Northern Marianas are known as Chamorros.

Contrasts of culture

Customs differ by island group, with strong allegiances within each group to local folklore, ancestors, leaders, and social structure. Isolated islands have produced their own local adaptations and inventions—such as different ways of assembling canoes. Social organization may be matrilineal in one group, caste conscious in another, and chief-dominated in a third.

Architecture. The ways of the modern world have influenced today's Micronesian house builders. Traditional construction methods and materials have been supplanted by tin, plank, plywood, and concrete.

Occasional devastating typhoons menace all buildings. In some island districts, many families now dwell in typhoon relief houses—plywood rectangles supplied by the government.

Despite modernized construction and destructive typhoons, thatch-roofed huts and traditional architecture still exist. Distinctive examples are the men's houses of Yap and Palau.

Language. Nine distinct languages and many dialects are spoken in Micronesia. The Chamorros, in the Northern Marianas and Guam, and the Palauans speak a language similar to Malay. The language of Yap, Ulithi, Truk, Ponape, Kosrae, and the Marshall Islands is considered to be Micronesian. The Kapingamarangian and Nukuoroan people in the Ponape district speak a Polynesian tongue. You'll also find English and Japanese spoken.

Dress. Except in the Yap district, traditional dress generally has disappeared from the district center islands. Shirts, T-shirts, and trousers are male garb. Most women wear bright print dresses.

(Continued on page 112)

In the Yap district men commonly wear the *thu* (loin cloth), while women can still be seen in voluminous Yapese grass skirts.

Religion. Either Catholicism or Congregationalism is followed by a large percentage of Micronesians. Other religious groups represented included Episcopalians, Jehovah's Witnesses, Lutherans, Mormons, and Seventh-Day Adventists.

A subsistence economy

Copra is the main cash crop in Micronesia's basically subsistence economy. The sugar cane fields and pineapple plantations developed by the Japanese were allowed to revert to jungle after the war. Attempts are now being made to diversify agriculture and to develop a fishing industry.

Supplementing the receipts from agricultural products is income generated by government and tourism—and on Guam, the military.

Guam

The largest land mass between Hawaii and the Philippines is Guam, hub of United States activity in the North Pacific. Although about one-third of the island's real estate is occupied by the military, there's still plenty of open space for island residents (112,000 including the military population).

Located at the southern end of the Marianas chain, Guam covers an area of 541 square km/209 square miles. A hilly island, it has savannalike expanses punctuated by jungle-filled valleys and ravines. Bays, beaches, and rocky cliffs mark its rugged coast. Guam offers the visitor a year-round warm climate, warm surf, uncrowded beaches, and a number of resort hotels.

Guam has become a pleasant stopover point for travelers returning from a temple tour of the Orient. For many Americans and Japanese, it holds memories of World War II. Guam has become a favorite for Japanese honeymooners—a tropical haven for them in terms of reasonable flight time and air fare.

Getting there and getting settled

Guam gained a reputation as a "crossroads of the Pacific" during the days when Spanish galleons plied the hemp routes between Acapulco and Manila. Today a number of international air carriers schedule regular flights to Guam International Airport from the Orient, Southeast Asia, South Pacific, and United States. From the airport it's a 5-km/3-mile taxi ride into Agana, the island's main town. Many hotels have courtesy cars for airport pickup.

Some passenger/cargo liners also stop at Guam.

In and around Guam. Since the island has no public transportation and taxis are relatively expensive, the best way to see Guam is to rent a car or take a tour. Local operators offer a variety of tours. Motorbikes and bicycles are also available for rent.

If you are touring Guam on your own, you'll want to obtain a copy of the sightseeing map issued by the Guam Visitors Bureau. The map is keyed to 150 route signs placed by the GVB to guide visitors to places of interest. The GVB office is located on O'Brien Drive West near Saylor Street.

Where to stay. Guam offers a number of new resort hotels along Ipao Beach on Tumon Bay, about 10 minutes from the airport. Amenities include restaurants, shops, and various water sport and beach activities. Beachfront hotels include the Fujita Guam Tumon Beach Hotel, Guam Continental, Guam Dai-Ichi, Guam Hilton, Guam Hotel Okura, Guam Reef Hotel, and Terraza Tumon Villa.

Away from the beach area near downtown Agana, you'll find the Cliff Hotel, Micronesian Hotel, and Magellan Hotel.

Dining pleasures. You'll find a surprisingly wide choice of cuisine—Japanese, Indonesian, Chinese, Italian, Korean, Polynesian, German, Spanish, and American—at Guam restaurants. Dining spots you might want to try are Kurumaya Restaurant for teppan-style cooking, Istemewa for Indonesian dishes, Kim Chee's Cabana for Korean specialties, Salzburg Chalet for Austrian cooking, Don Pedros for Spanish fare, and Po Po's for Polynesian delicacies.

Inquire at your hotel if any of the villages on Guam plan a fiesta during your stay. Usually held in honor of a village patron saint, these weekend, all-day affairs offer a great variety of local foods. You can sample barbecued ribs, red rice (colored with achote seed), taro, yams, chicken kelaguen (with lemon, onions, and coconut meat), roast pig, and bananas baked in coconut milk. Some hotels hold fiesta-type dinners regularly.

Shopping bargains. Guam's duty-free port status makes it a bargain center for international products. You can buy pearls, cameras, electronic equipment, watches, perfumes, liquor, and tropical resort clothing and sportswear. Shoppers find good selections of merchandise both in hotel shops and in Agana's stores.

At the public market on Marine Drive near Paseo Park you can browse for local handicraft items including shell products, ceramics, woodcarvings, and stick dolls.

Most stores are open Monday to Saturday from 10 A.M. to 9 P.M. and on Sunday from noon to 6.

A recreational playground. Water sports are the most popular recreational activities in Guam. An average year-round temperature of 28°C/82°F makes swimming, surfing, and water-skiing pleasant.

Snorkelers take advantage of miles of shallow reef-protected waters. Skin divers enjoy exploring shipwrecks in Apra Harbor—the German vessel *Cormoran* was scuttled here during World War I, and the Japanese ship *Tokai Maru* sunk during World War II. Snorkelers can rent or buy equipment at Agana stores, diving centers, and hotel shops. The Coral Reef Marine Center, International Divers, and Marianas Divers all rent diving gear.

You can rent sailboats and canoes at hotel stands along the beach on Tumon Bay.

Reeling them in. Game fish including tuna, skipjack, mahi mahi, and sailfish abound in the waters off Guam. Charter fishing boats can be hired at the boat basin in

FESTIVAL TIME

Residents of Micronesia observe all the national holidays of the United States. In addition, they celebrate a number of annual local events.

Almost every month, one or more of the villages on Guam holds a religious festival honoring its patron saint. These festivals usually include a parish procession on Saturday, and a special mass and community feast on Sunday. To learn about village fiestas during your visit, check with the Guam Visitors Bureau upon arrival.

Other major celebrations in Micronesia include the following:

January—April

New Year's Day. On January 1 the New Year is celebrated throughout Micronesia with family gatherings and feasts.

Saipan Laguna Regatta. In mid-February sailboat races off Saipan draw Pacific-wide participation.

Discovery Day. Ferdinand Magellan's 1521 landing at Umatac Bay is celebrated at Umatac village on Guam on March 7.

Marianas Covenant Day. The people of the Northern Marianas honor this public holiday on March 24.

Annual Saipan Ocean Swim. People from all over the Pacific congregate to compete in this swim meet held in Saipan's lagoon in March or April.

May—August

Law Day. On May 1 Micronesians gather for speeches, ceremonies, and sports events.

San Jose Fiesta. In early May the people of Tinian and Saipan honor the patron saint of the people of San Jose with processions, feasts, sports contests, and dances.

San Isidro Fiesta. Saipan's patron saint also is honored in May with religious ceremonies, a feast, and traditional songs and dances in Chalan Kanoa village.

Liberation Day. In addition to celebrating United States' independence on July 4, the people of Saipan commemorate their liberation from the Japanese. Events include beauty contests, a parade, dances, and sports and carnival events.

Micronesia Day. The 1965 founding of the Congress of Micronesia is observed throughout Micronesia on July 12.

Guam's Liberation Day. On July 21 the people of Guam celebrate the shaping of Guam's history, the 1944 liberation from the Japanese, and the 1977 constitutional convention. Activities include athletic events, contests, and concerts.

Palau District Annual Fair. In August, a week-long fair in Koror features sports events, parades, traditional music and dance performances, and displays of Palauan-made shell, wood, and woven handicraft items.

September—December

Fiesta of San Francisco de Borja. In early October Rota honors its patron saint with food, music, dancing, cockfights, mass, and a silent procession.

United Nations Day. Most districts celebrate the founding of the United Nations with parades, sports events, and traditional dances on October 24.

All Saints Day and All Souls Day. On November 1 and 2, Micronesians clean and decorate graves and hold mass.

Feast of the Immaculate Conception. Guam's patron saint is honored on December 8 with a fiesta and Roman Catholic mass and a procession in Agana.

---

central Agana and the charter pier in Merizo at the southern end of the island.

Land sports. Athletes who prefer to keep both feet on dry land can play tennis at a number of courts throughout the town. Many courts are lighted for night play.

Guam's two golf courses open to the public are the Country Club of the Pacific and Windward Hills Golf and Country Club, both with 18-hole courses. They are located between Talofofo and Yona on Guam's southeastern coast—about a 30-minute drive south from Tumon Bay.

Horseback riders can rent saddle horses at M.J. Riding Academy in the Talofofo River Valley. If you like, join one of the 2-hour horseback tours into the jungle and along the beach.

Strolling around Agana

Agana, Guam's main town, is located about midway along the west coast of the island. Once a sleepy village, today Agana is caught in an era of scrambling growth. Dozens of new buildings line Marine Drive, the main road into town from the airport.

Although much of downtown Agana is now new, you still catch glimpses of the island's architectural heritage on a short stroll through the downtown area.

Dulce Nombre de Maria Cathedral. Begin your walk at Guam's largest cathedral, located off O'Hara Street several blocks east of Marine Drive. The church was built on the site of an earlier structure destroyed during World War II.

Skinner Plaza. One block south of the cathedral, you come to Skinner Plaza dedicated to Guam's first civilian governor—Carlton Skinner. Bordered by flame trees, the park has a fountain and two monuments to local war heroes.

Spanish bridge. Continuing south another block from the plaza, you'll find an old Spanish bridge in a parklike setting. Built in 1800 and restored after World War II, the bridge was once part of a road leading from a Spanish fort at Umatac to Agana.

Plaza de Espana. Now return to the Plaza de Espana, located next to the cathedral. In this park, you'll see some of Guam's best examples of early Spanish architecture. For 160 years Guam was ruled from buildings on this site.

The Azotea is all that remains of the Spanish Governor's Palace; once his back porch, the veranda today still is used on special occasions. The small, round building with wrought ironwork nearby was called the "Chocolate House"; it dates from 1736. Here the wives of Spanish governors served hot chocolate to elite guests.

Guam Museum. You'll discover an interesting collection of artifacts reflecting Guam's history in this small museum located behind the Azotea. Built in 1736, the building was originally a guardhouse. The museum is open from 1 to 4:30 P.M. daily except Saturday.

Latte Stone Park. Located across the street from Plaza de Espana, this park honors an ancient civilization. The rough-hewn limestone columns called *latte* (pronounced lah-*tee*) stones are believed to be foundation supports for early Chamorro houses. The stones were moved to this park from the Fena River area in south central Guam.

Government House. If you hike up the hill from Latte Stone Park, you'll come to the present governor's official residence. The home is open to the public Tuesday and Thursday from 9:30 to 11 A.M.

Fort Apugan. Adjacent to Government House stand the remains of a Spanish fortress built in 1800 (also called Fort Santa Agueda). During World War II, Japanese guns commanded the harbor from this high site. The fort offers visitors a panoramic view of the Agana area.

A trip around Guam

You can see even more of Guam's historical sights on a day excursion from Agana around the southern end of the island. On this loop trip, you'll wind along spectacular coasts, travel over mountain passes, and meander through valleys dotted with banana plantations. Besides seeing ancient Spanish ruins and charming Chamorro villages, you'll be reminded of the impact of World War II on this tiny island. You'll see invasion beaches at Asan and Agat Bay; Japanese bunkers; and coastal defense emplacements.

Agat stone bridge. Just south of Agat near Nimitz Beach, a sign directs you to the ruins of a stone bridge built in the 1700s. It was part of the old Spanish coastal road to Umatac.

Umatac. At Umatac, a small Chamorro village clusters along the shores of a cove. A monument honors Ferdinand Magellan, who discovered Guam in 1521 and reputedly landed here. Visit the ruins of Fort Nuestra

Señora on the hill overlooking the town. The old Spanish sentry box still stands above the bay.

Merizo. Located near the south end of the island, Merizo boasts the oldest Spanish building continuously occupied in Guam—the parish house alongside the village church. It was built in 1856.

Merizo is a water sports base where you can arrange for boats to take you water-skiing, scuba diving, fishing, or sightseeing along the coast or out to nearby Cocos Island (a good picnicking and sunning spot). Glass-bottomed boats operate out of Merizo for nearby coral garden viewing.

Inarajan. Returning along the east coast, you pass through Inarajan, a town whose Spanish influence is evident in its narrow streets and old buildings.

The villagers have recreated a century-old Chamorro village in the area. In bamboo and palm-thatched huts, village elders demonstrate "life crafts" such as making salt from seawater, weaving hats and mats, and grinding corn. This replica village is open every afternoon.

Two Lovers' Point. Back on the west coast of Guam, the road north from Agana takes you past the hotels on Tumon Bay to the turnoff for Two Lovers' Point. From this clifftop you'll have an excellent view along the coastline. According to island legend, two lovers jumped to their death from the 102-meter/334-foot cliff rather than live apart.

The Northern Marianas

The Northern Marianas stretch northward from Guam for about 644 km/400 miles. Largest islands in the group—and the only ones with airstrips—are Saipan, Rota, and Tinian. Other populated islands include Pagan, Agrihan, and Alamagan. Total population of the district is 15,000.

A few basic facts

Several local airlines provide regularly scheduled service between Guam and Saipan, Rota, and Tinian. Saipan is the end of the line for Nauru Pacific Lines cargo/passenger ships out of San Francisco. Field trip vessels also make irregular stops in the Northern Marianas.

Island transportation for visitors is confined mainly to car rentals and organized tours. There is no public transportation. Bikes and jeeps can also be rented.

Places to stay. Saipan offers a variety of large, resort-type accommodations and smaller hotels. You can choose from the Saipan Grand Hotel, Hafadai Beach Hotel, Marianas Hotel, Royal Taga Hotel, Saipan Continental Hotel, and the Saipan Inter-continental Island Inn.

Rota's moderately sized hotels include Blue Peninsula Hotel, Rota Hotel, and Rota Pau-Pau Hotel. On Tinian you can stay in small establishments such as the Fleming Hotel (7 rooms), Orinesia Hotel (8 Japanese-style rooms), and Tinian Center (4 rooms).

(Continued on page 117)

Yapese women *dressed in voluminous grass skirts relate traditional tales in song and dance. Distinctive customs, architecture, and dress characterize the culture of Yap.*

Ponape woman *squats in partially dammed stream to wash clothes. Numerous swift-flowing rivers drain island's lush, mountainous slopes.*

Recreation. All the islands are noted for beautiful, secluded beaches and warm lagoon waters. Popular sports include scuba diving, sailing, swimming, waterskiing, and fishing.

Saipan has a 9-hole golf course. You'll find tennis courts on some islands, but bring your own racket.

Shopping. While browsing in shops, look for local craft items like shell handbags and necklaces, and woven products.

Saipan, the largest island

Largest of the Northern Marianas, Saipan covers an area of 122 square km/47 square miles. The island is bounded on the west by gentle, reef-protected beaches, on the east by a rugged rocky coast, and on the north by dramatic inland and coastal cliffs. Many of Saipan's palm trees were destroyed during the war. The island is now extensively covered with a mass of *tangan-tangan*, a nondescript tree that holds soil in place.

Touring Saipan has a special poignancy. Here you'll see many relics of World War II—tanks, landing craft, gun emplacements, ghost towns, the old Japanese command post, and war memorials.

Garapan. Now overgrown by tangan-tangan, this village was once a major seaport for the Japanese with a population of about 15,000. You still can see the ruins of the prewar Japanese hospital and old Japanese jail where Amelia Earhart may have been imprisoned.

Command post. Near the northern end of Saipan above Marpi Point, you can see the concrete-reinforced natural cave which was the final Japanese command post on the island to fall to American forces in one of the most bitterly fought amphibious battles of World War II.

From here you can also view Suicide Cliff and Banzai Cliff. Hundreds of Japanese, including entire families, plunged to their deaths from these cliffs rather than be taken prisoner during the 1944 battle for Saipan.

Several memorials, recently erected by the Japanese, now stand atop the cliffs.

Tinian, Saipan's neighbor

From Saipan, you can travel to Tinian just 5 km/3 miles to the south. Crumbling airstrips at the northern end of the island are reminders of Tinian's importance during World War II.

From one of these airstrips the B-29 *Enola Gay* took

NAN MADOL
A World of Mysterious Islets

In terms of age, engineering achievement, and sheer mystery, the ancient ruins of Nan Madol off the coast of Ponape rank alongside the great stone heads of Easter Island, the ancient *maraes* (temples) of Tahiti, and the *menehune* fish ponds of Hawaii.

Nan Madol is a series of artificial islets built on the tidal flats and reef bordering Temwen Island, one of Ponape's small satellite islands. Scientists believe that the islets were built in the early 13th century by the Saudeleurs, a dynasty of Ponape rulers.

Using slabs and log-shaped pieces of basalt, the Saudeleurs built royal houses, temples, tombs, ceremonial halls, an administrative center, artificial lake, playing field, special bathing rooms, feast houses, and pools to keep fish, turtles, and eels. The size of the complex is amazing: the islets stretch along the flats for more than 2 km/1 mile. Manmade channels wind through the complex; they are navigable by boat at high tide, traversable by foot at low tide.

For 16 generations the Saudeleurs reigned over Ponape before they were succeeded by the Nahnmwarki dynasty. The last residents of Nan Madol probably left the islet city 300 or 400

years ago. Since then, descendants have lived on Temwen Island. The life and activities of the rulers of the two dynasties still pervade the folklore of present-day Ponapeans.

Visitors reach Nan Madol by boat from Kolonia in about 40 minutes. Schedule your trip to take full advantage of high tide. Tide charts are available at the hotels and docks. Plan to spend at least a half day touring Nan Madol.

Fishermen *haul nets into shallow water along Saipan's shore. Reef-protected western coast of island offers long stretches of empty beach. Rugged cliffs, rocky shores, and secluded pocket beaches mark eastern shore.*

Rusting wreckage *of Japanese fighter plane lies half buried in coral sands on Elato Atoll in Caroline Islands southeast of Yap. Atoll dwellers paddle outrigger canoes to visit neighboring islets.*

off to drop the atomic bomb on Hiroshima in August 1945. A peace memorial now marks the plane's departure point.

At the southern end of the island, you'll find remnants of an earlier era in Tinian's history. The House of Taga, near the island's main village of San Jose, includes some of the best-preserved Micronesian latte stones.

The island's central plateau supports a flourishing beef cattle industry.

Rota, a tiny island

Tiny Rota—only 83 square km/32 square miles—is located between Guam and Tinian. A quiet island with good beaches, it also has historic reminders.

An ancient Chamorro village at Mochon Beach near the northern tip of the island has latte stones. Nearby is a latte stone quarry.

The Caroline Islands

Lying south of Guam, the Caroline Islands stretch from the Palau district in the west to the Kosrae district in the east. Other island districts include Yap and Truk.

A few basic facts

Air Micronesia provides regularly scheduled service to the district centers. Ships of the Nauru Pacific Line stop at Ponape and Truk on their route between San Francisco and Saipan. Field trip vessels also make irregular stops at various islands in the group.

Rental cars are available at hotels in the district centers, but roads can be rough. Motorbikes and four-wheel-drive vehicles also may be rented. Local operators sponsor sightseeing tours by bus and boat.

Places to stay. On Yap, accommodations are available at two small hotels—the ESA Hotel and Rai View Hotel. Palau visitors can choose from a variety of hotels on Koror, most of them small. They include the Barsakesau Hotel, New Koror Hotel, Palau Continental, Royal Palauan Hotel, Ngerchong Boat-tel, Peleliu Inn, and Winty's Hotel.

Truk's hotels, all on Moen Island, include the Bayview Hotel, Christopher Inn, Hotel Maramar, and Truk Continental. All of Ponape's accommodations are small—Blue Rose Inn, Cliff Rainbow Motel, Hifumi Inn, Kawaii Inn, Hotel Nan Madol, Hotel Pohnpei, Sokehs Diamond Head Hotel, South Park Hotel, and The Village.

Shopping for craft items. Palau is known for finely carved, wooden storyboards, an ancient art still maintained by skillful craftsmen. In Koror you can see prisoners carving them at the jail.

Other craft items of special note include carved wooden dance paddles and war clubs from Ponape, and grass skirts from Yap.

Recreational activities. Water sports are popular throughout the Caroline Islands. Skin divers head for Truk Lagoon and the islands of Palau. Tennis players find courts on both Koror and Ponape. Deep-sea fishing is excellent in many areas.

Yap, where traditions remain

Heading southwest from Guam, you'll come to the Yap district in the Western Carolines. The district center of Yap is actually four islands separated by narrow sea channels. Reminiscent of New Caledonia, Yap is noted for its red earth, fine beaches, and palm groves. Its interior stretches of dry uplands are clothed in grass, ferns, and scrub. Colonia is the island's urban center. Yap's road system is not lengthy, but the roads are good.

Least developed of any of Micronesia's island groups, the Yap district also seems the least interested in such development. Traditional culture is deeply ingrained in the Yapese way of life—customs, architecture, and dress have remained unchanged for centuries.

In local villages you can see examples of Yap's famous, doughnut-shaped stone money and some of the traditional *falus* (men's houses).

Falus. A number of well-preserved falus still stand in various parts of the main island. Centuries old in design, they rest on stone foundations, the floor a short distance above the ground. Open sided to allow the cooling trade winds to sweep through, the falus have steep, thatched roofs towering 15 meters/50 feet high. Symbolic decorations mark the thatch above the entrance.

Stone money. Northernmost in the cluster of Yap's four islands is the one claiming to have the largest piece of stone money: 4 meters/12 feet in diameter. Balabat village, on the south edge of Colonia, has Yap's largest stone money bank. You'll also find two falus in the same area. The quiet village of Dalipebinaw, on the west coast of the main island, claims to have some of the region's oldest and most valuable stone money.

Palau, world of green islets

In the Palau district you'll see a fascinating collection of black-green, jungle-clad hills, coastal mangrove swamps, and a seemingly endless number of clear, placid channels threading between countless islands.

Travelers flying into the Palau district (a 3-hour flight southwest of Guam) land on the big island of Babelthuap, then travel south to the neighboring island of Koror, the district center.

Seeing Koror. Busy Koror has a varied array of stores, handicraft shops, nightclubs, boat docks, and busy fisheries. Sprawling over flatlands and across undulating hills, the town is nearly submerged in lush greenery.

While in Koror, visit the local museum, housed in the former Japanese Communications Center. Its collection includes artifacts from many Micronesian islands, World War II relics, and some fascinating photographs of the Koror area as it looked at the height of its development under the Japanese.

You'll also find an *abai* (Palauan men's house) on the grounds of the museum. The Palauans decorate the thatch above the abai entrance with intricately carved and decorated storyboards. These long wood planks illustrate scenes from local legends.

Palau's Floating Islands. South of Koror are Palau's Floating Garden Islands—land masses that resemble huge green pin cushions. About 200 islands lie in clusters, creating a labyrinth of channels and protected bays. The best way to see the islands is by boat.

Rounded limestone knobs undercut by centuries of tidal action, the Floating Garden Islands are smothered in trees, shrubs, and vines that grow in an impenetrable mass right to the waterline. Few of the islands are inhabited because of the dense growth, the steep rise of rock from the water, and the sharp undercut that makes landing on most islands extremely difficult.

Visiting Babelthuap. Despite Babelthuap's intriguing appearance, most Palau visitors bypass Babelthuap en route to Koror.

On Babelthuap you can explore fascinating caves, some a part of island lore, others used as hangars for Japanese seaplanes. Island villages have preserved Palauan culture in an almost unchanged state. You'll discover jungle waterfalls that may be among the most beautiful in the tropical Pacific and stone pillars marking the ruins of what may have been a giant abai large enough to shelter more than 1,000 people.

Most of Babelthuap's attractions must be reached by boat, since little remains of the old Japanese road system.

Truk, a fascinating lagoon

In the eastern Carolines, a collection of verdant islands lie within the protective reef enclosing Truk Lagoon. Roughly triangular in shape, the lagoon measures 64 km/40 miles at its widest point and encloses an area of 2,130 square km/822 square miles. This lagoon and the marine world beneath its surface are Truk's key attractions. Arriving travelers land on Moen Island, but most of Truk's interesting spots are found elsewhere.

Exploring the lagoon. For the scuba diver, the lagoon holds a dual fascination: the natural world of coral and tropical fish counterbalanced by submerged World War II wreckage. More than 60 ships of the Japanese Imperial fleet were sunk in the lagoon during a surprise bombing attack in February 1944.

The superstructures of some of the hulls rest just below the water surface, and some masts jut above the water. Nondivers can share a little of this underwater world by snorkeling or cruising over the wrecks in a glass-bottomed boat.

Because the lagoon has been declared a monument, salvage and souvenir taking of relics are prohibited by law. Divers should obtain a permit from the Truk Office of Tourism before diving around the ships.

Excursion to Dublon Island. Since Truk was Japan's major Micronesian naval installation, the Japanese developed the area with airfields, seaplane ramps, underground hangars, submarine pens, huge docking facilities, hospitals, extensive communications installations, gun emplacements, and roadways.

Before the war, more than 40,000 Japanese lived on Dublon Island, the Japanese naval command headquarters. If you take a boat excursion to the island today, you'll discover that the jungle has reclaimed much of the prewar development. Trees and vines nearly cover the remains of the roads and buildings.

On a walking tour from the docks, you'll stroll along one of the overgrown roads past the ruins of a Japanese hospital, an elaborate geisha house, and other installations that partially survived the war.

Ponape, a mountainous island

One high island—Ponape—and eight atolls comprise the Ponape district, located in the easternmost part of the Carolines.

Compared with other Micronesian islands, Ponape is large: 303 square km/117 square miles. Ponape Island is actually the slightly submerged remains of a classic, shield-shaped volcano, now encircled by a coral reef that protects a narrow lagoon.

Its rugged central mountains, 17 of which rise above 488 meters/1,600 feet, taper off to the sea. Cutting their flanks are long, deep valleys marked by turbulent rivers and dramatic, cascading waterfalls.

Dense, mossy rain forests, almost perpetually in the clouds, clothe Ponape's upper elevations. The island's lowlands are planted with breadfruit and coconut trees. Extensive mangrove swamp areas border the coastline; some of the swamps are planted in taro.

Kolonia, the only town. Ponape's only town is Kolonia (not to be confused with Colonia on Yap), the government and commercial center for the district. Rising across the lagoon that fronts the town is the profile of Sokehs, a soaring promontory sometimes called the "Diamond Head" of Ponape.

In and near Kolonia, you'll find a few fragmentary mementos of former governing powers: a moss-covered Spanish fort, an agricultural station begun by the Germans, an encircling road and fortifications built by the Japanese.

Ponape's cultural center. A visitor can easily spend a half day or more at Ponape's Nett Cultural Center. Inspired by Hawaii's Polynesian Cultural Center, a young Ponapean returned to his homeland and organized a cultural center for Ponape with the cooperation of the people of his community.

Visitors arrive at the center by canoes that they paddle themselves. At the center—a simple collection of thatched sheds set in a shady spot beside the river— you'll see Ponapeans demonstrate local dances and handicrafts. They'll make and serve you some *sakau,* Ponape's tongue-numbing, potent brand of *kava* (see page 61).

Other sights. A prime target for Ponape visitors is Nan Madol. For more information on this intriguing ancient city, see page 117.

The Marshall Islands

The Marshall Islands—a collection of 29 low-lying atolls and 5 small coral islands—lie east of the Caroline Islands and the Marianas. Total land area covers only about 181 square km/70 square miles.

A few basic facts

Air Micronesia and Air Nauru provide regularly scheduled air service to Majuro, the district center. Seaplanes and small trading vessels operate from Majuro to other islands in the Marshall group.

You'll find taxis at the airport. You can explore the island by rental car or on a tour.

Accommodations. Majuro has only three small hotels—the Hotel Ajidrik, the Eastern Gateway Hotel, and the Hotel Majuro.

Buying craft items. Favorite souvenirs are local woodcarvings such as small canoes and stick charts. Charts of this type were used in ocean navigation by early Micronesians.

Recreational possibilities. Swimming, shell collecting, snorkeling, scuba diving, and fishing are prime attractions on Majuro. Visitors can rent small boats from hotel concessionaires. Cruisers may be chartered for deep-sea fishing trips.

Touring Majuro

Located near the southern end of the Marshall Islands, Majuro is the major tourist center for the group. Majuro Atoll itself is a meandering thread of reef and palm-studded sand surrounding a huge turquoise lagoon.

Outside the reef, the ocean waves pound endlessly; inside, the calm waters of the lagoon lap gently on the white sand beaches. The lagoon itself sparkles like a lake. At its highest point, the land surrounding the lagoon is only a few feet above sea level.

Majuro's strip of land is only a kilometer/½ mile wide at its widest point, but it stretches so far along the western edge of the lagoon that Majuro boasts the longest road in Micronesia. Beginning near the airport, the road extends 56 km/35 miles to the beautiful little mission village at Laura Point on Majuro's northern tip.

Know Before You Go

The following practical information will help you plan your trip to Micronesia.

Entry/exit procedures. United States citizens need only proof of citizenship. Other visitors will need a current visa and passport.

Travelers arriving from an infected area will need smallpox, yellow fever, and cholera inoculations. Typhoid, paratyphoid, and tetanus shots are also recommended. (Since health requirements change from time to time, check with your local public health department before leaving on your trip.)

There is no airport departure tax.

Currency. The United States dollar is used throughout Micronesia. The recent exchange rate is approximately US$1 = Australian $.87 and New Zealand $.92.

Tipping. On Guam a 10 to 20 percent tip is expected. Tipping is beginning to be customary on other Micronesian islands.

Time. Because the islands of Micronesia are scattered across a great expanse of the Pacific Ocean, they are included in several time zones. Agana, Guam, the principal arrival point in Micronesia, is GMT (Greenwich mean time) +10. For example, when it is noon Sunday in Agana, it is 6 P.M. Saturday in San Francisco, 2 P.M. Sunday in Auckland, and noon Sunday in Sydney.

Weather and what to wear. Micronesia's islands share a common tropical climate: hot, with high humidity. Temperatures rarely drop below 21°C/70°F or exceed 32°C/90°F, but humidity can make them seem higher. The fall and winter months—November to April north of the equator—are the best months to visit. The rainy period can extend from May to October. Typhoons are possible almost any time, but usually occur only once or twice a year.

Lightweight summer clothing is worn throughout the year in Micronesia. Short shorts are considered inappropriate in some of the more remote areas. Don't forget to pack sunglasses, suntan lotion, and a plastic raincoat for sudden showers. You'll need beach shoes for reef walking and insect repellent to ward off mosquitoes.

For more information. For more information on Micronesia you can write several different sources.

Information on Guam is available from the Guam Visitors Bureau, P.O. Box 3520, Agana, Guam 96910. For general information on Micronesia, contact the Office of Tourism, Department of Resources and Development, Trust Territory of the Pacific Islands, Saipan, Northern Marianas 96950. Local Continental Airlines (Air Micronesia) offices also can provide information on Micronesia.

For information on the individual island groups, write the Marianas Visitors Bureau, P.O. Box 861, Saipan, Northern Marianas 96950; Marshall Islands Tourist Commission, Majuro, Marshall Islands 96960; Palau Tourist Commission, Koror, Palau 96940; Ponape Tourist Commission, Kolonia, Ponape 96941; Truk Tourist Commission, Moen, Truk 96942; and Yap Tourist Commission, Colonia, Yap 96943.

OTHER ISLANDS

Easter Island, Lord Howe Island, Norfolk Island
Nauru, Gilbert Islands, Tuvalu

In addition to the varied and fascinating tropical islands already described, the South Pacific offers other interesting off-beat destinations. Each year inveterate island collectors go out of their way to visit these "untouched" islands.

Relatively undeveloped islands just beginning to experience tourism include Easter, Lord Howe, Norfolk, Nauru, the Gilberts, and Tuvalu. Each offers the traveler different experiences, yet all feature simple but comfortable accommodations, limited island transportation, and a pace of life geared to a relaxing visit.

Most of these islands are some distance from well-traveled routes, but a visit to one or more of them can become the highlight of a South Pacific journey. Here are brief overviews of some of these intriguing destinations.

Easter Island

At the southeastern tip of the Polynesian triangle lies windswept Easter Island, one of the South Pacific's most isolated destinations. Surrounded by limitless ocean, Easter Island is regarded by some travelers as one of the loneliest islands in the world. Its closest neighbor is Pitcairn Island, 1,900 km/1,181 miles to the west. Chile, Easter Island's governing country, lies 3,701 km/2,300 miles east on the South American continent.

Triangular in shape, Easter Island—called Rapa Nui in Polynesian—is 117 square km/45 square miles of rocky grasslands, extinct volcanic cones, and steep ocean cliffs. Looming like ancient sentinels, the famed stone statues gaze with brooding eyes over this desolate landscape.

Easter Island is a vast storehouse of archeological treasures. Nearly 1,000 of these huge monoliths (called *moai*) dot the island; some are over 18 meters/60 feet high. The island also contains hundreds of petroglyphs and cave paintings, and the foundations of ancient buildings. Scientists still are trying to unravel the mystery of the island's ancient civilization and its culture.

Migration, discovery, and exploitation

Some scientists theorize that during ancient migrations two separate groups of Polynesians—the "Long Ears," who wore jewelry that elongated their ear lobes, and the "Short Ears"—arrived and settled on Easter Island.

The more artistic Long Ears carved the statues. Some scholars feel that the Long Ears wanted the Short Ears to do their manual labor—hauling the heavy statues and clearing the island of rocks. The two groups eventually fought and the Short Ears killed off the Long Ears. The victors then toppled many of the statues, and carving ceased.

When the first European navigator—Dutch Admiral Jacob Roggeveen—arrived on Easter Sunday, 1722, many of the statues had been toppled. In 1770 Felipe Gonzalez claimed the island for the King of Spain. Other explorers to visit the island were Captain James Cook in 1774 and French navigator Jean La Pérouse in 1785.

Six Peruvian slave ships arrived at Easter Island in 1862, and their crews hauled more than 1,000 islanders off to work Peru's guano islands. Most died en route. When the 15 survivors were finally released to return home, they brought smallpox with them. Within a short time an epidemic reduced the island's remaining population of 4,000 to a few hundred.

In 1888 Chile annexed Easter Island. Today's 1,800 residents mainly live off the desolate land, growing vegetables and fruit inside small gardens walled against the drying effects of the constant winds. Fish, pigs, and sheep provide other dietary staples. The island's main industry is sheep ranching. Since the island has no rivers or streams, water is sometimes scarce.

Hanga Roa, the island's only village, is located not far from the airport.

Visiting Easter Island today

LAN-Chile, the Chilean airline, stops at Easter Island on regularly scheduled flights between Chile and Tahiti

Brooding *stone statues
(called* moai) *gaze over lonely,
rolling hills of remote
Easter Island, easternmost
outpost of Polynesia.*

Gilbert Islander *carries
outrigger canoe from thatched
boathouse. Small boats
provide main transport between
scattered islets and atolls.*

and Fiji. Easter Island visitors stay in the modern 60-room Hanga Roa Hotel or at a local family's guest house.

Horses provide the most popular form of local transportation. They can be rented in the Hanga Roa village area. The island has few motor vehicles, and car rentals are expensive.

Visitors can explore the island independently or join a full or half-day guided tour.

Statues and other sights

Whether you take a tour or explore on your own, you'll find a number of interesting sights. At Ahu Akivi, northeast of Hanga Roa, you'll see seven statues that were replaced on their *ahu* (stone platform) during a 1960 restoration project.

On the eastern side of the island, you'll find Rano Raraku. From the crater walls of this extinct volcano, islanders obtained the stone which they fashioned skillfully into huge statues with elongated ears and jutting chins. The statues remain as they were left—some half carved, others completed. They stand in groups or alone, both inside and outside the crater; some are upright, some haphazardly tilted, some sprawled on the ground.

Besides the island's statues, you can see the ruins of ancient huts—their long, boat-shaped stone foundations still intact. The island also contains hundreds of petroglyphs and cave paintings.

For more information on Easter Island, write Director, Public Relations, LAN-Chile, Aeropuerto de los Cerrilos, Santiago, Chile.

Lord Howe Island

Qualifying as a hideaway is Lord Howe Island, 670 km/416 miles northeast of Sydney. The friendly islanders move at a relaxed pace—and so will you when you visit this small island. A dependency of the Australian state of New South Wales, Lord Howe is 11 km/7 miles long and 3 km/2 miles wide. Many island visitors return regularly every year for a vacation.

An interesting topography

Aside from its peace and quiet, Lord Howe Island is distinguished for its coral reef—the most southerly one in the world. Two massive mountains dominate the south end of the island. Heavily forested, the island has fine stands of Kentia (or Howea) palms and banyan trees.

Lord Howe Island derives its name from the lord who was Secretary of State for the Colonies in the British Cabinet in 1788, the year the island was discovered by Lieutenant Lidgbird Ball.

Visiting the island

Regular air service connects Lord Howe with Sydney and Brisbane in Australia and with Norfolk Island.

Since Lord Howe has few motor vehicles, the best method of island transportation is a bicycle. Rentals are available.

Tour opportunities feature glass-bottomed boat trips and around-the-island bus excursions. Other activities you might want to try are deep-sea fishing, swimming, scuba diving, snorkeling, tennis, mountain climbing, golf, and lawn bowls.

Accommodations on Lord Howe Island include a number of simple lodges and motels, some apartments, and a few cottages.

For further information about the island, write the Lord Howe Island Tourist Centre, 8th Floor, 275 George Street, Sydney, N.S.W. 2000.

Norfolk Island

Lying 1,448 km/900 miles off the east coast of Australia, Norfolk Island possesses an interesting but not always pleasant past.

At first glance the tiny island resembles Cornwall. Just 8 km/5 miles long and 5 km/3 miles wide, it is reminiscent of England in its greenness, its pastoral qualities, and its peaceful atmosphere. Rugged basalt cliffs edge the island's irregular coastline; inland, cows and horses roam the rolling green hills. The native Norfolk Island pines, many of them planted by convict laborers, majestically crown the ridges and mark the roadways.

A former penal colony

Life was not always as peaceful on the island as it is today. When Captain James Cook discovered Norfolk in 1774 it was uninhabited. However, a few weeks after the founding of Sydney, Australia, in 1788, a small convict settlement was established on Norfolk Island for felons of the British Empire. This settlement was difficult to supply, and it was abandoned in 1814.

The island became a penal settlement again in 1825, when hardened criminals were sent to Norfolk Island. Tales of brutality, floggings, executions, and violence in the penal colony spread throughout the Pacific. By 1855, surviving prisoners were shipped to Tasmania and the penal settlement was closed.

As a result of overcrowding on Pitcairn Island, descendants of the mutineers of *Bounty* fame migrated to Norfolk Island to settle in 1856. Norfolk became a Territory of the Commonwealth of Australia in 1913. The administrative center is located at Kingston on the island's southern coast.

Many of today's 1,600 island residents are descendants of the first settlers from Pitcairn. These friendly, hospitable people live in modest wooden houses tucked amid groves of Norfolk pines. They tend gardens yielding bananas, yams, melons, potatoes, oranges, and peaches. Norfolk residents speak English and a language called Norfolk—a combination of west country English and Tahitian.

Discovering Norfolk's attractions

Norfolk Island can be reached easily by plane from Auckland, New Zealand; Sydney and Brisbane, Australia; and Lord Howe Island. On the island, you can rent a car or bicycle, or tour by taxi. Horses are also available for inland excursions. Local tour operators offer glass-bottomed boat cruises and around-the-island trips.

Accommodations range from self-contained apartments to small hotels and lodges, inns, and guest houses.

At the south end of the island near Kingston you'll find walls and buildings built by convict labor during the penal settlement era. Many of the fine colonial Georgian buildings have been restored and are now used for government administrative offices. You'll also see the remains of high prison walls topped with broken glass, the gallows gate, the guard's barracks, officer's baths (Roman-style), and Bloody Bridge (where many prisoners died). The epitaphs on the headstones in the prison cemetery tell of the harshness of this era in Norfolk Island history.

On Douglas Drive near the airport, you'll discover remnants of the island's Melanesian Mission established in the late 18th century. All that remains today is the vicarage and handsomely designed St. Barnabas Chapel —an architectural gem with stained-glass windows and handworked timbers. The Mission moved to the Solomon Islands in 1920.

For further information on Norfolk Island, write the Norfolk Island Tourist Board, P.O. Box 211, Norfolk Island, South Pacific 2899.

Nauru

The Republic of Nauru—just 21 square km/8 square miles in area—is one of the smallest sovereign states in the world. Located about 644 km/400 miles west of the Gilberts, Nauru is distinguished from other South Pacific islands by having one of the highest per capita incomes in the world. This income is derived from the mining of phosphate deposits that cover about 85 percent of the island.

The land and its people

Island residents live in a narrow green belt along the shore. Less than a kilometer/½ mile inland lies a barren, phosphate-rich plateau. After the phosphate has been mined, grotesque coral pinnacles remain, giving the area an appearance of devastation. In the shadows of late afternoon, the pinnacles resemble stark gravestones. Acre upon acre of coral pillows—rising to 18 meters/60 feet—are all that remain after the phosphate has been ripped away.

The Nauruans who live on this mineral-rich island are friendly, humorous, helpful people. Every man, woman, and child receives an annual income of several thousand dollars plus free health services. Workers from other South Pacific islands and the Orient actually mine the phosphate. The government invests excess money earned from phosphate mining for security against the time when the phosphate deposits are exhausted.

Taking a trip to Nauru

The Republic of Nauru has its own airline, Air Nauru, that operates regular flights linking Nauru with a number of other Pacific islands as well as Australia, Japan, the Philippines, and Hong Kong. The country also has its own passenger/cargo line, Nauru Pacific, which sails regularly between San Francisco and islands in Micronesia.

The island's only hotel is the 32-room Meneng Hotel. Arriving travelers must have confirmed hotel reservations or confirmation of home-stay accommodations.

For further information on Nauru, write the Secretary for Island Development and Industry, Republic of Nauru; or Nauru Consulate General, 110 Sutter Street, San Francisco, CA 94104.

Gilbert Islands and Tuvalu

Until recently the Gilbert Islands and Tuvalu (formerly the Ellice Islands) were one British Crown Colony. They have now separated into two colonies, each working toward independence from Britain.

The three island groups of the Gilberts have a total land area of only 684 square km/264 square miles. Smaller in area, Tuvalu covers only 26 square km/10 square miles. Nearly all the islands are low lying, coral atolls rising just a few feet above sea level.

The people of the Gilberts are predominantly Micronesians who speak both Gilbertese and English. The Tuvaluans are Polynesians; they speak both English and their own Polynesian dialect. The people of both countries must eke a living from the sparse land of the atolls, which are nothing more than bits of coral rock covered with hard sand. The islands' scanty soil is just enough to grow taro, coconut, and pandanus. The rest of their food must come from the sea.

Travelers reach the Gilberts and Tuvalu on regularly scheduled flights from Fiji and Nauru. Gilbert Island visitors stay at the Otintai Hotel at Bikenibeu on Tarawa and the Abemama Hotel on Abemama Island. Tuvalu accommodations are available at the small Vaiaku Langi Hotel on Funafuti.

The remoteness of these islands makes them an interesting place to visit. Visitors can go fishing, swimming, picnicking, or shell collecting. There are also World War II battlegrounds to explore. During your visit, you'll learn how the islanders have adapted to an atoll existence.

For more information on the Gilbert Islands, write to the Ministry of Natural Resource Development, P.O. Box 77, Bairiki, Tarawa, Gilbert Islands, Central Pacific. You can get more information on Tuvalu by writing to the Ministry of Commerce and Natural Resources, Tuvalu Government, Vaiaku, Funafuti Island, Tuvalu.

Additional Readings

Battleground South Pacific by Robert Howlett with photos by Bruce Adams. Rutland, Vermont, and Tokyo, Japan: Charles E. Tuttle Co., 1970. A pictorial presentation of well-known World War II combat areas in the South Pacific.

A Descriptive Atlas of the Pacific Islands by T. F. Kennedy. New Zealand: A. H. & A. W. Reed Ltd., 1974. A comprehensive atlas including maps of Polynesia, Melanesia, Micronesia, Australia, New Zealand, and the Philippines.

Easter Island by Bob Putigny with photos by Olivier de Kersauson, Michel Folco, and Jean-Paul Duchêne. Papeete, Tahiti: Les Éditions du Pacifique, 1976. Color photos and text cover this remote Polynesian island.

Explorations of Captain James Cook in the Pacific, As Told by Selections of His Own Journals, 1768–1779 edited by A. Grenfell Price. New York: Dover Publications, Inc., 1971. An account of the explorer's journeys in the South Pacific.

Fodor's Australia, New Zealand, and the South Pacific edited by Robert C. Fisher and Leslie Brown. New York: David McKay Company Inc., 1978. A travel guide containing facts about many South Pacific countries.

Guam: Past & Present by Charles Beardsley. Rutland, Vermont, and Tokyo, Japan: Charles E. Tuttle Co., 1964. This general handbook tells of the island's discovery, history, culture, and geography.

Isles of the South Pacific by Maurice Shadbolt and Olaf Ruhen. Washington, D.C.: The National Geographic Society, 1968. Color photographs and text cover the islands of Polynesia and Melanesia.

Men From Under the Sky by Stanley Brown. Rutland, Vermont, and Tokyo, Japan: Charles E. Tuttle Co., 1973. A historical account of the arrival of the first westerners in Fiji.

Micronesia: The Breadfruit Revolution by Byron Baker and Robert Wenkam. Honolulu, Hawaii: East-West Center Press, 1971. The islands of the Marshalls, Carolines, and Marianas are covered through text and photographs.

Moorea by James Siers. Wellington, New Zealand: Millwood Press, 1976. A photographic guide to the history, people, and sights of this French Polynesian island.

New Guinea by Milton and Joan Mann. Tokyo, Japan, and Palo Alto, California: Kodansha International Ltd., 1972. A first-hand account of travels through Papua New Guinea.

Pacific Islands Year Book edited by Stuart Inder. Sydney, Australia: Pacific Publications, 1978. A standard reference book on the islands of the Pacific.

Pan Am's World Guide. New York: McGraw-Hill Book Co., 1978. An encyclopedia of travel containing basic facts on many South Pacific countries as well as Europe, Africa, the Middle East, Orient, Asia, North, Central and South America, and the Caribbean.

Papua New Guinea Handbook and Travel Guide edited by Stuart Inder. Sydney, Australia: Pacific Publications, 1978. A standard reference guide to this South Pacific country.

Polynesia in Colour by James Siers. Rutland, Vermont, & Tokyo, Japan: Charles E. Tuttle Co., 1970. Text and photographs cover Fiji, the Samoas, Tonga, the Cooks, New Caledonia, and Tahiti.

Rarotonga by James Siers. Wellington, New Zealand: Millwood Press, Ltd., 1977. The people of the Cook Islands are portrayed in color photos.

Samoa in Colour by James Siers. Rutland, Vermont, and Tokyo, Japan: Charles E. Tuttle Co., 1970. Photographs and text tell of the Samoan people and their islands.

Samoa, A Photographic Essay by Frederic Koehler Sutter. Honolulu, Hawaii: The University Press of Hawaii, 1971. Color photographs and detailed captions depict Samoan daily life.

South Pacific by Jack and Dorothy Fields. Tokyo, Japan, and Palo Alto, California: Kodansha International Ltd., 1972. A pictorial with photographs and text covering 14 island groups in Melanesia, Micronesia, and Polynesia.

South Pacific Travel Digest by Charles and Babette Jacobs. Palm Desert, California: Paul Richmond and Co., 1978. A guide to sights, transportation, hotels, restaurants, and shopping in the South Pacific.

Tahiti and Its Islands by Bob Putigny with photos by Bernard Hermann, Michel Folco, Erwin Christian, and Claude Rives. Papeete, Tahiti: Les Éditions du Pacifique, 1976. A colorful portrayal of French Polynesia's islands in photos and text.

Tin Roofs & Palm Trees, a Report on the New South Seas by Robert Trumbull. Seattle & London: University of Washington Press, 1977. A portrait of the South Pacific's emerging island states.

Setting sun *streaks the Pacific sky with vibrant tones of gold, pink, and purple as lone stroller walks along the shore.*

Index

Note: Names of individual countries appear in boldface.

Airport departure tax. *See* individual countries—Know Before You Go
American Samoa. *See* Samoas
Architecture, Pacific, 32. *See also* individual countries

Boating, 22, 47, 66, 79, 103, 112, 121

Caroline Islands, 119–120
Babelthuap, 120
Colonia, 119
dress, local, 111–112
Dublon Island, 120
economy, 112
festivals, 113
geography, 111, 119
government, 108
history, 106, 108
hotels, 119
Know Before You Go, 121
Kolonia, 120
Koror, 119
language, 111
map, 116
Moen Island, 120
Nan Madol, 117, 120
Nett Cultural Center, 120
Palau, 119–120
Palauan men's houses, 119
Palau's Floating Islands, 120
people,111–112
Ponape, 120
recreation, 119, 120
religion, 112
shopping, 119
sightseeing, 119–120
stone money, 119
storyboards, 119
tourist information, 121
transportation, 119
Truk, 120
Yap, 119
Yap men's houses, 119
Climate. *See* individual countries—Know Before You Go
Coconut palm, 101
Cook, Captain James, 5, 14, 16, 17, 26, 42, 50, 58, 74, 81, 82, 122

Cook Islands, 13, 50–53
Aitutaki, 53
Ara Metua, 53
Avarua, 53
economy, 50
entertainment, 52
festivities, 50
food, 52
geography, 50
history, 50
hotels, 52
Know Before You Go, 53
map, 52
people, 50
Rarotonga, 53
recreation, 52
religion, 50
shopping, 52
sightseeing,52–53
tourist information, 53
transportation, 50, 52

Currency. *See* individual countries—Know Before You Go
Customs allowances. *See* individual countries—Know Before You Go

Diving and snorkeling, 22, 36, 47, 52, 65, 79, 87, 95, 103, 109, 112, 117, 119, 121

Easter Island, 122, 124
Entertainment, 6. *See also* individual countries
Entry regulations. *See* individual countries—Know Before You Go

Festivals. *See* individual countries

Fiji, 56–57, 58–73
Bau, 69, 71
Beachcomber, 72
Blue Lagoon Cruises, 72
Castaway, 72
Coral Coast, 71–72
cruises, 68, 72
Dick's Place, 72
dress, local, 60, 61
economy, 61
entertainment, 64, 67, 71
feasts, 64, 72
festivals, 65
firewalking, 69, 71–72
food, 64, 67, 71
geography, 58
government, 60
Grand Pacific Hotel, 68
history, 58, 60
hotels, 63–64, 67, 71, 72, 73
island retreats, 72
King's Road, 72
Know Before You Go, 73
Labasa, 73
language, 63
Lautoka, 66–67
Levuka, 71
Mana, 72
map, 60
model villages, 68–69
museum, 68
Nadi, 66–67
parks and gardens, 68
people, 60–61
Plantation, 72
plants and animals, 58
public markets, 64, 66, 68
Queen's Road, 71–72
recreation, 64–66
Savusavu, 72–73
shopping, 64, 68
sightseeing, 66–73
sports, local, 61
Suva, 67–69, 71
Taveuni, 73
Toberua, 72
tourist information, 73
transportation, 61, 63, 68, 71, 72, 73
Treasure, 72
Vanua Levu, 72–73
Victoria Parade, 68
Viti Levu, 66–72
Yaqona (kava), 61, 64

Fishing, 22, 36, 47, 52, 65–66, 79, 95, 103, 112–113, 117, 119
Fcod, 6. *See also* individual countries
French Polynesia. *See* Tahiti

Geography, 4, 11, 55, 106. *See also* individual countries

Gilbert Islands, 125
Golf, 22, 36, 47, 52, 66, 87, 95, 103, 113, 117

Guam, 112–114
Agana, 113–114
dress, local, 111–112
economy, 112
festivals, 113
fiestas, 112, 113
food, 112
geography, 111, 112
government, 108
history, 106, 108
hotels, 112
Inarajan, 114
Know Before You Go, 121
language, 111
Latte Stone Park, 114
map, 116
Merizo, 114
people, 111–112
Plaza de Espana, 114
public market, 112
recreation, 112–113, 114
religion, 112
shopping, 112
sightseeing, 113–114
tourist information, 121
transportation, 112
Two Lovers' Point, 114
Umatac, 114

History, 5, 11–12, 55–56, 106, 108. *See also* individual countries
Hotels, 6. *See also* individual countries

Inoculations. *See* individual countries—Know Before You Go

Kava, 35, 46, 61, 64, 120

Lord Howe Island, 124

Map, general, 8–9. *See also* individual countries

Marshall Islands, 120–121
dress, local, 111–112
economy, 112
festivals, 113
geography, 111, 120
government, 108
history, 106, 108
hotels, 121
Know Before You Go, 121
language, 111
Majuro, 121
map, 116
people, 111–112
recreation, 121
religion, 112
shopping, 121

Marshall Islands *(cont'd.)*
sightseeing, 121
tourist information, 121
transportation, 121
Melanesia, 54–105
Micronesia, 106–121

Nauru, 125

New Caledonia, 57, 74–81
Amedée Island, 80
Anse Vata, 80
aquarium, 80
Baie des Citrons, 80
Baye, 81
Canala, 80
dress, local, 76
economy, 77
entertainment, 78
feasts, 78
festivals, 79
food, 78
geography, 74
government, 74
Grande Terre, 80–81
history, 74
hotels, 78, 81
Isle of Pines, 81
Know Before You Go, 81
language, 76
Lifou, 81
Loyalty Islands, 81
map, 76
Maré, 81
Nouméa, 79–80
Ouen Island, 80
Ouvéa, 81
people, 74, 76–77
Place de Cocotiers, 80
Plaine des Lacs, 80
plants and animals, 74
public market, 80
recreation, 79
religion, 76
shopping, 79
sightseeing, 79–81
sports, local, 76–77
Thio, 80
tourist information, 79, 81
transportation, 77–78, 80, 81
Yaté, 80

New Hebrides, 57, 82–89
art gallery, 88
cruises, 88
dress, local, 84
economy, 84
Efate, 87–88
Espirito Santo, 88–89
festivals, 87
food, 86–87, 88
geography, 82
government, 82
Havannah Harbour, 88
history, 82
Hog Harbour, 88
hotels, 86, 88, 89
John Frum movement, 89
Know Before You Go, 89
land diving, Pentecost Island, 85, 87
language, 84
Luganville, 88
map, 84

New Hebrides (cont'd.)
  people, 84
  plants and animals, 82
  Port Vila. *See* Vila
  public market, 88
  recreation,87
  religion, 84
  Santo. *See* Espirito Santo
  shopping, 87
  sightseeing, 87–89
  sports, local, 84, 88
  Tanna Island, 89
  tourist information, 89
  transportation, 85–86, 88, 89
  Vila, 87–88
  wild horses, 89
  Yasur volcano, 89

Norfolk Island, 124–125

Northern Marianas, 114, 117, 119
  Banzai Cliff, 117
  dress, local, 111–112
  economy, 112
  Enola Gay, 117, 119
  festivals, 113
  Garapan, 117
  geography, 111, 114
  government, 108
  history, 106, 108
  hotels, 114
  House of Taga, 119
  Know Before You Go, 121
  language, 111
  map, 116
  people, 111–112
  recreation, 117
  religion, 112
  Rota, 119
  Saipan, 117
  shopping, 117
  sightseeing, 117, 119
  Suicide Cliff, 117
  Tinian, 117, 119
  tourist information, 121
  transportation, 114

Pacific migrations, 5, 11–12, 55, 106

Papua New Guinea, 57, 90–97
  Asaro mud men, 96
  Bougainville, 97
  Bulolo, 96
  Chimbu bush plays, 96
  dress, local, 92
  economy, 92
  entertainment, 94
  feasts, 94
  festivals, 95
  food, 94
  geography, 90
  Goroka, 96
  government, 90
  haus tambaran, 97
  Highlands, 96
  Highland Show, 96
  history, 90
  hotels, 94, 95, 96, 97
  Know Before You Go, 97
  Kundiawa, 96
  Lae, 96
  language, 92, 93
  Madang, 96
  mainland, 95–97
  map, 92
  Maprik, 96–97
  Mt. Hagen, 96
  New Britain, 97
  people, 90, 92
  plants and animals, 90
  Port Moresby, 95–96

Papua New Guinea (cont'd.)
  public markets, 95, 96
  recreation, 95
  religion, 92
  Sepik Explorer cruises, 96
  Sepik River, 96
  shopping, 94–95
  sightseeing, 95–97
  sing sings, 94, 95, 96
  Sogeri Plateau, 96
  tourist information, 97
  transportation, 92–94, 96, 97
  Trobriand Islands, 97
  Wau, 96
  Wewak, 96–97
People, 5–6, 11, 55, 106. *See also*
    individual countries
Plants and animals, 4. *See also*
    individual countries
Polynesia, 10–53

Reading list, 126

Samoas, American and Western,
    13, 30–41
  American Samoa, 36–37, 39
  Apia, 40
  dress, local, 33
  economy, 33–34
  entertainment, 35, 37
  etiquette, Samoan, 35
  feasts, 35, 37, 40
  festivals, 34
  foods, 35, 37, 40
  geography, 30
  government, 33
  history, 30, 33
  hotels, 34, 37, 40, 41
  Know Before You Go, 41
  language, 33
  Manono Island, 41
  Manu'a group, 39
  map, 36, 37
  Mulinu'u, 40
  Pago Pago, 39
  people, 33–34
  plants and animals, 30
  public market, 39
  recreation, 36
  religion, 33
  Sadie Thompson, 39
  Savai'i, 41
  shopping, 36
  sightseeing, 39–41
  sports, local, 34
  Stevenson, Robert Louis, 40
  tourist information, 41
  transportation, 34, 37, 39, 40, 41
  Tutuila, 36–37, 39
  Upolu, 40–41
  Western Samoa, 40–41
Snorkeling. *See* Diving

Solomon Islands, 57, 98–105
  Bloody Ridge, 104
  dress, local, 102
  economy, 102
  entertainment, 103
  feasts, 103
  food, 103, 105
  geography, 98
  government, 100
  Guadalcanal, 104
  Henderson Field, 104
  history, 98, 100
  Honiara, 104
  hotels, 103
  Iron Bottom Sound, 104
  Know Before You Go, 105
  Langa Langa Lagoon, 105
  language, 102

Solomon Islands (cont'd.)
  Lau Lagoon, 105
  Malaita, 104–105
  map, 100
  people, 100, 102
  plants and animals, 98
  public market, 104
  recreation, 103
  Red Beach, 104
  religion, 102
  shell money, 105
  shopping, 103
  sightseeing, 104–105
  sports, local, 102
  tourist information, 104, 105
  transportation, 102–103, 105

Tahiti, 12–13, 14–29
  Australs, 29
  Bastille Day, 19, 21
  Bora Bora, 28
  dress, local, 17
  economy, 17, 19
  entertainment, 21, 24–25, 27, 28
  Fare, 28
  feasts, 21, 27
  festivals, 21
  firewalking, 29
  food, 20–21, 27
  Gambiers, 29
  Gauguin, Paul, 26–27
  geography, 14
  government, 16
  history, 14, 16
  hotels, 20, 24, 26, 27, 28, 29
  Huahine, 28
  Know Before You Go, 29
  language, 17, 19
  Le Truck, 20, 25, 26
  Maeva Village, 28
  Manihi, 29
  map, 16
  maraes, 27, 28
  Marquesas, 29
  Moorea, 27
  Papeete, 22, 24–25
  people, 16–17, 19
  plants and animals, 14
  public markets, 22, 24
  Raiatea, 28–29
  Rangiroa, 29
  recreation, 22
  religion, 17
  shopping, 21–22
  sightseeing, 22–29
  sports, local, 19
  Tahaa, 28, 29
  Tahiti, 22, 24–27
  Tetiaroa, 24
  tourist information, 24, 29
  transportation, 19–20, 24, 26, 27,
    28, 29

Tahiti (cont'd.)
  Tuamotus, 29
  Uturoa, 28
Tennis, 22, 36, 47, 52, 66, 79, 87, 95,
    103, 113, 119
Time, local. *See* individual
    countries—Know Before
    You Go
Tipping. *See* individual
    countries—Know Before
    You Go

Tonga, 13, 42–49
  blowholes, 48
  dress, local, 44
  economy, 44
  entertainment, 46
  Eua Island, 48
  feasts, 46
  festivals, 47
  flying foxes, 48
  food, 46
  geography, 42
  government, 42
  Ha'amonga Trilithon, 48
  Ha'apai Group, 49
  history, 42
  hotels, 46
  Hufangalupe, 48
  Know Before You Go, 49
  language, 42
  map, 44
  Neiafu, 49
  Nuku'alofa, 48
  Pangai, 49
  people, 42, 44–45
  Port of Refuge, 49
  public market, 48
  recreation, 47
  religion, 44
  Royal Chapel, Palace, 48
  Royal Tombs, 48
  shopping, 46–47
  sightseeing, 47–49
  sports, local, 44–45
  tapa, 45, 46
  terraced tombs, 48
  Tongatapu, 47–48
  tourist information, 49
  transportation, 45
  Vava'u Group, 49
Transportation, 6. *See also* individual
    countries

Tuvalu, 125

Visas. *See* individual
    countries—Know Before
    You Go

Western Samoa. *See* Samoas

Photographers

Dave Bartruff: 43 bottom, 54, 75 top. **Jack Cannon:** 10, 59 bottom. **Joan Erickson:** 62 top. **Jack Fields:** 2, 31 all, 35, 51 top, 75 bottom, 83 all, 86, 94, 99 all, 107, 110 bottom, 115 all, 118 bottom. **Shirley Fockler:** 18 top, 23 all, 26, 38 right, 46, 51 bottom, 91 top, back cover top right. **James Gebbie:** 43 top, 91 bottom. **Jane Keator:** 67, 70. **Milt and Joan Mann:** 110 top, 123 bottom. **Richard Rowan:** 15 top, 78. **Elliott Varner Smith:** 7 bottom, 62 bottom, 102, 118 top, back cover top left. **Joan Storey:** 7 top right, 18 bottom, 59 top, 126, back cover bottom. **Darrow M. Watt:** 15 bottom. **Basil Williams:** 7 top left, 38 left, 123 top.